AF576946

AMERICAN BOOKS ABROAD

TOWARD A NATIONAL POLICY

AMERICAN BOOKS ABROAD

TOWARD A NATIONAL POLICY

Edited by
William M. Childs and Donald E. McNeil

With a Foreword by
Ambassador Jeane J. Kirkpatrick

The Helen Dwight Reid Educational Foundation
Washington, D.C.

Published by
Helen Dwight Reid Educational Foundation
4000 Albemarle Street, N.W.
Washington, D.C. 20016

Library of Congress Cataloging-in-Publication Data

Childs, William M. 1922-
American books abroad.

Bibliography: p.
Includes index.
1. Book industries and trade—United States. 2. United States—Commercial policy. 3.Books—Marketing. 4. Books and reading—Developing countries. 5. Book industries and trade—Developing countries. 6. Export marketing. I. McNeil, Donald E., 1926- II. Title.
Z479.C48 1985 338.4’70705 85-17540
ISBN 0-916882-05-5

To Louis A. Fanget

Pioneer and Moving Force Behind So Many U.S. Overseas Book Programs

Friend and Mentor
With Appreciation and Warm Regards

Since its founding in 1957, the Helen Dwight Reid Educational Foundation has been interested in and has supported the free flow of knowledge and ideas among all countries. Helen Dwight Reid was a teacher and scholar with strong interests in education abroad. She served in the international division of the former U.S. Office of Education and was an education officer with the Agency for International Development. Her work and experiences in international education confirmed her belief in the value of American books in educational development around the world.

Most officers and board members of the foundation are also from the academic world and are writers of textbooks and other education-related materials. Many of their works have been republished and translated around the world and they have all had extensive experience in the international community of scholars and educators. They share Helen Reid's belief, therefore, in the importance of American books and journals to foreign education and the growth of knowledge in the developing world especially. For this reason, the Reid Foundation has viewed with considerable concern the inability of the U.S. distribution system to make American books and journals more widely available to readers in other countries.

Foundation officers and board members travel frequently and as scholars and writers visit bookstores and libraries in countries around the world. They are dismayed to find so few serious American books and journals available to scholarly counterparts overseas. American books are not as readily available to them as one would hope and expect. This lack is not a recent development; clearly exports of American books to Third World countries have declined over the past two decades, and scholars have never been able to find an adequate range of serious works relevant to their interests even in the developed world.

It is a national tragedy that the U.S. government decided in precisely this same time frame to sharply curtail its support of overseas book and library programs. The U.S. Information Agency once aided publishers around the world in the translating and reprinting of between 10 and 12 million American books a year. In 1984, less than one half million were produced under USIA programs. Clearly something has gone wrong.

For this reason, we were pleased to be asked by USIA Director Charles Z. Wick to undertake the study of American books abroad and of the barriers preventing American books from reaching overseas markets. As scholars, teachers, writers, and publishers, Reid Foundation staff and associates have been especially concerned over the inadequate dissemination of American ideas to overseas scholars, writers, professionals, educators, and students and have welcomed the opportunity to be a part of the U.S. Books Abroad project.

Evron M. Kirkpatrick, President
Helen Dwight Reid Educational Foundation

Contents

Foreword

It is endlessly ironic that the Soviet Union, which affirms the power of economics over culture and matter over mind, should sponsor a vigorous program of publishing and distributing *books* world-wide while the United States, which embodies and promotes freedom, should invest little effort and few resources in their production and distribution.

Books are basic tools of both democracy and development. The invention of the printing press contributed more to the expansion of human freedom than any other technological event. Printing presses made the Bible generally available and sparked the Reformation. Books have been intimately associated with every major revolution since that time, including our own struggle to form a new, independent nation. In this century, the *idea* of national independence inspired the anti-colonial leaders to demand independence, and undermined colonial governments serving confidence and rectitude. New ideas of oppression articulated by Karl Marx spurred on V. I. Lenin and his Bolshevik colleagues and today inspire communist leaders around the world.

Supporters and detractors alike call those who today rule the Soviet Union and act in its behalf Marxists; believers of Marxist *ideas* propel the tanks, helicopters, the guerrillas.

A civilization embodies a distinctive way of being human—a pattern of beliefs, values, and habits that shape our purposes and actions and give meaning to our experience. We Americans are part of a liberal democratic civilization that at its core affirms the value of the individual—and his or her capacity for freedom and responsibility.

We believe people are capable of choices, that is, of exercising freedom. We believe that freedom is the principal engine of innovation and progress. After all, human behavior is purposive. People act to achieve purposes. Their purposes reflect their beliefs about what is desirable and possible, what is true and false, what is noble and base, about how things may be achieved and avoided.

Books have a lot to do with freedom. They communicate ideas, they offer alternative ways of perceiving, interpreting, knowing.

Repressive governments, seeking to control their subjects, turn to censorship because they understand that papers, pamphlets, and books communicate alternative ways of seeing the world and acting in it. In his essay *On Liberty*, John Stuart Mill emphasized the unity of freedom of thought and expression, asserting that "The liberty of expressing and publishing opinions may seem to fall under a different principle, since it belongs to that part of the conduct of an individual which concerns other people, but, being almost of as much importance as the liberty of thought itself and resting in great part on the same reasons is practically inseparable from it." (J.S. Mill, *Essay on Liberty*).

Books both express opinions and stimulate them.

There are at least three reasons that it is appropriate for the United States government to take an interest in the production and distribution of books abroad: because they communicate who we are, because they are useful tools in promoting development, and because they are essential to democracy.

Communicating with other nations about who we are as a people is very important. What people in another country think about us will in the long run shape their attitude and policies toward us. The citizens of our democratic allies will not value the alliance if an insubstantial number of them believe there is no difference between the United States and the repressive Soviet dictatorship. Democractic peoples will value their relation with the U.S. if they understand that our government is a constitutional democracy, and that the American people are committed to a government of law and freedom. The various contemporary arguments suggesting there is no significant moral difference between the U.S. and the U.S.S.R. are damaging and false. They cannot be countered in one or two speeches, however brilliant. They can be ignored only at our peril. Errors, distortions, outright lies left unanswered are then taken for truth. There is, moreover, a world-wide disinformation industry that works to confuse and mislead others about our society, economy, politics, government, history, and future intentions. This disinformation supplements simple mistakes. There is a national interest in the wide availability of materials and information that provide an accurate picture of our pluralistic democratic society. The U.S. government has a legitimate interest—even a duty—to insure that books communicating a fair picture of America are available abroad.

Second, books are the basic tools for communicating information on development. More than its factories, machines, communications, and transportation systems, development is modernity. Technological, scientific, and economic development require work forces and citizens who have acquired the information skills, attitudes, and habits associated with modernity. People become modern through learning. Books and educational exchange are the foremost tools of modernization. Technical and economic assistance programs that focus on things more than ideas and information will fail to do more than achieve temporary amelioration of problems afflicting the less developed countries. They will fail to deliver the help of which we are capable.

Third, books are the basic media for communicating ideas of freedom and information about democratic governments.

The classics and handbooks of Marxism-Leninism are available at low cost all over the world. The Soviet Union gives high priority to mass production and distribution of their handbooks of misinformation about history, politics, economics, arms. The classics of democracy are esoteric items in most countries. Yet there are many rulers and many peoples who could profit enormously from *The Federalist Papers*, or a dozen other classics of American democracy. Democratic ideas are important tools of U.S. foreign policy. It should be as high a priority for the U.S. government to spread ideas of democratic self-government, national independence, pluralism, and self-determination as it is for the Soviets to spread the virus of class war and repression.

For these reasons and many more, I believe the U.S. should do far more to promote production and distribution of appropriate books to foreign audiences.

Information is the cheapest, safest, and finally, the most important instrument of foreign policy. We can fight ignorance and even animosity with information, lies and truth, repression with the example of diversity and freedom.

As Donald McNeil describes later in chapter 16, the Soviet Union is the most active and aggressive book publisher in the world, producing vast quantities of largely propagandistic books on the philosophies of Marx and Lenin, on communism, and on Soviet life in general. These books are translated into all major languages and widely distributed in the developing and developed world—including the United States. The British, French, German, and Spanish governments all support their publishing industries in getting books which explain their peoples, societies, governments, and policies in a proper perspective to readers and governments of other countries.

The time has come where we should have a national policy on book publishing and distribution abroad. This volume is clearly a significant contribution to that objective.

Ambassador Jeane J. Kirkpatrick
September 1985

INTRODUCTION

America's "Neglected Ambassadors"

A silent, far-reaching, and corrosive problem plaguing United States foreign policy today is the inadequate use of American books abroad, an inadequacy especially problematic at a time when the U.S.S.R. has been sharply stepping up its use of Soviet books in other countries. Government officials, American publishers, and other knowledgeable observers, including academicians and professionals, have reported a growing disparity between the shrinking number of books available overseas that support America's national interests and the growing number emanating from the Soviet Union to be found in other countries. These observations are confirmed by a U.S. Information Agency (USIA) study[1] showing that the Soviets published some 74.5 million books in languages not native to the U.S.S.R. in 1982, a foreign language publishing effort for which there is no comparison anywhere. For example, few books are published in the U.S. in Spanish despite the presence here of 20 million Hispanics; the U.S.S.R., with *no* Spanish market at home, published 11.6 million books in that language in 1982. The same USIA research report notes that the Soviets had increased exports of their books by 250 percent over the past decade while U.S. exports rose by only 25 percent during this period.

During the same decade, USIA officials were de-emphasizing that agency's overseas book and library programs. Principal factors in their decisions leading to the decline in use of books in overseas programming were

[1] William F. Freeman, with Scott Righetti. *Soviet Book Exports 1973–82*. (Washington, D.C.: USIA 1984.)

(1) preference for newer, high-tech communications techniques that were very expensive, forcing budgetary adjustments disadvantageous to book and library programs; (2) failure of some senior USIA officials to appreciate the importance attached to books by writers, journalists, scholars, and other opinion leaders both here and abroad; and (3) dissatisfaction with the uneven results of some book programs, problems due to handling by inexperienced personnel and overloading of the already inadequate distribution pipelines in some instances. These latter breakdowns eroded confidence of some USIA senior officials in the book program, resulting in a lessened top management support for books.

By the early 1980s the U.S. book world had become conscious of the inadequate presence of the American book abroad. Responding to warning calls from the publishing industry, U.S. government officials and other members of the book community, the Center for the Book in the Library of Congress took the initiative and commissioned the late Curtis G. Benjamin, publishing consultant and retired president of the McGraw-Hill Book Company, to prepare a study. Its purpose as Mr. Benjamin writes in his introduction "is to provide a document that endeavors to stimulate renewed and wider awareness, first, of the dire need for U.S. books in less developed countries, and, second, of possible ways and means by which this need may be met. . . ."[2]

National Security Council Director Robert C. McFarlane, commenting on Curtis G. Benjamin's insightful study, wrote the following to USIA Director Charles Z. Wick: "Statistics have graphically demonstrated in Curtis Benjamin's book . . . that the United States has unilaterally disarmed in this field."[3] It becomes clear that, as a consequence of our government's own neglect and an aggressive Soviet book export policy, the U.S. is steadily losing ground. A serious book gap exists, in the Third World especially, which the U.S.S.R. clearly intends to help fill. The Soviet's recorded export trade is complemented by an unreported international trade through foreign language editions published outside of the U.S.S.R. with Soviet subsidy, books readily observable in the marketplaces of the world although not tabulated by research to date. Whatever the Soviet numbers on foreign subsidies in 1982, and experts believe they are larger than the official export figures given in the USIA study, the one-half million books published abroad with USIA support in that year do not begin to compete internationally.[4]

---

[2] Curtis G. Benjamin, *U.S. Books Abroad: Neglected Ambassadors*. (Washington, D.C.: Library of Congress, 1984).

[3] Memorandum from NSC Director Robert D. McFarlane to USIA Director Charles Z. Wick, April 4, 1984: "U.S. Books Abroad." NSCD-130 (Appendix 1).

[4] "Books Published Abroad in Translation and in English, 1982" (Washington, D.C. Book Programs Division, USIA, 1983). Books published with USIA assistance remained at substantially the same level in 1983 and 1984 reports.

Responsibility for American failure to adequately address the book gap cannot be assigned exclusively to "unilateral disarmament" by government agencies, however. Other factors beyond anyone's control include the high price of American books, the deterioration or stagnation of much of the world's economy, shortages of a rapidly strengthening dollar, and inadequate publishing and bookselling infrastructures in most of the Third World, all of which are discussed in later chapters of this study. Such problems have widened the book gap, with the result that American books are not as readily available in book markets around the world as they could and should be. The book gap results also from insufficient attention to Third World markets by the American publishing industry itself, and failure of the private sector to break away from a sometimes isolationist and often provincial preoccupation with domestic markets.

What the book gap means, stated most simply, is that while the ideas and philosophies of other countries and societies are reaching readers around the world in increasing numbers every year, those of the U.S. are not. For example, as we approach the 200th anniversary of the ratification of the U.S. Constitution, there are few copies of *The Federalist Papers* in English, or at best in no more than two or three other languages available in bookstores abroad. Moreover, it speaks volumes for our neglect that while four communist leaders (Lenin, Brezhnev, Marx, and Mao Tse-tung) are listed among the world's first *15* most frequently translated authors in the *UNESCO Statistical Yearbook*,[5] no American philosophers of democratic thought such as Thomas Jefferson, Thomas Paine, John Adams or even Abraham Lincoln appear. Of the 192 authors listed by UNESCO as most frequently translated, John Kenneth Galbraith, with 177 translated editions, is the only American writer on the list who is not a literary figure such as Mark Twain, Jack London, Ernest Hemingway, etc.

Except for scientific and technical textbooks and some reference works, very few serious American works concerning American society, culture, thought, and policies can be found in libraries, universities or bookstores outside the U.S. It must be pointed out here that there is an assumption on the part of many in government, and indeed, in much of the American publishing industry itself, that the absence of such American works around the world is limited to developing countries. The Reid Foundation Study Group has found that this is simply not the case. A foreign writer, scholar, professor, student, or general reader in Western Europe experiences as much frustration trying to find American books in the social sciences and humanities as does his or her counterpart in Latin America or Africa (see chapter 12).

---

[5] "Authors Most Frequently Translated," *UNESCO Statistical Yearbook, 1983*, Section 7.17. (Paris: UNESCO, 1984).

USIA Director Charles Z. Wick established a USIA Book and Library Advisory Committee in 1981 to counsel him on the book gap. In November, 1982, he issued a new book program rationale for USIA that stated "serious American books in English or in translation on themes of concern to USIA are essential to the agency's mission in public diplomacy" and then noted that "such books face a major challenge abroad . . . their distribution and readership have declined steadily in the Third World for many years, while there is evidence that other nations, including the U.S.S.R., have increased significantly the distribution of their books and, thereby, their philosophies."[6]

There is no doubt that a shift in USIA book program policy direction was long overdue. Even so, Director Wick's book program rationale promised no early action and stated: "In itself, this rationale calls for no immediate new expenditures, although it provides the conceptual foundation for an expansion of our book programs as funds become available. Certainly, as soon as possible, we hope to amplify these programs to provide support to our posts' cultural and information activities and to compete adequately with other major powers." In other words, USIA announced its firm commitment to supporting the role of the book in public diplomacy in 1982, but admitted that it currently had neither funds nor resources to adequately fulfill that commitment.

However, Director Wick's USIA book policy statement did stimulate action outside USIA. The Center for the Book in the Library of Congress quickly seized the initiative in 1983, establishing an ad hoc coalition of publishers, librarians, writers, and government representatives that consulted on the previously cited study on declining American book exports by the late Curtis G. Benjamin. That study reviewed the ill-fated history of American book programs between 1948 and 1983 and issued a call to action to immediately address our neglect in getting U.S. books abroad, noting that "in the end, a book costs less, lasts longer, and penetrates more deeply than any other means of international communication of information and ideas."

Within a short time of the publication of Mr. Benjamin's work in January, 1984, as we have noted, the National Security Council took note of the problem. On April 4, 1984, NSC Director McFarlane, citing that report, wrote his memorandum to USIA Director Wick asking that USIA immediately assemble a task force and prepare a study and plan for dealing with declining exports of American books. Declaring that "the book gap is serious," Mr. McFarlane wrote "the time is right for a major new commitment to the provision of U.S. books abroad. The power of ideas has been projected through the written word. Whether we are dealing with the 'war of ideas' or looking at the problem in terms of fostering the 'infrastructure of democ-

[6] Charles Z. Wick, "Rationale, USIA Book Promotion and Translation Programs" (Washington, D.C.: USIA, 1982)

racy'—twin goals eloquently stated by the President in London in June, 1982—we must compete" (Appendix 1).

Wick responded immediately ordering that a comprehensive study of all facets of American book exports, including USIA's and other government agencies' overseas book programs, be undertaken. He asked his USIA Book and Library Advisory Committee to form a task force, technically a subcommittee, composed of representatives from private publishing firms, academia, libraries, nonprofit book-related institutions, and quasi-public and public institutions, and charged members with the task of making recommendations. To support the work of that task force, which finally numbered 43 specialists and professionals from the book world and related fields (Appendix 2), the Helen Dwight Reid Educational Foundation was asked to prepare this study of American books abroad especially geared toward examination of the barriers preventing American books from reaching overseas markets.

A distinguished group of citizens responded to the NSC/USIA call to action and gave generously of their time, talent, and experience for more than six months as members of the U.S. Books Abroad Task Force. They guided and commented on this Reid Foundation study and then prepared recommendations, their "Task Force Report," for Director Wick (see the text of the full report at the end of this study). This is only a beginning. We hope these efforts will call the attention of the public policy community, research and educational institutions, the book world (including the publishing industry), scholars and writers, the media, and other concerned citizens to America's negligence in allowing the book gap to develop in the first place and in allowing it to continue until now without adequate response. And we hope especially that the study will mobilize informed opinion and help frame a national policy aimed at eliminating the book gap.

William M. Childs
Project Director

Acknowledgements

The editors are not the many who have owed so much to so few, to paraphrase Churchill, but rather the few with so many to thank that we fear we may overlook some, which would be inadvertent but an injustice nonetheless. We thank our friends and colleagues in the book world not just for their help and counsel in our preparation of the study itself and in the rewriting and editing of the manuscript, but more for what they have taught us about publishing over the years of our pleasant and rewarding association with them.

Our judgement tells us not to single out any one of them for special mention but our gratitude—to say nothing of our conscience—overrules. We owe more than would be apparent without special mention of Dan Lacy for his generous and enormously sound advice and counsel throughout our study. We confess that there is much more of his thinking and approach in the following pages than the reader is likely to discern.

Leonard H. Marks, as the personal representative of USIA Director Charles Z. Wick, gave generously of his time and we are indebted to him for helping sharpen our own perceptions and focus. Paul E. Feffer, president of Feffer and Simons, Inc., a 30-year veteran export representative and chairman of both the USIA Book and Library Advisory Committee and the U.S. Books Abroad Task Force, with his keen knowledge of and rich experience in international marketing was an invaluable information source as well as a loyal supporter and inspiration throughout the long months of investigation and writing.

Leo N. Albert, former chairman of the board, Prentice-Hall International, Inc., with his years of managerial and executive experience in international publishing and his leadership role over the years in international copyright and anti-piracy crusades gave unstintingly of his time and will find more of his thoughts and ideas in the following pages than he is probably aware he contributed.

One who reads very much by publishing professionals will soon find a familiar name on acknowledgements pages. We, too, are grateful to Datus C. Smith, Jr., for his sage and experienced counsel and unstinting support throughout the U.S. Books Abroad project. He has been a teacher and friend from the days of our early associations with him in the USIA/Franklin relationships. John Y. Cole, executive director for the Center of the Book in the Library of Congress, whose sponsorship of the late Curtis Benjamin's earlier study which started the project bearing the title of his book, was a friendly supporter. We thank him as we do the Librarian of Congress, Dr. Daniel J. Boorstin, for his hosting in January, 1985, of the U.S. Books Abroad reception which gathered all of the involved book world participants to hear him and USIA Director Charles Z. Wick speak on the importance of addressing "America's Neglected Ambassadors."

Those Task Force members and professional observers who consented to author or co-author some of the following chapters are especially appreciated. Their contribution and counsel extended beyond their particular chapters to other sections of the study for which we thank them all: John P. Dessauer, Lois Spice Haig, Kenneth T. Hurst, Dan Lacy, William R. Lofquist, Leonard H. Marks, Howard R. Penniman, and Theodore M. Waller, all of whom have short biographies in the Contributors section at the end of this volume. Space limitations force us to do injustice to each of the other Task Force members who are at least listed in Appendix 2 at the end of this volume.

USIA Director Charles Z. Wick became involved at the outset of the U.S. Books Abroad project and gave support throughout. Members of his book and library program divisions were supportive and particularly helpful in supplying reports, documents, and related materials: Dr. Guy Story Brown, Jerry L. Prillaman, and Richard D. Moore, who served as rapporteur and scribe of the Task Force report which is reprinted at the end of this volume, Robert O. Jones, Pamela K. Roe, and Cynthia M. Banks. At the Department of Commerce, almost a mini task force made intelligible the complex world of foreign trade economics and finance, but special appreciation is due to John T. Sullivan. And back in the private sector, the AAP's Saundra Smith provided materials thought by others to be no longer in existence, while Carol Risher kept us informed on fast breaking 1984 copyright events. The AAP International Division Chairman, Pierre Balliett, vice president and director of Houghton-Mifflin's International Division, was personally forthcoming and supportive while also assuring our access to the other AAP members through both meetings and communications.

We cannot end this inadequate recognition of all the help and support we received from so many colleagues and friends of the book world without special acknowledgement of the encouragement and support of Evron Kirkpatrick, president of the Helen Dwight Reid Educational Foundation. He made the staff and facilities of the Foundation freely available and made us feel at home in the foundation. Cornelius W. Vahle, director of the Foundation's journal publishing division, Heldref, and former director of a book review and bibliographic service under contract with USIA at the zenith of its overseas book and library programs, was invaluable as historian for so much of the chapters recounting and examining them. Joyce Horn was first draft editor and typist, Ed Taylor kept us editorially in line with syntax, grammar, and often just a less convoluted way of expressing our ideas; Carol Gore must be given credit for the layout graphics; Joanne Reynolds guided us through production; and Louise Dudley coordinated us and all of the above. Judy Getrich prepared the important but sometimes underappreciated index.

Finally, we bow to tradition and save to the last the warm words of acknowledgement and appreciation for the support our families gave us throughout what must have seemed to them an eternity which we owe them. The long evening and weekend hours during which we closeted ourselves in our dens, losing ourselves in the problems of the study were forgiven—but must be repaid! We thank our wives, Betty Childs and Priscilla McNeil, for their patience, their support, and their good nature.

PART I

THE AMERICAN BOOK WORLD

1

The U.S. Book Industry Today

John P. Dessauer

We speak of book publishing as an industry and as a profession. Both designations are certainly appropriate. Book publishing is a business conducted, for the most part, for profit. But its practitioners—at least those who do it honor— have motivations that transcend their profit interest. They know that books are no mere commodity, no mere items for consumption that leave their readers much as they find them. Books, like other vehicles of information and sources of entertainment, can change, influence, elevate, demean, exalt, or depress those who expose themselves to them.

What books are and can be depends heavily on the judgment, integrity, taste, and acumen of those who select and produce them—their publishers. Thus publishers play a vital role, not only in the marketplace, but within the culture and civilization of which they are a part, and what makes book publishing a profession as well as a business is the conscious pursuit by publishers of their responsibilities. They wield influence with pride, caution, and conscience. They make decisions with the awareness that they are injecting live matter into the cultural bloodstream.

As industries go, book publishing is small, accounting for only $10.2 billion in revenues in 1984, according to *Book Industry Trends 1985*. Some 49 percent of this total, furthermore, represented sales to schools, college students, libraries, and other institutions, and only 51 percent ended up in the hands of general customers. Some observers predicted that books and other

---

Reprinted from *Book Publishing: What It Is, What It Does* by John P. Dessauer with permission of the R.R. Bowher Company, Copyright 1981. Excerpts updated June 1985 by the author. 2nd ed. rev. (New York: R. R. Bowker, 1981).

printed means of information and entertainment would suffer a decline. The very reverse has occurred. While the audiovisual scene has grown dramatically, books and periodicals have also seen gains. The reason is that as the thirst and capacity for knowledge increase, so does the use of the many and varied means of satisfying them. The same individual, responding to different needs and moods, may find it opportune to read during one hour, then see a live play, and watch some television in between.

Books in History

Books in one form or another are as old as civilization. We encounter them in ancient Mesopotamia as clay tablets and in ancient Egypt as papyrus rolls. Rolls were also the form they took in Greece and Rome, where bookselling already flourished and the "scriptoria" or copying establishments plied a vigorous trade. The format of books as we know them dates from the first century A.D. when the codex, a volume of parchment pages bound on one side, was introduced. A massive and often beautiful object, the codex remained the characteristic book of the Middle Ages. The religious and secular works then produced, mostly in monasteries, were often duplicated assembly line style with copyists, proofreaders, and illustrators each fulfilling separate, coordinated functions. The Reformation and Counter-Reformation proved—thanks to the invention of type—to be potent stimuli to reading and the publication of books. Not only were the Scriptures made available in the vernacular and widely distributed, but religious controversy found in the newly established printing presses ready means for spreading argument and counterargument far and wide. If the distribution of a great many books was thus encouraged, so was a good deal of suppression, confiscation, and burning. Censorship became a way of life. Even John Milton, who in 1644 wrote the *Areopagitica*, a ringing defense of freedom to publish, later became censor for the Commonwealth. But literacy gained ground, embracing by one estimate 60 percent of the population of sixteenth-century England.

During the eighteenth century the common people in the Western world shared a growing belief that they could acquire learning through reading. Women had attended the common schools; the farmer or artisan as a man of letters was no longer a rarity. This was the era of the founding of the great encyclopedias, such as the *Britannica* in England. But if book production was substantial in the eighteenth century, with two million titles issued worldwide, the nineteenth century was a period of even more significant development. Some eight million titles were published. By 1900 a best-selling novel would sell 600,000 copies in the English-speaking world. Urbanization, industrialization, and the impetus given to universal education by the growth of democratic influences were among the principal factors in this growth.

The contemporary era for the book dates from World War II. Not that some of the trends, phenomena, and practices shaping the present scene had not been initiated before. But the educational boom and the general prosperity in the postwar period are among the principal factors contributing to the shape and character of today's publishing world. The war itself played a role in changing conditions in the industry. In a patriotic and enlightened move publishers made available thousands of "Armed Forces Editions" of their books to the military in the field. Books thus became companions and solace, entertainment and relaxation, to countless individuals, many of whom might otherwise never have acquired the habit of reading. As these volumes were paperbound they also helped pave the way for the incipient paperback revolution. The war, furthermore, brought on the beginning of the college explosion: the era in which higher education was to become the perceived birthright of the masses. The veterans who flocked into college classrooms under the G.I. Bill established a precedent which, partly a success and partly a failure, has nevertheless become an article of national faith and commitment. The veterans purchased a great many books with government funds, thus giving college publishing its first big postwar shot in the arm.

Shortly after the war's end the new era in paperbound books was born. The titles which Pocket Books, Bantam Books, New American Library, and others that soon joined them were disseminating were not only different in format, size, and price—they used new channels of distribution which books had never before found open to them. Books were displayed on newsstands and cigar counters, in drugstores, railroad terminals, etc. The market they created was in large measure new and previously untapped.

Quite a different paperbound development occurred soon after, during the early 1950s in the traditional book field when trade paperbacks made their appearance. These titles of serious nonfiction and literary classics, while enjoying a certain vogue with the general consumers, found their prime markets in education. Most were used in college courses. During the late fifties, when secondary school programs were upgraded, high schools also contributed to their consumption. In fact, as time went on, both trade and "mass market" paperbacks enjoyed increased educational uses.

The Changes in the Sixties

By the early 1960s journalists, economic forecasters, and Wall Street analysts began to make ecstatic predictions for the future of education, for the use of leisure time, and, by implication, for book publishing. They succeeded in whetting the appetite of investors and corporations searching for ways to diversify their holdings. Publishing stocks, particularly those of educational companies, became glamour holdings. And conglomerates began to woo every independent publisher whose future promised to throw off even a modest share of the forecast earnings. A major segment of the industry found itself in merging, acquiring, or more frequently, being acquired.

These mergers and acquisitions have had a profound effect upon the book field. They made resources available without which the industry probably could not have capitalized on its opportunities and fulfilled its obligations to educational and consumer audiences alike. They brought new management and business acumen to the field which had been seriously lacking and which, in many instances, resulted for the first time in orderly budgeting, forecasting, planning, and fiscal arrangements. But in many cases they also placed the power of ultimate decision and policy-making in the hands of people unfamiliar with books, their peculiarities, and their markets.

What liabilities were being engendered by these changes were not readily apparent, during the prosperous sixties. From 1963 to 1969 publishing industry sales increased by 59 percent, from $1.7 billion to $2.7 billion. Many factors worked together to benefit the various segments of the industry. Research projects supported by government and foundation grants encouraged acquisition of professional books; generous federal and state budgets, bringing unaccustomed affluence to colleges, universities, and their faculties, augmented sales of scholarly materials.

There was, in addition, the factor of growing export and foreign sales. The postwar scholarly and scientific community had embraced English as the international language, and American publishers were reaping some large benefits. Translations and the leasing of publishing rights to foreign publishers were also growing phenomena. Soon American publishers of professional and reference materials saw the advantages of founding their own subsidiary companies abroad, thus enjoying the best of both worlds. (See the next chapter for a discussion of the growth of these overseas subsidiaries.)

It could not last. The 1970s ushered in some substantial reverses. General economic conditions initially declined, then recovered only sporadically. Enrollments in elementary schools turned downward. Taxpayers' revolts curtailed school budgets. College enrollments, too, began to decline even as state legislators cut appropriations for higher education. Federal support for schools, libraries, and research were reduced. The pace of book industry growth was expectedly slowed. From 1969 to 1972 sales increased by only 11 percent, from $2.7 billion to slightly over $3 billion, hardly more in some segments than could be accounted for by inflationary factors. Understandably, textbook and other educationally related sales suffered above-average reverses.

But if the boom era had come to an end, the industry had matured significantly during this period, and many of the gains appeared to be permanent. Large numbers of new readers had come into the fold. Lower education had been upgraded and higher education expanded to a larger segment of the population with related advances in book consumption. Even if consistent readers and book buyers still represented only a minority, or more accurately a group of cultural minorities, these minorities had grown substantially, and a larger universe of occasional book buyers now surrounded the hard core of loyal devotees.

Recession and Inflation in the Seventies

These gains did not prevent the industry from being affected by the recession and inflation in the mid-seventies. In fact, its very progress had made the book field more vulnerable. A greater number of occasional purchasers meant that more patrons could fall by the wayside during lean times. The number of consumer books sold, particularly mass market paperbacks, fell off during 1974–1975. Dollar revenues fared a great deal better, but only because substantial book price inflation set in at about the same time.

Countering a trend that had prevailed for more than a decade, when book price inflation had stayed well below general consumer commodity levels, the price dam broke in 1974 under the pressure of drastic increases in the cost of paper, skyrocketing guarantees paid to authors, rising operating expenses, and shortsighted profit objectives. Book prices were suddenly inflating at rates significantly higher than the general consumer price index, and expectedly general consumers and institutions found their resources inadequate to keep up with the rapidly rising cost of books. Many schools and libraries were particularly hard-hit because their book budgets had already been cut to austerity levels.

The industry might have fared even worse had it not been for some favorable developments in the retail market where the two major chains, B. Dalton and Waldenbooks, embarked on sizable expansion programs, and where an unprecedented number of independent booksellers were entering the field. Although the rapid proliferation of these outlets led to competition for the same limited consumer dollars in many cases, expansion unquestionably arrested what might otherwise have been a disastrous decline in industry sales.

A Broad Perspective

Book publishing, as we have noted, is both a cultural activity and a business. Books are vehicles of ideas, instruments of education, and vessels of literature, but the task of bringing them into existence and of purveying them to their readers is a commercial one requiring all the resources and skill of the manager and entrepreneur. It is appropriate, therefore, to describe book publishing as a cultural industry. It is important to recognize the dual character and demands of book publishing because its success depends on it. Both the environment in which they function and the qualifications of their practitioners reflect this duality; in both instances we must consider cultural and business requirements if our enterprise is to flourish.

Book buying, though a growing phenomenon in America, is not a consistent habit with a majority of the population. Sales figures of individual books are most revealing. When a national best seller, after going through hardcover and paperbound editions, sells two million copies, the industry rejoices. Yet such a sale represents a purchase by less than 1 percent of the population. The average hardcover trade book published may sell up to 10,000 copies, the average "mass market" paperback perhaps 100,000. The designation "mass market" for that paperback may be justified when comparing it with the hardcover volume—but in relation to the total potential market it is something of a fiction.

Unfortunately, many editorial and marketing concepts the industry has formulated in recent years are based on the assumption that books are a mass commodity. Thus, the best seller, which supposedly will reach a mass audience, receives major emphasis; the more specialized book, appealing to a more limited market, is given less attention. Yet all the evidence suggests that in aggregate the industry receives the bulk of its income and support from book buyers who indulge specialized interests and tastes. To the extent that the emphasis on imagined "mass" interests neglects these buyers, the industry is cutting off its nose to spite its face.

The single greatest challenge facing American book publishing—the goal that would most enable it to reach its potential—is simply to reach effectively the people willing to buy books. This would entail emphasizing editorial choices aimed at satisfying the real interests of consumers as well as the development of adequate means of placing books into their hands. Specialized books are rarely available in retail outlets, are difficult to obtain even by mail, and take interminable time to arrive when ordered. Uncounted book sales are lost in this country every day because willing buyers cannot find what they want.

Publishing and Education

Closely related to the general cultural climate as an environmental factor for book publishing is the state of education. Many stresses currently trouble this field: broad public disillusionment with what are perceived to be its failures; demands for greater accountability by educators; rising costs coupled with public reluctance to meet them. Educators themselves are anxious to introduce methods that will improve performance, centering mostly around greater individuation in approach to students.

Recently two trends in the choice of educational materials have been challenging the traditional textbook: the use of general books, particularly paperbacks, and the employment of audiovisual and other nonprint media. Many educational publishers have diversified their products and are in a position to respond effectively to these trends. But industry sales figures suggest that although textbooks have lost some ground, the attrition is far smaller than the lively rhetoric would lead one to believe. If a significant trend has emerged it seems to be that in the majority of schools and colleges the textbook will remain the principal tool of instruction.

This is not to suggest that the textbook is not going to change as conditions change. Certainly new emphases in instruction—including, one must own, new fads—will influence the content and appearance of text materials. We are witnessing more softbound texts, more consumables (materials on which the students work directly and which they, therefore, use up), more modular packages (kits consisting of small units). What is of the essence, however, is that from all appearances printed materials especially designed for the classroom—or for individualized instruction within formal educational settings—remain the favored choice of educators and students alike.

Divisions of the Industry

The products publishers develop, the markets to which they are addressed, and the methods used to reach those markets are the principal criteria by which the industry has divided itself into certain categories. Such divisions as trade, text, professional, or mass market paperback publishing have come about naturally because houses engaged in these activities share common editorial objectives and economic concerns.

Trade books are designed for the general consumer and are sold, for the most part, through bookstores and to libraries. They may be hardbound or paperbound and include works for both adults and children. Typical trade books are hardcover fiction, current nonfiction, biography, literary classics, hobby books, popular science books, art books, books for self-education, such as those in foreign languages, books on sports, music, poetry, and drama.

Professional books are, as the designation implies, books directed to professional people and specifically related to their work. AAP surveys distinguish among three major areas of professional-book publishing: *technical and scientific* books which treat subjects in the physical, biological, earth, and social sciences as well as technology, engineering, and the trades; *medical* books designed for physicians, nurses, dentists, hospital administrators, veterinarians, pharmacists, etc.; and *business and other professional* books addressed to business people, lawyers, librarians, or other professional individuals not covered under the technical, scientific, and medical categories.

Mail order publications are books created for the general consumer and marketed by direct mail. The principal differences between book club and mail order publications programs are that the latter are originated by the publisher who does the marketing and the publications are distributed without the specific commitments by the purchaser which characterize book club memberships.

Mass market paperbacks are softbound books on all subjects whose predominant distribution is through "mass" channels: newsstands, chain stores, drugstores, supermarkets, and the like. Many are reprints of hardcover trade books; others are originally published in this format. It is often difficult to discover the differences between trade and mass market paperbacks. (Sometimes the originating publisher's imprint provides the only clue.) Generally mass market paperbacks use less costly paper and employ covers more likely to attract the "mass" audiences than do their trade counterparts. Yet they, too, enjoy large secondary markets in trade outlets (book and department stores) and in educational settings.

University press books provide an instance where the content of titles and the methods used in their distribution are disregarded in their classification, and the sole criterion employed is the originating source. University presses, which are, for the most part, not-for-profit departments of universities, colleges, museums, or research institutions, publish mostly scholarly materials or titles of regional interest. However, occasionally they produce trade books and textbooks as well which are then categorized here rather than in the area that content and market would dictate.

Elementary and secondary textbooks are hardcover and soft-cover textbooks, workbooks, textbook-related tests, manuals, maps, and similar items all intended for classroom use and equipped with specific pedagogical features which distinguish them from consumer-oriented materials such as trade juveniles. The industry refers to producers of these materials as "elhi" publishers.

College textbooks include hardcover and soft-cover textbooks, pamphlets, reprints, course-related texts, and other materials and certain audiovisual items such as films, slides, and cassettes. "College" here embraces all higher education from junior colleges to postgraduate level. The upgrading of secondary school programs has created an interesting additional market in high schools for college publishers. Government, industry, and libraries also account for some of their sales.

It is noteworthy that nearly every division of the industry enjoys substantial markets outside its primary sales focus. This growing phenomenon is of relatively recent origin. Prior to World War II, product and market distinctions were nearly synonymous: trade books sold almost exclusively through bookstores and libraries, elhi textbooks to schools, college textbooks to students of higher education. The advent of the mass market and the growing practice in education of supplementing texts with other books have served to blur what were once fairly precise market lines.

Industry Activities and Associations

The record of the book field in dealing with its common problems is a strangely mixed one. On the one hand some publishers' groups have maintained good information services and statistics for many years, and textbook publishers in particular have established effective joint relations with national and local governments. Trade-book publishers have often united in battling censorship. But only in 1970 did general and textbook publishers join in one industry association, and the organizations representing publishers and retailers have barely begun to attack their most serious common difficulties, such as inadequate distribution.

Book people are often known and admired for their rugged individualism, which stands them in good stead when they must make difficult editorial decisions. Unfortunately the same staunchness of spirit often makes them less than wholly receptive to the needs and possibilities of cooperation. Here as in other ways the influx of new management and ownership has been an advantage.

The Association of American Publishers (AAP) was created by the merger of the American Book Publishers Council and the American Educational Publishers Institute and is organized into divisions corresponding generally to the historic groupings described earlier. In carrying out its tasks AAP has cooperated with other publishers groups such as the Evangelical Christian Publishers Association, the Information Industry Association, the Association of American University Presses (AAUP), and the Children's Book Council. AAP has also joined forces with the American Booksellers Association and the National Association of College Stores in exploring possible solutions to the industry's critical marketing and distribution problems. And it has continued the long-established relationship of the publishing community with the Book Manufacturers' Institute in developing and promulgating specification standards, particularly in the textbook field.

One of the most significant developments of recent years, the introduction into the United States of the International Standard Book Numbering System (ISBN), also enjoys AAP sponsorship, along with that of the American National Standards Institute and the R.R. Bowker Co., which administers the program. This system, to which most major book-producing nations now subscribe, assigns a unique number (the ISBN number) to every title which also identifies its country of origin and publisher. Numbers have also been assigned to institutions and dealers who purchase books and other materials, so that all ordering, invoicing, and record keeping now lend themselves readily to standardized computerization.

Steps are being taken by a number of industry firms to capitalize on these and similar system advances. A major move in this direction has been the formation of the Book Industry Systems Advisory Committee (BISAC), a committee of the Book Industry Study Group (BISG). The founding of BISG in 1976 was itself a major development. Primarily a research organization, BISG enrolls the major trade associations serving the industry as well as individual firms from the publishing, manufacturing, retailing, wholesaling, library, and supplier sectors of the field. The group regularly releases reports which have included market research studies, economic analyses, reviews of technological developments, and industry forecasts.

Other industry organizations and activities that should be noted here are the American Library Association (ALA), the Authors League of America, the American Institute of Graphic Arts (to which book designers belong and which sponsors annual exhibits and awards for excellence in the field), the Council for Periodical Distributors Associations (wholesalers handling mass market paperbacks), and the National Book Critics Circle which sponsors annual awards for outstanding titles. *Literary Marketplace*, the directory for the industry, lists all such book trade organizations and gives details for the above and others.

One certainly hopes that the impetus toward a common approach to shared problems which the growing activities of these organizations have provided will continue to be felt. As a cultural industry the book field is far too dependent on public attitudes and public policy to afford its members the luxury of autocratic isolation.

What Does the Future Hold?

Can books survive in our electronic age?

This question is actually easier to answer in the 1980s than it was a decade ago. For books have not only survived the predictions of their early death, which have been current since the days of MIT's Project Intrex, but have recently shown unprecedented growth particularly in general consumer markets. Based on government and industry data, I estimate in 1984 that per capita consumer expenditures on books rose by 12 percent in constant (1967) dollars and 11 percent in units between 1979 and 1983 and will increase by an additional 38 percent in constant dollars and 35 percent in units by 1988. This growth is occurring simultaneously with the electronic revolution, confirming the judgment that books and electronic media can prosper fruitfully side by side.

Why should we ever have thought otherwise? The history of civilization is one of growing complexity; each age has offered mankind an expanding range of tools for progress or retrogression. The basic inventions, those responsive to fundamental human needs and desires, such as writing and the wheel, have survived this long evolution. Books have been among the survivors because they offer great practical advantages and deeply satisfying experiences which even our electronically oriented society continues to prize. The BISG 1978 *Consumer Study* reported that the most active book readers were also among the most active TV watchers. Many of the most successful current professional titles deal with computers and other electronic subjects.

What of the fear of excess concentration in publishing? Largely groundless. Never in the history of the industry has the number of new houses grown to the degree evident during the past decade. True, many of the imprints are very small, hardly significant in an assessment of mainstream publishing in the United States. Yet a respectable number of these new houses has been able to gain industrywide attention for their output, and enough titles from small houses have achieved best-seller status in consumer, professional, and educational markets to reassure all but the most confirmed doomsayers. In fact, it is surprising that such gloomy forecasts should ever have been given credence in the book industry, where the rugged individualism of most practitioners is the best safeguard against undue domination by commercial interests.

Consumer markets will prosper more than educational and institutional ones, where rising costs and shrinking resources have diminished the purchasing power of libraries and schools. Even in this area, however, I see grounds for optimism. Libraries and schools rank too highly in the esteem and affection of most Americans to allow them to subject these vital institutions to permanent deprivation. Already, we are witnessing significant improvements in the funding of materials purchased by public libraries and schools.

Does the future, then, look altogether bright? Will book publishing be able to enjoy an easy, comfortable prosperity? Possibly. Much will depend on publishers themselves. Will enough of them find the determination and cooperative spirit necessary to resolve the industry's debilitating distribution problems? Will enough commit themselves to meaningful marketing efforts, or will they continue to act as though their responsibility ended when a book was physically produced? Will enough publishers be genuinely selective and judicious in their decisions to publish, thus curtailing the serious overproduction which now clogs the industry's pipeline?

Time will tell. The opportunities are great, not only for commercial success but for cultural achievement. This ancient profession may yet realize its potential on our shores, in the service of American society.

2

U.S. Publishing on the International Scene

Dan Lacy

The presence of American books abroad, either as exports from the United States or as overseas reprints, adaptations, and translations, is now achieved almost entirely due to private sector market mechanisms. More than a billion dollars a year are spent to make those books available abroad, and this money is provided almost entirely by *foreign* governments, institutions, and individuals who buy our books and/or rights to publish them. That fact is an extraordinary tribute to the quality and usefulness of American books abroad and to the interest of other countries in American culture, ideas, and technology. It is in marked contrast to the situation with respect to Soviet books. Their presence outside the Soviet Union is achieved almost entirely at the cost of the Soviet government itself, thrusting them upon audiences who have little interest in them.

Since this extraordinary market performance must be the base on which any supplementary governmental program is planned, it is essential to understand the structure and organization of the U.S. publishing business through which the international market is served.

Except in the case of Canada (which in some ways is an extension of the U.S. domestic market) the predominant flow of exports from the United States is composed mainly of professional books, and college and university textbooks in science, technology, and medicine, books which have values justifying their relatively high overseas prices and are in fields in which English is internationally used. Companies that are major publishers of such books in the United States, such as CBS (including Holt, Rinehart & Winston, and Saunders), Harper & Row, Macmillan, McGraw-Hill, Prentice-Hall, and John Wiley & Sons, have extensive overseas establishments. One major company, for example, has subsidiary publishing companies in Canada, Mexico, Panama, Colombia, Brazil, the United Kingdom, West Germany, Spain, Portugal, India, Japan, and Australia, a branch in France, a major distributing center in Singapore, and sales representatives covering most other countries. Other similar companies have comparable, if not always as extensive, overseas organizations.

Publishers primarily concerned with trade books, scholarly works, children's books, and elementary and high school textbooks, for which the export demand is smaller, use other means of export sales promotion. Especially in Canada, a local publisher may be retained as a general agent, representing the entire list of titles from a particular U.S. publisher. More frequently, a U.S. export sales agency, simultaneously representing a number of publishers, will be engaged to promote and market the publisher's output abroad. One major U.S. publishers' export representative firm has well over 200 American publisher clients. Larger university presses sometimes have a collective foreign representation in principal markets, using export representatives elsewhere. There are also export jobbers in the United States, who buy and stock American titles in their own warehouses, and sell them abroad at their own risk. Conversely, there are importing jobbers in some countries, especially Japan, who have offices in the United States and buy at their own risk to supply the domestic markets in their own countries or regions.

Other publishers, especially firms with specialized interests, may rely primarily on mail promotion to overseas libraries and professionals and fill mail orders directly from the United States. Separate arrangements may also be made for individual titles, under which a stock of bound copies or, more often unbound sheets to be bound abroad is sold to a foreign, usually British, publisher, who is given exclusive right to market the edition in a specified area. In the case of British publishers, the exclusive sales area may include all or most of the countries of the British Commonwealth.

A great variety of promotional tactics is necessary to make American books known in overseas markets. Publishers mail their catalogs and other promotional materials to foreign libraries, wholesalers and principal booksellers and to selected professors and other specialists, directly or through their overseas subsidiaries or marketing representatives. Sales representatives call on principal accounts. Major customers abroad may subscribe to *Publishers Weekly, Choice,* or other bibliographical services. A principal means of promotion is the international book fair, of which the largest is held annually at Frankfurt, West Germany. There are in addition many regional fairs (i.e., at Dresden and Warsaw), and specialized fairs, (i.e., the Children's Book Fair at Bologna, Italy). As a result of this extensive and vigorous effort by American publishers, in the years since World War II the United States has become the largest exporter of books in the world. However, exports alone can do only part of the job. Exporting can bring American ideas, culture, and technology to foreign countries through the purchase of books by libraries, universities, scholars and other specialists. However, the actual dissemination of American ideas, culture, and technology *within* other countries is much more difficult and more rarely accomplished.

There are many reasons why this is so. Books from the U.S. are, with the exception of mass market paperbacks, almost always too expensive for widespread individual purchase. Except for advanced works in science, books in the English language must be translated if they are to reach their intended audiences in most of the world. Frequently, even in English-speaking countries, American books must be adapted and published to meet local standards and needs—for example, by converting U.S. measures to the metric system, or by substituting local statistics and references to local legislation, regulation, fiscal policy, etc., in an economics textbook.

Hence, if American books are to reach a wide audience, including students and other individual purchasers, they must be published in inexpensive overseas editions (see chapter 6), translated and/or adapted as necessary. The larger U.S. publishers mentioned above may do this through their foreign subsidiaries. Among them, they publish many of their titles in French, German, Spanish, Portuguese, Arabic, Japanese, Afrikaans, and various languages of India and Africa, as the market demands. Spanish language editions are especially frequent. Also especially important are paperback, relatively inexpensive English-language editions of college textbooks, issued by most large college publishers exclusively for foreign sale. These may be overruns of domestic editions, separately bound and shipped abroad for sale, or they may be printed abroad using the offset printing films of the American edition with cheaper paper and binding.

Publishers without overseas subsidiaries (and indeed many that do have such subsidiaries) may have their books brought out in foreign editions, including English reprints, translations, and adaptations, by foreign publishers. The right to issue such editions is acquired by the foreign publisher from either the American publisher or the author. Authors of trade books (fiction, poetry, popular nonfiction) often retain world rights to their books and arrange through their literary agents for overseas editions. Authors of other types of books (textbooks, reference works, scientific, technical, and professional books) are more likely to authorize the publisher of the American edition to arrange foreign rights sales. The grant of rights to a foreign publisher is usually exclusive for a given language or marketing area. For example, a U.K. publisher licensed to bring out a British edition of an American novel will usually have the exclusive right to publish and sell the book not only in Great Britain but in all or most of the countries in the British Commonwealth. Similarly a French or Spanish or Mexican publisher licensed to publish a French or Spanish translation will usually have the exclusive right to publish and market the work in that language throughout the world.

This market-driven system is very efficient in serving commercially attractive markets. It produces, at foreign, not American, expense, a vast flow of American books in the form of exports, overseas editions, adaptations, and translations, in whatever format and language best serves the users' needs. Powerful commercial incentives assure that every commercially feasible market is actively explored and served. Competition assures efficiency and cost-effectiveness. Every book exported or republished abroad, is sent in response to active user demand and, hence, will be read and used.

However, such a market-driven system fails to meet many needs. It responds only to those needs of foreign users that can be expressed as active demand in the marketplace. It does not meet the needs of American foreign policy with regard to economic development or public diplomacy, when those needs do not express themselves in the marketplace. Government policy with regard to American books abroad should be specifically addressed to, and in generally only to, those areas of market failure.

Failure of market mechanisms to bring American books to those who need or desire them, and to the audience that would serve the public interest of the United States, occurs for three principal reasons:

1. the inability of those whom we would like to have American books to pay for them;
2. what we might call "frictions" in the market mechanism; and
3. the inadequacy of an infrastructure of publishers, booksellers, libraries, and educational institutions responsible for the dissemination of books within foreign countries.

All three of these sources of market failure are interrelated, and tend to be most serious in those countries in which economic under-development and political instability create special problems for American foreign policy, including economic development policy.

Lack of Adequate Funds

American books cost more abroad because of the higher marketing, shipping, and inventory costs and the typically long delays in payment. Added to this is the apparent over-valuation of the dollar in foreign trade. As a result, even in prosperous, highly industrialized countries the price of American books is an impediment to their import, and less expensive overseas editions are required if broad markets are to be reached. In less developed countries, like most in Latin America, the price even of local editions becomes a limitation; and in the poorest countries, like many in Africa, only donated books or very cheap subsidized editions are likely to reach into even the highly literate fraction of the population.

Lack of means has an indirect effect as well. Private U.S. publishers are not motivated to direct their marketing efforts toward countries that offer only unrewarding opportunities. Publisher sales calls, mailings, and participation in book fairs and exhibits are fewer. Subsidiaries, and local warehouses and inventories, are unlikely to exist. Even when a buyer in such a country has some means for a limited purchase of books, he may still encounter special difficulties resulting from the general unattractiveness of the market in that country.

"Frictions" in the System

The great variety and flexibility of the systems for selling American books abroad, and the profusion of sources for bibliographical information about them, heighten their effectiveness in reaching sophisticated and rewarding markets. But these very characteristics of the systems also create difficulties for all users, and become a major source of confusion and frustration to less sophisticated foreign purchasers of books or rights.

A foreign bookstore or wholesaler wanting to order American books, for example, will need to order directly from the United States in the case of some publishers, and from a particular foreign subsidiary in the case of others. To purchase books from one publisher, for example, importers in Asia order from Singapore, except in Japan where they buy from Japanese trading houses; those on the European continent order from Hamburg, as do those in Israel; those from sub-Saharan Africa, except South Africa, order from the United Kingdom, as do those in the Middle East, except Israel, and North Africa, unless the books are French titles, which are ordered from Paris, with most importers having the option of buying from a U.S. exporting jobber rather than directly from the publisher—unless, of course, it turns out that exclusive right to the title in the importer's country has been licensed to a British publisher, from whom it must be ordered.

A second point of "friction" in the movement of American books results from shipping delays. It takes weeks to fill most foreign orders from the United States by ocean freight, and air freight is very expensive. Publishers with a large export business, export representatives, and foreign subsidiaries may maintain inventories in a number of warehouses abroad. This reduces but does not eliminate shipping delays; and inventories stocked abroad are necessarily limited to titles in relatively active demand.

A foreign publisher, especially one in a less developed country, who wants to acquire rights to produce a translation or other local edition of an American book faces even greater "frictions." As noted, the power to license such editions may rest in the American publisher, or it may have been retained by the author. The exclusive right to publish in that country or in that language may already have been granted to another publisher. (For example, the right to publish in Portuguese sought by a Brazilian publisher may already have been granted to a publisher in Portugal.) Moreover, the American publisher or the agent of the American author may place rights with foreign literary agents. (For example, for Spanish language rights to a particular U.S. book, a publisher in Buenos Aires, Mexico City, or Madrid may have to negotiate with an agent in Barcelona.) Sophisticated publishers in major publishing centers have continuing contacts with American publishers and agents, and find the diversity of channels efficient and easy to deal with; however, to a less sophisticated publisher in a Third World country the process of acquiring rights may represent a seemingly impossible maze, made more impenetrable by his unfamiliarity with publishing practices, standard royalties, etc., among mainstream publishers, and by the further fact that he himself may represent a little known or unknown enterprise with which an American publisher, author, or agent is not eager to do business.

All of these sources of difficulty are much greater in Third World countries beset by lack of funds. In unrewarding markets, American publishers do not find it economically feasible to provide the extensive mailings, bibliographical tools, participation in book fairs and exhibitions, and frequent visits by informed travellers needed to reduce these "frictions" inherent in a market-driven system.

Lack of an Adequate Infrastructure

The third major cause of market failure is the absence in many poorer countries of an infrastructure of publishers, booksellers, and libraries adequate for the effective dissemination even of local editions throughout the country. Hence, in many areas, U.S. technical assistance to local publishers, booksellers, and librarians should be an important component in any government program to make American books more widely available abroad. Such programs should use and strengthen, not bypass and hence undercut, the existing commercial and library structures.

It is clear that the extensive and effective market-driven system of bringing American books to foreign readers must be our primary reliance, just as the experience of participants in that system was essential to completion of the U.S. Books Abroad Task Force project. In addition to their hands-on experience, U.S. book professionals have acquired irreplaceable ongoing contacts and collaborations with foreign counterparts through international associations formed since World War II. The International Publishers Association (IPA), the International Federation of Library Associations (IFLA), International Bookseller Federation (IBF), and the International Reading Association (IRA) are among the best known. U.S. government programs should only be aimed at strengthening, extending, and supplementing that market-driven system, especially in poorer Third World countries. We should continue to rely on market incentives, but help to reduce the financial and informational barriers that prevent the market from functioning effectively. The following chapters suggest ways of doing this.

3

Copyright Law and the Protection of Intellectual Property

Donald E. McNeil

Book piracy, the unauthorized publication of copyright-protected material for commercial gain, is a growth stock in international black markets. Technology that yesterday was viewed by media prophets as potentially capable of displacing the book in the cultural-informational matrix emerges now as a threat to legal book commerce through the power to duplicate. Presses are available, at modest cost, that allow quick and inexpensive reproduction in small quantities that a decade ago would have been considered uneconomical. Other advances make possible instant satellite transmission of text to distant printing plants. In sum, the creation of a worldwide interconnected book industry is now a possibility for the benefit of all; such development is, however, threatened by the spread of piracy that disrupts normal trade by unfair and illegal competition.

It is at best a source of ambivalent pride for the U.S. that, while book pirates respect no language, English books make up the majority of pirated works, and the biggest share of these pirated English works is American. The fact that English has become a world language only makes piracy more attractive, since printers using photo offset equipment need not set type and have potential markets everywhere. The U.K. Book Development Council estimates the value of pirated English-language books at $1 billion per year, and 75 percent of that loss is believed to be borne by American copyright holders, their publishers, and their legitimate foreign licensees. If this estimate is valid, the annual U.S. loss to pirates exceeds America's total 1984 book exports by almost $110 million. Although the estimate includes piracy of items other than books, the U.S. Copyright Office believes that the U.S. alone is losing $1.5 billion annually to pirates through lost foreign earnings. Addressing the piracy problem is, therefore, a moral and economic imperative for the U.S. in both the public and the private sectors.

The stimulation of individual intellectual creativity is a fundamental premise of democratic governments, and is of crucial importance to the advancement of democratic culture. The right of the individual to profit from the tangible expressions and manifestations of his or her creativity for a period of time, a right protected by the state, is essential to innovation and the advancement of society. It is a principle embedded in the U.S. Constitution (Article I, Section 8) and the first U.S. copyright law, enacted May 31, 1790. Unfortunately, while that 1790 act protected the works of U.S. citizens and others who resided here, it specifically excluded from protection the works of non-residents other than citizens. For more than a century, that exclusion was the essence of U.S. international copyright policy. In its 1984 report to Congress,[1] the U.S. Copyright Office notes that the "infant industry" concept, balance of payment deficits, abuse of power by foreign copyright holders, and most other reasons given today by Third World countries desiring easier access to foreign copyrighted materials were first heard from the U.S. in response to nineteenth-century pressure from other countries to protect the copyrights of foreign nationals in the U.S.

International pressure and the demands of some American copyright holders produced the Copyright Act of March 3, 1891, America's first provision for foreign copyright protection but a law that by no means could be described as international in scope. The president was authorized to extend U.S. copyright protection to nationals of other countries, when he found that such foreign governments gave U.S. authors protection equal to that provided to their own citizens. This bilateral approach served American copyright needs adequately until 1956, when the Universal Copyright Convention of 1952 (UCC)[2] came into force, with the U.S. a signatory to it. Bilateral U.S. copyright relations had been established with 38 countries between 1891 and 1956.[3] The U.S. now has relations via the UCC with 71 countries. American relations with 61 other countries are listed by the U.S. Copyright Office as "unclear," meaning that they involve countries that gained independence

---

[1] U.S. Copyright Office, *To Secure Intellectual Property Rights In World Commerce,* a report to the Subcommittee on Patents, Copyrights, and Trademarks of the Committee on the Judiciary of the U.S. Senate and to the Subcommittee on Western Hemisphere Affairs of the Committee on Foreign Affairs, U.S. House of Representatives, dated September 21, 1984. (Washington, D.C.: U.S. Copyright Office 1984). Multilith.

[2] Universal Copyright Convention of 1952, *Copyright Laws and Treaties of the World* (Paris: UNESCO-WIPO, n.d.).

[3] Copyright Office Circular R38A, July 31, 1983, provides the status of U.S. relations with other countries, on a country-by-country basis. (Washington, D.C.: Copyright Office, 1983).

since 1943 and may be honoring obligations incurred under their former political status, but with whom we have not established copyright relations. Some 17 of these 61 countries are signatories to the Berne Convention, and give U.S. works protection indirectly, through the "back door" to Berne that will be discussed later. U.S. relations with five countries continue to be covered by bilateral agreements. With 17 countries, the U.S. has no direct or indirect copyright relations at this time.

Bilateral copyright policy characterizes a country that recognizes specific markets for its own copyrights, and seeks protection for its copyrights in those markets by offering reciprocal protection for the copyrights of citizens of those countries. Hence, the Copyright Act of 1891 was followed quickly by bilateral agreements between America and the United Kingdom, Belgium, Denmark, France, Italy, Portugal, and Sweden—all countries where American literature was becoming popular. Such an approach left the copyrighted material of other countries, from which we continued to regard ourselves as net importers, open to U.S. piracy. At the same time, the formalities required to obtain copyright protection under U.S. law were such that, in practical terms, not all rights holders of countries with whom we had bilateral agreements actually pursued protection. Similar formalities hampered U.S. copyright holders seeking protection in countries party to these agreements, but did not arouse sufficient American interest to bring about further reciprocal changes in copyright laws.

The demand for American works that induced this country to change its copyright approach from a bilateral one to a multilateral one resulted from the aftermath of World War II. Devastation produced by the war left American science and industry virtually unchallenged as world leaders. The foreign demand for American technology required texts and materials with which to understand, use, and eventually reproduce that technology. Warfare had also weakened the international colonial system, and newly independent countries seeking national identities of their own sought out the literature with which to understand the American. American copyright owners saw that the market for U.S. literature was now global, particularly in English but also in translation, and that only a global approach to copyright reciprocity would protect American works. Hence, the U.S. was very interested in the Universal Copyright Convention of 1952, which came into being with strong American support. For a variety of reasons, including the necessity for changes in U.S. copyright law that America was not yet prepared to make, the creation of a new convention was favored over ratification of the Berne Convention for the Protection of Literary and Artistic Works that had been in existence since 1896.[4] In the case of some countries already signatory to the Berne Conven-

[4] Berne Convention for the Protection of Literary and Artistic Property, 1896, *Copyright Laws and Treaties of the World* (Paris: UNESCO-WIPO, n.d.).

tion, a primary reason for signing the UCC was to obtain better protection for their copyrights in American markets, protection they had sought for years by urging unsuccessfully that the U.S. ratify the Berne agreement. (For example, France stated that it would not ratify the UCC until the U.S. had done so.)

The Berne Convention was the work of European countries that had tried the bilateral approach to protection for many years with limited success. It differs from the UCC in that it places greater emphasis on certain basic rights of the author, e.g., to ensure protection of those rights in all countries as quickly as possible, the Berne Convention requires that registration formalities in signatory countries be minimal. The U.S. has resisted becoming a party to the Berne Convention for the reasons previously discussed, although the enactment of the U.S. Copyright Act of 1891 may in part be considered a response to the Berne agreement five years earlier. Through the revision of American copyright law in 1909 and the complete revision of 1976, the U.S. has also been motivated by practical reasons to bring its copyright law into closer conformity with that of Berne signatories. The Department of State has long favored U.S. ratification of the Berne Convention[5] and the current administration is expected to once again seek congressional ratification in 1985.

New attention is being focused on ratification of the Berne Convention, in light of the U.S. withdrawal from UNESCO as of December 31, 1984. While meetings of the World Intellectual Property Organization (WIPO), which provides the secretariat for the Berne Convention, are not without debates on the right of access to developed world copyrights by Third World countries, the proceedings of WIPO are deliberative and the organization actively seeks to provide education on the need for copyright law. The politicization of UNESCO is, of course, a major reason given for U.S. withdrawal from that organization, and UNESCO provides the secretariat for the UCC. The Department of State and the Copyright Office have assured the American copyright industries that American participation in UCC deliberations will not be affected by U.S. withdrawal from the parent body. They point to the fact that the U.S. was just reelected in 1984 to a new six-year term on the Intergovernmental Copyright Committee (ICC), the deliberative body on UCC matters. Nevertheless, among discussants who favored the U.S. withdrawal as well as among those who oppose it, there is a feeling that the U.S. situation is tenuous enough—the ICC is not the only UNESCO body in which copyright arises as a problem—that the time is right to reconsider ratifying the Berne agreement.

Ratification of the Berne Convention has actually been favored by many in the U.S. copyright industries since long before America's current problems

---

[5] Report of the U.S. Copyright Office.

with UNESCO began: indeed, some in the industry favored ratification before World War II and the UCC occurred. Some 17 of the countries with whom America has unclear copyright relations are signatories to the Berne Convention. Since 1976 our copyright law has been essentially the same as that of the Berne agreement, although differences on formalities of registration and on the U.S. manufacturing clause limiting protection of the works of Americans first published abroad remain to be accommodated by Berne countries or modified by the U.S. Meanwhile, America has been receiving at least partial protection under the Berne agreement through a "back door provision," a back door that publishers believe may be about to close as a result of America's lack of reciprocity and the growing impatience of Berne signatories. Back door coverage is essentially arranged by simultaneous first publication of an American book in the U.S. and in a country signatory to the Berne Convention (most often Canada). Such publication automatically gives the work protection in Berne countries. Some copyright industries represented at the September, 1984, meeting of the State Department's International Copyright Panel, Advisory Committee on Intellectual Property, stressed that the new U.S. status vis-a-vis UNESCO only adds strain to already difficult relations with media producers of Berne signatory countries in reprint and translation rights negotiations. While those at the meeting accepted the assessment of the UNESCO withdrawal by the Department of State as having no impact on U.S. copyright relations immediately under the UCC, they strongly backed Berne ratification in 1985. Other industry associations not present expressed the same views by telegrams and letters read at the panel meeting.

Pressure by developing countries for easier access to Western copyrights is based, they say, on their need for Western material to aid their national development. Such countries usually say they do not have the dollars with which to purchase copies of a Western book; they are unable to purchase translation or reprint rights because of the same currency shortages. In addition, the price of imported U.S. books is too high and the royalties asked for particular English-language reprint rights are out of reach, in their view. (Much international debate involves what is a "reasonable" royalty.)

Parallel Stockholm meetings of UCC and Berne countries in 1967 led to special concessions on rights access in principle, at the behest of Third World countries, that were later spelled out in codes adopted at parallel meetings in Paris in 1971 and incorporated in the Berne and Universal Copyright conventions. These concessions, considered by some Western copyright holders as the taking of property without due process, were in modifications to the two conventions that allowed for "compulsory licensing" by developing countries. Either when depositing its ratification of the Paris Acts or thereafter by a deposit, a developing country can inform the secretariat of the appropriate convention that the country intends to substitute a system of non-exclusive and non-transferable licenses for the exclusive rights intended by the two conventions. This translates into the right of a developing country government to grant a local license for the publication of a foreign book without the expressed permission of the foreign copyright holder. To some critical commentators, this was an unwise step away from protection of the author's complete rights to publication of his or her own works, copyright's fundamental purpose. For others, such licensing was a necessary compromise, meeting the demands of developing countries while maintaining protection of copyrights essentially intact.

The concessions take the form of power to grant licenses, not to deny that copyright exists. A developing country wanting to take advantage of these concessions must amend its national copyright statutes and regulations to comply with the conditions stipulated in the Paris Acts. These conditions must be met before a compulsory license can be issued. Evidence must be presented that the book has not been distributed in the would-be licensing country by the copyright holder or his licensee at a price reasonably related to that normally charged in the country for books of its kind. The book must have been in print for a period of years, the length of this period varying according to language and whether the work is a reprint or translation. The prospective licensee must show that a reasonable effort has been made to obtain rights from the copyright holder and that those rights have been refused, or that the owner has asked an unreasonable royalty. The compulsory license is granted by the government of the developing country when these conditions have been met. The copyright holder is informed of the license and of the royalty that has been determined to be a "reasonable" one. In theory at least, sales of a book reprinted pursuant to the Paris concessions are limited to the country in which the compulsory license is issued, and the work cannot be exported.

To ensure that these stipulations are followed before a compulsory license is issued, International Copyright Information Centers (ICIC) were established in the developed countries to assist Third World publishers attempting to obtain rights without resort to compulsory licensing procedures. From 1972 to 1975 the U.S. center, with the acronym INCINC, operated from the Franklin Book Programs office. Since 1975, INCINC has been located in the Washington office of the Association of American Publishers (AAP), with that association funding the operation. Government assistance in the funding of the office has been proposed several times by the AAP, without success. Alternatively, the AAP has suggested that INCINC be made part of a government agency, as are similar centers in other developed countries. The Government Advisory Committee on Book and Library Programs (GAC) endorsed the latter proposal in April, 1977, and the Copyright Office was recommended as the operating agency: however, the transfer did not occur.

Some eight countries are reportedly considering the adoption of compulsory licensing under the Paris Acts by amendment to their copyright law. (India has enacted the law, but not yet clarified the regulatory procedure to be followed.) INCINC Director Carol Risher (also director of copyright and new technology for the AAP) described for the Reid Foundation Study Group the process necessary to identify copyright holders and contact them on behalf of Third World publishers, and to follow up when a publisher receives no answer or a refusal of rights, both necessary steps before a compulsory license can be legally pursued. INCINC also becomes involved in debates on what is a "reasonable" rate: e.g., is any U.S. rate reasonable, when the American copyright offer is compared to that of a Soviet book offered free of charge? (The distinction between privately held rights and those controlled by the state becomes clear in such situations.)

Despite presentations at international meetings, advertising in appropriate foreign publications, and promotion of services through U.S. embassies, INCINC reports that requests for rights assistance have been and continue to be minimal, primarily because compulsory licensing regulations have not been developed as expected. If U.S. efforts to stop piracy using economic leverage (discussed in this chapter) are effective, providing assistance to Third World publishers who wish to legitimately acquire rights will require promotion of and assistance to INCINC both at home and abroad. It can be assumed, in that regard, that the enactment of compulsory licensing arrangements will be one form of reaction in developing countries to decreased access to pirated books. That, in turn, would produce a flow of requests to INCINC that the present staff (of one) cannot possibly handle. Therefore, INCINC questions become critical ones, on which Task Force advice is needed. Where will the funding come from for staff and programs of an activated INCINC? Where in the private, independent, or governmental sectors should INCINC be located? If INCINC is the logical organization to undertake other rights-related activities discussed in chapters 11 and 12 as needing a "home," its status requires considerable thought. As noted, other ICICs are administered by governments.

Piracy was suggested at the outset of this paper as a growth industry. It is a lucrative profit-making enterprise as well, despite the efforts of some to characterize it as a "Robin Hood" operation, caring for the academic needs of poor students and the demands for low-priced editions of an expanding, newly literate audience with very limited incomes. Whatever may be said about the very real need for legitimate low-priced editions of American books, it should be stressed that the price of pirated editions is low because the pirate has photo offset technology on his side; he has none of the editorial costs of the publisher from whom he steals; he pays nothing to the individual(s) whose creativity produced the work; he profits from the promotion of the legitimate version of the book. Yet, there is little evidence that he relates his prices to the market in the manner of legitimate publishers. For a popular book, the pirate's price may be only slightly less than that of the original foreign edition and, in certain rare instances, may be even higher. In sum, as one Third World publisher observed, "the problems of distributing pirated works point to people with considerable business acumen, capital, and international connections, not the bookstore with a multilith who will produce a single copy of a book for you at a penny per page." They are not "Robin Hoods." In fact, book pirates work with far better profit margins than the original publishers, and could afford to sell at much lower prices than they do.

Legitimate authors, booksellers, and publishers in Third World countries are as affected by piracy as their counterparts in the developed world. If the bookseller imports a book at legitimate prices, or if the publisher legitimately acquires rights to foreign books for local publication, they find themselves unable to compete with pirated products that appear locally, or are imported from some of the major identified piracy states. (Singapore, Korea, and Taiwan are the primary pirates, as newly industrialized countries. Just behind them come India, Indonesia, Iran, Malaysia, the Philippines, the Dominican Republic, and Nigeria.) The development in a country of a domestic community of writers, poets, and intellectuals also suffers, as legitimate publishers of domestic writings cannot compete with the prices of pirated foreign books.

Since copyrights involve civil as well as criminal law, foreign publishers and importers have brought damage suits against pirates in local courts, sometimes with support from the original foreign copyright holder, in the case of U.K. or U.S. publishers. In Pakistan, a country where piracy was at one time almost an official industry, the publishers and booksellers association has removed known pirates from their membership; bookseller members may boycott all titles from a recognized pirate, and not just the illegal ones; association publishers refuse to sell books to retailers and other distributors who persist in stocking pirated works. There are variations on these approaches in other countries—such as cooperation on identifying pirates, and their outlets for foreign publishers, so that boycotts can be organized or suits brought—that underscore the importance of acting in concert with legitimate publishers abroad and the importance of avoiding unilateral actions that damage allies.

One important element of copyright law that reenforces the need for cooperation is the fact that the equal treatment principal is the basis of all copyright law, i.e., the same protection is given to the rights of a foreign author as is given to the rights of a country's citizens. The stroke of a legislative pen can therefore diminish the rights of a native population in the interest of ensuring access to similar foreign works without violating *any* conventions. This potential weakness in copyright law could, if acted upon in any extensive way abroad, do great damage to all copyright relations. Special attention is given to it in the recent report of the President's Advisory Commission on Industrial Competitiveness, which concludes that a rewrite of copyright treaties may be necessary to ensure that U.S. copyright holders receive a basic, fair treatment without regard to how a country treats its own intellectuals.[6] As the commission notes, this is not a theoretical concern in view of the new informational technologies. Japan recently declared that computer software is *not* copyrightable, affecting its own producers but by ready extension making American software available without royalty payment.

Coping with pirates is also a matter for joint public sector and private industry action. In the U.S., the American Copyright Council has been formed, by producers and licensees of copyrights, to educate the American public on copyrights and their importance, so that citizens will understand the legislation and international action that may be necessary to protect American copyrights in new technological fields. The International Intellectual Property Alliance is a coalition of U.S. copyright industry associations (for books, records, films, computer software, etc.) formed in mid-1984 to express common concerns about piracy to the U.S. government and to work with government agencies and Congress in dealing with the problem. The alliance presented a report to President Reagan on May 1, 1985, not yet accessed by the Reid Foundation Study Group, which asks for high level coordinated approaches to a problem it says has reached "crisis proportions."[7]

The International Committee for the Protection of Intellectual Property Rights (ICPIPR) was formed at meetings during the Frankfurt International Book Fair in October, 1984, and consisted initially of publishers from six countries who agreed to form a common front against the pirates. American and British publishers are among these six along with, among others, Mahmud Mirza of Pakistan, well known for his pro-copyright stance and a discussant of the Reid Foundation Study Group concerning the anti-piracy efforts in Pakistan described previously. An extensive reporting form has been drafted by the ICPIPR to provide present and future members with a uniform reporting system on pirates and booksellers handling pirated works, where possible providing information on pirates' country of origin. (Legitimate publishing in Pakistan and India is threatened as much by pirates in Singapore as it is by any illegal domestic producers.) The major copyright producers of English-language books in the U.S. and the United Kingdom have created war chests with which to bring civil suits against major pirates in their own home countries, including those countries where there are no copyright laws but there are tort laws covering damages and/or unfair business practices.

---

[6] Report of the President's Commission on Individual Competitiveness, *Global Competition: The New Reality* 2 Vols (Washington, D.C.: Government Printing Office; 1985). See especially Appendix D: "A Special Report on the Protection of Intellectual Copyright."

[7] "U.S. Coalition Suggests Anti-Piracy Actions," *Publishers Weekly,* April 26, 1985, p. 17.

There are limits to what can be practically accomplished through civil action by the private sector, however, and this is particularly true of suits in distant courts by foreign copyright holders. Such actions are expensive, uncertain as to outcome in the case of foreign complaints before a national court, and interminable in many countries where civil dockets are reportedly more backlogged with cases than those of U.S. courts. Viewing piracy as a criminal act that a local government will aggressively punish is the most effective long-range approach to this continuing problem. That, of course, requires a willingness with respect to copyright protection that is not always present in Third World countries. Action by legitimate publishers and producers of copyrightable material, who are citizens of the country in which the piracy occurs, to influence a particular government is one way to obtain stronger criminal sanctions. In Pakistan, for example, publishers propose seeking a court ruling to the effect that copyright is theft as defined by Islamic law, and thus its punishment should be that dictated by the Koran for theft. Since Islamic Gulf states do not have copyright laws, it is believed that a favorable decision in Pakistan would have a ripple effect in more conservative Islamic countries.

Piracy has never previously been of such concern to so many in the executive and legislative branches in the U.S. as it is now, when America's balance of trade is so critically negative, and all agencies of both arms of government are addressing the need for expanded foreign trade. A U.S. International Trade Commission (USITC) study of counterfeiting[8] established that the estimated monetary loss to U.S. industry abroad due to deceptive imitation and patent, trademark, and copyright infringements is $8 billion per year. Hence, the alliance of U.S. copyright industries previously cited is finding many more attentive ears in Washington as the U.S. trade deficit grows. Piracy, it is agreed, must be stopped, even as efforts are made to expand legitimate U.S. copyright trade. Governmental bodies now focused on copyright include the Working Panel on Copyright of the Cabinet Council on Commerce and Trade (the council is chaired by the U.S. President or Secretary of Commerce), the Department of State Advisory Committee on Intellectual Property's International Copyright Panel, the Office of the U.S. Trade Representative Trade Policy Staff Committee on Intellectual Property, and the National Security Council.

What the copyright industries and the government were particularly interested in during 1984 was U.S. government influence on other governments through bilateral and multilateral trade agreements, as well as assistance and development programs that might influence foreign copyright

---

[8] *The Effects of Foreign Product Counterfeiting on U.S. Industry,* (Washington, D.C.: USITC, 1984).

policy.[9] The Caribbean Basin Economic Recovery Act (P.L. 98-67; 97 Stat. 369), enacted by Congress in 1983 in pursuance of President Reagan's Caribbean Basin Initiative (CBI), presaged 1984 copyright activity by requiring that the adequacy and effectiveness of copyright laws in countries requesting beneficiary designation under CBI be a consideration in the designation process. Foreign governments seeking CBI beneficiary status must demonstrate the adequacy and fairness of their laws. The cited 1984 Copyright Office report identifies the *ineligibility* of American copyrights for protection, and the *inadequacy* and *ineffectiveness* of protection as areas with which the U.S. government should concern itself internationally. The president of the U.S. must certify the adequacy of the laws of CBI applicants in determining whether an applicant state is eligible for CBI assistance.

The General System of Preferences Renewal Act of 1984, in extending tariff concessions for developing countries through mid-1993, also places emphasis on protection of U.S. intellectual property rights as a consideration in General System of Preferences (GSP) negotiations. GSP concessions give duty-free status to certain Third World products, thus enabling eligible countries to compete effectively in U.S. markets with the prices of industrialized countries. The 1984 renewal act gives the president discretionary powers over extension of preferential status to additional developing countries, renewal of status, and revocation or diminishment of GSP privileges in the case of countries already on the schedule, if such countries do not give reasonable and effective protection to U.S. copyrights. GSP requirements that any one developing country's trade with the U.S. on a specified product cannot exceed 50 percent of total U.S. imports of that product can be waived by the president under the terms of the extension act under certain circumstances: e.g., as an incentive for a country to improve its copyright protection. This new GSP legislation also requires the executive branch to develop a catalog over the next two years concerning the status of copyright protection in GSP countries and deliver it to Congress. Several newly industrialized countries identified as major exporters of pirated intellectual property (Singapore, South Korea, and Taiwan) will be faced with the choice of either losing concessions, in one case valued at $150 million, or revising their copyright laws.

The Trade Agreement Extension Act of October, 1984, also enacted by Congress in the closing days of its 1984 session, underscores the seriousness of the U.S. government's plan to counteract piracy through economic relations. Revisions of the act in this 1984 renewal state that any law, policy, or practice which denies adequate and effective protection to U.S. copyright holders is "unreasonable" and "unjustifiable." Section 302 (19 U.S.C. 2412)

---

[9] The 1984 U.S. Copyright Office study and the newly released May, 1985, report of the International Alliance both address economic approaches at length.

of the act provides that any interested party can petition the U.S. Trade Representative alleging acts by a foreign government with whom we have economic relations that negate such protections. The purpose of such a petition is to request an investigation of the allegation that, if found valid, must then be the subject of trade agreement negotiation. This legislation places particular emphasis on the cooperative efforts of U.S. publishers and their legitimate foreign partners to systematically identify acts of piracy, providing a remedial use for information.

On the procedural and administrative side (e.g., action that can be taken without new legislation) the Commerce Department has officially communicated to all embassies the importance of copyright to U.S. trade interests and instructed commercial attachés and officers to monitor the local marketplace on a continuing basis, to identify pirated works and communicate information about them to the Commerce Department for action. A handbook on copyright law and piracy for embassy use is being prepared as a joint effort of the American copyright industries, the International Alliance, and the Commerce Department. The new anti-piracy economic weapons that Congress has provided to the executive branch make this collection of information by the Commerce Department a practical base for concerted public and private action.

Many discussants to the Reid Foundation Study Group believe that because of USIA's special status as a link between American and foreign cultural communities the agency should limit its copyright-oriented activities to an informational and educational role, and not become involved in the government's direct monitoring of civil and criminal piracy activities. An example of the educational involvement by USIA that book industry discussants favor was its production of a videotape on piracy (in cooperation with the AAP) to be shown at book fairs and other international events attended by publishers and foreign government officials concerned with copyright. Initial showings, in September, 1984, at the Barcelona International Book Fair (Liber '84) and, one month later, at the USIA national stand at the Frankfurt International Book Fair, produced positive reactions from foreign publishers, including requests for additional showings in their countries. However, showing such a tape at those two fairs was preaching to the already converted in a sense; a greater test of the videotape's effectiveness will come at Third World book fairs and events in 1985.

As response to this tape suggests, USIA is particularly well suited to the communication of American views on copyrights to scholarly, educational, and cultural communities, since these groups and the various media make up the agency's primary audiences. The American Copyright Council, mentioned herein as the private sector institution focusing on increasing domestic appreciation of the importance of copyright, is likely to have programs and materials adaptable to USIA needs. In the long run, such an educational effort by the agency may be its most effective function.

Discussants on copyright feel that USIA's response to the National Security Council should also include assurance that the agency's officers understand that U.S. law precludes their participation in any cultural or informational activity in which improperly licensed American copyright materials are used and that they should communicate this position to foreign groups with whom they work. There has been no new USIA policy statement on copyright for more than two decades, and the applicability of copyright in annual country program plans is no longer mentioned in instructions on country plan preparation sent to USIA posts. Some discussants stress that copyright education of USIA officers must be a prime agency objective in connection with its book programs.

While this study has described the importance of copyright law in America's international trade and political relations and the encouraging steps that are being taken to curb piracy, it is important to stress that illegal publication is but a symptom resulting from the more fundamental problems of U.S. books abroad—the shortages of affordable American books in Third World countries and the continuing difficulty in obtaining American books facing these countries. Economic sanctions against piracy are, in fact, not likely to accomplish their objectives without great resentment, unless the other elements of an effective U.S. book program described in this study are implemented. Suggesting that many thieves steal because they are needy is not intended to apologize for or excuse piracy, nor should antiquated nineteenth-century copyright laws and situations in the U.S. or any other country be considered acceptable today as justification for new generations of pirates. However, barring stolen goods only emphasizes that there must be a concerted effort to eliminate genuine need legitimately.

It is suggested that the U.S. Books Abroad Task Force and other groups concerned with copyright should consider specifics of this chapter for recommendation and/or implementation—e.g., U.S. accession to the Berne Convention, enhancement of INCINC's activities, and an active role for USIA in the area of copyright education among its foreign constituencies and its overseas book programs. Undoubtedly, the Task Force will also want to endorse the economic approaches to halting piracy that government and industry have jointly developed and also recommend expansion of such activities into political and cultural areas. In the previously cited September, 1984, study, the Copyright Office recommended to Congress that, either bilaterally or multilaterally, the U.S. should seek to clarify its relations with those 61 countries identified by the Copyright Office as ones with which our copyright relations are "unclear"—ultimately through their signature accession to the UCC or Berne Convention, but immediately through bilateral agreements still provided for in the U.S. Copyright Act of 1976. Additionally, it is suggested that America's goal in this area should be worldwide recognition of copyrights and universal protection, including those countries with whom the U.S. today has no copyright relations at all. As one publisher observed, there is no longer any country that is not a market for the books of other nations.

PART II

ECONOMICS AND FINANCE

4

Government Export Financial Support Programs

Donald E. McNeil

Viewed strictly as commodities that contribute to a favorable trade balance, books have not been significant enough in export sales statistics to warrant the kind of attention given to glamor products such as those of high technology. Consequently, since concern about their political and cultural importance has been in remission in Washington for many years, there are now no government assistance programs outside of USIA aimed specifically at stimulating book exports and copyright sales. What is available is a matrix of tax incentives, special antitrust waivers, types of export insurance, loans, and loan guarantees intended to generally promote export activity with applicability to the U.S. book industry.

TAX INCENTIVES

The tax incentive programs identified in this study are institutional. Such programs call for the establishment of subsidiaries or independent companies devoted almost exclusively to the export segment of an enterprise that are eligible for tax deferrals and/or tax exemptions, for at least part of their export earnings. Such incentives are available in Domestic International Sales Corporations (DISC) and Foreign Sales Corporations (FSC). DISCs, as their name implies, are located in the U.S. and incorporated in the U.S. FSCs must be incorporated in a foreign country (one that the Treasury Department recognizes as having a satisfactory agreement with the U.S., for exchange of tax information), or in a U.S. possession other than Puerto Rico.

Domestic International Sales Corporations

Subject to modifications relative to income deferral and interest thereon that makes them "interest charge DISCs," provided for in the Tax Reform Act of 1984, DISCs are companies incorporated under the laws of any U.S. state or territory solely for the purpose of exporting property produced in the United States.[1] Export incentives in the form of tax deferral have been available to qualifying DISCs since they were created by Congress in 1971. To qualify for such deferrals, the DISC must, in addition to the domestic incorporation requirement: have only one class of stock; have outstanding capital stock with a par or stated value of at least $2,500; elect to be treated as a DISC by filing with the IRS and have shareholders pay income tax on income deferred as a result; and must satisfy the gross receipts and gross assets tests (i.e., at least 95 percent of the corporation's gross receipts must consist of *qualified export receipts,* and at least 95 percent of the corporation's assets must consist of *qualified export assets* as defined by the U.S. tax code).

Qualified export receipts are those derived from the sale or lease for use outside the U.S. of export property, or from the furnishing of services related or subsidiary to such sales or leases. Managerial services provided to an unrelated DISC, and interest on any obligation that is a qualified asset, are also export receipts. The property being sold or leased must be manufactured, produced, grown, or extracted in the United States. Generally, exports subsidized by the U.S. do not qualify. Clearly, the income from books produced in the U.S. and sold by a DISC does qualify as export receipts. However, DISC benefits are not allowed for copyright licenses and other intangibles.

Qualified export assets include inventories, export property, necessary operational equipment and supplies to the extent they are used for export, trade receivables from export sales, producers' loans, working capital, obligations of domestic corporations organized solely to finance export sales under Export-Import Bank (Eximbank) guaranty agreements, and obligations issued, guaranteed, or insured by the Eximbank or the Federal Credit Insurance Administration. (Insurance, loans, and guarantees are discussed later in this chapter.)[2]

The profits of a qualified DISC are not taxed to the DISC; shareholders are subject to tax on certain "deemed distribution" required by the tax code, and actual distributions out of deferred income, when it occurs. The maximum tax deferral benefit is 1.7 percent of gross receipts or 21.25 percent of combined taxable income. Retained earnings must be held in the form of qualified export assets as described above. Included in the list of qualified

---

[1] Internal Revenue Code, Sections 991–997, as amended by the Tax Reform Act of 1984, *Congressional Record,* June 22, 1984, H6634.

[2] *Ibid.*

export assets are inventory and accounts receivable. This makes possible, for example, more competitive pricing or credit terms for book buyers by a U.S. DISC, since accounts receivable can be financed by deferred taxes and income rather than interest-bearing loans.

The creation of DISC has, however, been a subject of dispute with other member states of the General Agreement on Tariffs and Trade (GATT),[3] who contended that DISC amounted to an illegal export subsidy. A GATT panel determined in 1976 that DISC did have some characteristics of an illegal export subsidy, pointing to the failure to charge interest on deferred taxes as the specific offending subsidy.

Although the U.S. did not concede that DISC violated GATT, the federal government did agree in December, 1981, to the adoption of the 1976 GATT Panel Report, subject to a GATT council decision that was understood to qualify the panel's findings. That 1981 decision provided that GATT signatories are not required to tax export income attributable to economic activities occurring outside their territorial limits. The decision report also stated that "arm's length" pricing principles should be observed in transactions between exporting enterprises and foreign buyers. Finally, the 1981 decision stated that the GATT does not prohibit the adoption of measures to avoid the double taxation of foreign source income. This did not resolve the dispute with the European Economic Community (EEC), which insisted that DISC was an illegal subsidy because it allowed indefinite deferral of direct taxes on income from exports earned in the United States. The EEC estimated that DISC provided more than $2 billion in subsidies for U.S. exports to member countries of the EEC alone over the 10 years since DISCs were created by Congress. The U.S. made a commitment to GATT to propose legislation that would address the concerns of GATT, although the U.S. did not agree with the EEC views on DISC.

In March, 1983, an administration proposal to Congress modified the DISC and also provided a territorial system of taxation for U.S. export firms as an alternative. The result was the Foreign Sales Corporation Act of 1984, providing for the formation of a new entity—the FSC—beginning January 1, 1985. The Tax Reform Act of 1984 incorporated the FSC provision into new sections 991 through 997 and section 291(a)(4) of the tax code. An exporter can keep its original DISC or start a new one, with enhanced deferral benefits for income derived on up to $10 million of export sales, provided an (tax deductible) interest charge at Treasury Bill rates is paid by its shareholders to the IRS on the accumulated tax deferrals. The details for operating the "interest charge DISC" have not been changed from those described for prior

[3] The basic multilateral agreement among major trading countries under which reciprocal efforts to reduce barriers to free trade are regularly initiated, monitored, and modified.

[4] Senate Finance Committee Report on the Tax Reform Act of 1984, Appendix D: Title V-Foreign Sales Corporations, Part A. "Present Laws" reviews DISC history.

DISCs, except that a new election will have to be made and reported to IRS for existing DISCs as well as new ones, and the tax year of the new DISC must match that of its majority stockholder. The DISC requirements were effective January 1, 1985. The tax treatment of the interest charged to DISC is different in that the income tax on 94 percent of its income may be deferred if the income is retained by the DISC in qualified assets, and no incremental rules will apply to the first $10 million of DISC deferrals. (There are no tax deferral benefits for the excess of exports handled by a DISC over $10 million.)

Foreign Sales Corporations

While DISC is retained under the 1984 tax reforms with enhanced benefits it is clear from the congressional committee reports on tax reform, material available from the Commerce Department, and discussants in the book trade, that the real intention of the enabling legislation is to focus tax incentives on Foreign Sales Corporations, which may be initiated beginning January 1, 1985. FSCs are incorporated under the laws of a foreign country with which the U.S. has a satisfactory agreement for exchange of tax information, or a U.S. possession defined as the U.S. Virgin Islands, American Samoa, Guam, or the Northern Marianas (not Puerto Rico). The FSC must have at least one director who is not a U.S. resident, and keep one set of its books of account (including copies of invoices) at its main offshore office. Like the DISC, the offshore corporation must file an election to become an FSC with the IRS.[5]

A list of 24 countries that exchange tax information with the U.S., and are thus eligible as locations for an FSC, was issued by the Treasury Department in November, 1984. The following treaty countries have been certified by the Treasury Department for FSC purposes at the time of this book's publication:

Australia	France	Netherlands
Austria	Germany	New Zealand
Barbados	Iceland	Norway
Belgium	Ireland	Pakistan
Canada	Jamaica	Philippines
Denmark	Korea	South Africa
Egypt	Malta	Sweden
Finland	Morocco	Trinidad and Tobago

Treaty parties not listed above may subsequently be certified at any time by the IRS, upon publication of a notice to that effect in the Federal Register. Would-be incorporators of an FSC will also want to investigate the incorporation laws of each IRS-certified country, the income tax rates on foreign

---

[5] Ibid.

corporations located there, and its proximity to particular markets, among other considerations, before deciding where to locate an FSC.

As described for the Reid Foundation Study Group by John T. Sullivan, Jr., director of the Office of Trade Finance, Department of Commerce,[6] an FSC can obtain corporate tax exemption on a portion of the earnings generated by the sale or lease of export property and services related and subsidiary to the export of such property. (The only pure service export related to the book industry that qualifies for the exemption is export management service for an unrelated FSC.) Manufacturers, non-manufacturers, and export groups such as export representatives and export trading companies can form FSCs. An FSC can function as a principal, buying and selling books for its own account (similar to a wholesaler), or as a commission agent for specific publishers. It can be related to a manufacturing parent or can be an independent merchant or broker.

The portion of FSC income exempt from U.S. corporate taxation will be 32 percent, according to Mr. Sullivan, if the FSC buys from independent suppliers or uses the tax code section 482 "arms length" pricing rules with related suppliers, e.g., a publisher shareholder in the FSC ownership. However, special administrative pricing rules (safe haven rules) are available, if the FSC is supplied by a related entity. The first such rule will allow FSCs to share the profit from export transactions on the basis of 23 percent allocated to the FSC and 77 percent allocated to the related supplier. If the FSC then conducts the required minimum of activity outside U.S. customs territory, 16/23 of its 23 percent of profit would be exempt from U.S. corporate taxation, equal to 16 percent of the total combined profit of the FSC and the supplier.

An alternative, particularly for FSCs with low profit-margin exports purchased from related suppliers, is for the FSC to take as its share of combined income 1.38 percent of gross receipts, not to exceed 46 percent of combined income. Then, 1.27 percent of those gross receipts, not to exceed 32 percent of combined income, would be exempt from corporate taxation, provided the FSC conducts the required minimum of "offshore" activity. (If shareholders of the FSC are corporations, the limit or exemption is 30 percent and 15 percent instead of the 32 percent and 16 percent stated above.)

Administrative pricing rules can also be used to determine the amount of commissions available to a commission agent FSC. However, under either of the administrative pricing rules, the commission agent or buy-sell FSC will be required to perform by itself, or by contract, all of the following activities, to the extent they are performed at all with respect to the export transaction in question: (1) solicit, negotiate, and make the contract of sale; (2) provide

---

[6] Letter of December 13, 1984, from John T. Sullivan to Donald E. McNeil, Reid Foundation, with enclosures.

advertising and sales promotion; (3) process customer orders and arrange for delivery; (4) provide for transportation; (5) assemble and transmit final invoices and receive payment; and (6) assume the credit risk. For FSCs generating more than $5 million in export sales to obtain the corporate tax exemption on qualifying income, some, but far from all of the above listed activities are required to be performed, either directly or by contract, outside the U.S. customs territory.

An FSC must perform the following three categories of "offshore" activity outside the United States customs territory (these are the only activities a qualified FSC must perform offshore):

1. Participate by itself, or by contract, in one of the three following transactions giving rise to qualified export sales—(a) solicitation of sale, (b) negotiation of terms of sale, and (c) making of the contract of sale;
2. Participate by itself, or by contract, in activities accounting for 50 percent of the aggregated direct costs of all five of the following, or accounting for 85 percent of the direct costs for each of two of the following—(a) advertising and sales promotion, (b) processing customer orders and arranging delivery, (c) transportation, (d) determination and transmittal of final invoice or statement of account and receipt of payment, (e) assumption of credit risk; and
3. To the extent they are performed at all, conduct the following activities completely outside the U.S. customs territory—(a) FSC shareholder and board of directors meetings, (b) disbursement of dividends, accounting fees, legal fees, and board of directors salaries, (c) maintain principal bank account.

An FSC that, along with any affiliated FSC, generates less than $5 million in foreign trading company gross receipts per year will not be required to undertake any activities outside the U.S. customs territory, except to incorporate offshore; have an office outside of the U.S. (that may be shared by others); have at least one director residing outside of the U.S.; maintain periodic statements of operations and summary statements of sales, as well as a complete set of records, in the U.S.; file an election to be a small FSC with the IRS.

FSCs present an export opportunity for those small and middle-sized book publishers who had long hesitated to tap foreign markets in the face of the complexities that the international marketplace represented. An FSC can be formed by a combination of up to 25 stockholders (read 25 companies) and, if their export experience is indeed limited, they can contract with another FSC to provide managerial services. Edward Malinowski, president of U.S.A. Book Expo and one who has enthusiastically followed development of the FSC legislation, recommends the U.S. Virgin Islands as a location for FSCs without significant foreign experience, and Mr. Malinowski believes that in not too many years such FSCs will be numerous in the book industry, creating a new U.S. corporate presence abroad. U.S.A. Book Expo is, as of this writing, the only book-related company formed to take advantage of export trading company (ETC) legislation (see below). The FSC Act provides that FSCs can be owned by export trading companies, among others, and thus offer a linkage of tax incentives with the special capital potential and wherewithal of the ETC legislation.

EXPORT TRADING COMPANIES

The export trading companies have a long commercial history. The Dutch, British, and—most recently—the Japanese have been highly successful in penetrating international markets through the consolidated marketing, financial, and managerial efforts made possible by ETCs. Hence, in the context of the continuing federal interest in seeing that American industries have available to them all legitimate approaches to maintaining and enhancing their competitive positions in international trade, Congress enacted the Export Trading Act of 1982.[7] President Reagan signed the legislation in October, 1982, in a special ceremony in San Francisco designed to call attention to the importance his administration places on this legislation as a way to increase our exports.

Like DISC and FSC laws, export trading company legislation represents special institutional concessions to the demands of international trade. In this legislation, the objective is not tax incentives. (ETCs can, as reported herein, themselves form FSCs to obtain those benefits.) Two major impediments to the formation of ETCs removed by the 1982 legislation were the uncertain application of U.S. antitrust laws to cooperative export activities, and restrictions against bank participation in owning or investing in ETCs.

ETC Objectives

The ETC Act has three major objectives: the capitalization of the export trade industry; suppression of fears concerning antitrust liability when involved in export activities; and tapping the potential of small and medium-size manufacturing and service firms by gaining economies of scale in the exportation of their goods and services through joint ventures, or by forming a large export trading company that can take title to these goods.

Under Title I of the ETC Act, the Office of Export Trading Companies, Department of Commerce, was set up to handle the day-to-day monitoring of these companies. Included in the functioning of this office are the basic responsibilities for promoting, educating, counselling, and facilitating contact

[7] Price Waterhouse and the Council for Export Trading Companies, *The Export Trading Company Guidebook* (Washington, D.C.: ITA, Commerce, 1984).

between producers and providers of trade facilitation services: for example, if a publisher wants to work with an existing ETC related to his field rather than developing one, the Commerce Department ETC office will provide names of all registered ETCs concerned with the book field.

Under Title II, bank holding companies have been allowed to invest in ETC ventures, and may hold up to 100 percent ownership. To add more working capital to the exportation of American goods and services the Eximbank has also introduced the Guaranteed Loan Program described below.

Under Title III, a certificate of review process was set up, establishing a written pre-clearance of defined export conduct which grants immunity from prosecution under state and federal antitrust laws. While these regulations cannot prevent private civil actions from being filed, they can discourage such actions by reducing the benefits one can gain through a civil action.

ETC Advantages

Department of Commerce officials believe that the act enables publishers to expand exports of their products in a number of ways. The first and most obvious is that the ETC enables competitors to take part in joint activities to facilitate exports that reduce overseas costs, while expanding fulfillment capabilities through combined efforts. Instead of competing against each other, publishers with complementary or related titles can develop strategies allowing these categories to complement each other in foreign markets. In addition, an ETC could facilitate the sale of translation and reprint rights by allowing interested foreign companies to contact one source rather than attempting to deal with each individual U.S. publisher. This could be an effective adjunct to efforts to fight piracy.

Other advantages cited in Commerce Department papers prepared specifically for this study include:

1. ETCs will generally assume the risks associated with international trade by taking domestic title to products and performing subsequent export operations. Economies of scale, often unavailable to small or medium-size firms individually, are generated by exporting large volumes of products from many sources at lower per-unit cost through an established network of foreign offices, transportation, insurance, warehousing, etc. Exclusive agreements could be signed with foreign distributors or agents in order to ensure proper representation in each market.
2. ETCs can monitor markets more efficiently and are better equipped to recognize potential opportunities. By virtue of their combined size, some ETCs may offer a wide range of products, secure more favorable prices, or develop additional marketing opportunities denied manufacturers acting alone. By combining orders, an ETC can bargain for lower freight, insurance, and storage costs than individual small-or-medium-sized pro-

ducers. An ETC, for example, could develop long-range agreements with a transportation company at a reduced cost, to carry a prescribed amount of books every year or month.

3. For book publishers, ETCs should be able to provide comprehensive market research at minimal expense per firm. The ability to share overseas market information among U.S. firms secure from antitrust actions is another strong incentive to engage in ETC operations.

It should be noted that many of these advantages are not considered "new" by some long in the book export business, and are already available to publishers through export representatives such as Feffer & Simons and Kaiman & Polon, and through large wholesalers such as Baker & Taylor and Key Books. It is likely that some of those service corporations will pursue FSCs and possibly ETCs, exporting companies doing so independently or in cooperation with publishers they represent.

Cooperation with the Eximbank

The U.S. Export-Import Bank (Eximbank) has just introduced a guarantee program that will enable export trading companies to obtain short-term pre-export loans that can be used to finance export-related activities when they cannot arrange such loans from the private credit markets.

Eximbank's new ETC Loan Guarantee Program has been developed in accordance with the provisions of the ETC Act of 1982, and should be especially helpful to small, medium-size, and minority exporters or producers. The guarantee may cover individual loans or revolving lines of credit to export trading companies for specific, export-related activities. Any financial institution or other public or private creditor will be eligible to apply for Eximbank's ETC Loan Guarantee. The terms of the guaranteed loan will generally be from one month to one year, but may be longer if necessary. The guarantee will cover 90 percent of the principal amount of the loan and interest up to the U.S. Treasury rate for similar maturities plus 1 percent to the date of default.

The applicant must demonstrate to Eximbank's satisfaction that the loan would not be made without Eximbank guarantee and that it will facilitate additional exports. Eximbank will require that the borrower provide collateral in the form of inventory of exportable goods or export accounts receivable. The value of the collateral must be equal to at least 110 percent of the loan value. Eximbank will not impose any interest rate ceiling on the lender, but will monitor the rates and fees being charged. Eximbank's guarantee fee will be 1 percent of the loan amount for maturities of 180 days or less, 1.5 percent for maturities of 181 days to one year, and 0.5 percent for each additional six months. The program will be administered by the bank's Exporter Credits and Guarantees Division.

Export Insurance, Loan Guarantees, Working Capital

The Reid Foundation Study Group established that eight government agencies are significantly involved in the promotion of U.S. exports through provision of business insurance, political risk insurance, loan guarantees, and working capital loans. The agencies are the departments of Commerce and Agriculture; the Agency for International Development (AID); the Office of the U.S. Trade Representative; the U.S. Trade and Development Program (Bureau of Private Enterprise Affairs, AID); the Export-Import Bank; the Small Business Administration; and the Overseas Private Investment Corporation. To attempt to catalog all of these agencies' programs, and list the other agencies that provide limited services for U.S. businesses seeking to export or invest abroad is beyond the scope of this report and its time constraints. In any event, *Washington's Best Kept Secrets* preceded us, a cooperative effort by the eight listed agencies. It is a primer on how to begin to tap Washington resources in almost any aspect of exports, from market research to finance.[8] In the areas with which this Task Force is concerned, the following characterizations are meant to be only indicative.

Export-Import Bank

The Working Capital Guarantee Program of the Eximbank was extended to ETCs pursuant to the 1982 ETC Act described above. Similar loan guarantee programs are available to individual private companies. Eximbank credit insurance policies are serviced by the Foreign Credit Insurance Association (FCIA), a group of 50 insurance companies. The private companies underwrite the commercial credit risks; Eximbank covers political risks and reinsures certain "excess commercial risks." Policies give protection for the riskiest part of asset portfolios: foreign receivables. With this insurance, businesses can have access to higher risk markets and compete with the credit terms of foreign businesses.

Political insurance covers expropriation, cancellation of licenses, and unexpected currency controls. The Eximbank says most publishers can get short term durable goods coverage. If not paid in 180 days, the exporter files a convertibility claim. He must then wait 365 days for payment. One Reid Foundation Study Group discussant says FCIA losses have been rising so fast that the association companies have become reluctant to insure, and are now asking the Eximbank to consider all or most failures as "excess commercial risks" and finance them directly. FCIA insurance rates are at 2½ percent of

---

[8] William A. Delphos, ed., *Washington's Best Kept Secrets, A U.S. Government Guide to International Business* (New York: John Wiley & Sons, 1984).

accounts receivable now in many cases, and some publishers indicate that they are self-insured because they cannot afford that rate.

Overseas Private Investment Corporation

Investments in businesses located in foreign countries are insured by the Overseas Private Investment Corporation (OPIC) against three major types of political risks: inability to convert local currency from profits, earnings, or return of capital (OPIC insures against adverse discriminatory exchange rates as well); expropriation; and war, revolution, etc.

OPIC direct loans are for ventures in the $100,000 to $4 million range, and are made to U.S. small businesses defined as smaller than the smallest firm on the *Fortune 1000* listing. Interest rates are at commercial equivalents, but vary according to the project's financial and political risk.

The OPIC Loan Guarantee Program is available to all businesses regardless of size. OPIC will issue a guaranty under which funding can be obtained from a variety of U.S. financial institutions. Interest rates are comparable to those of other U.S. guaranteed loans. The guarantee fee, ranging from 1½ to 3 percent, depends upon a project's commercial and political risk, not its country of location. Both commercial and political risks are covered.

The Contractors and Exporters Program provides insurance on political risks when foreign projects require standby letters of credit on bid, performance, or advance payment guarantees. This insurance protects against arbitrary or unfair drawing of such letters of credit. Protection is also available against the risks of currency inconvertibility, confiscation of tangible assets and bank accounts, war, and civil strife.

Feasibility study assistance provides up to 40 percent of such a study's cost (60 percent in the case of small business) on a reimbursable basis. For small businesses, funding is provided by an interest-free reimbursable grant. Repayment over two years is required only if the investor moves forward with the project. Small businesses may also apply for a grant of up to $5,000 to cover travel costs and per diem associated with visiting a country for the first time to assess its investment climate. For larger firms, a two-year loan is available at a rate generally equivalent to two-thirds of the prime rate. Such studies may be related by publishers to marketing needs in relationship to FSC.

Special grants and loans are available for training and educating host country nationals involved in OPIC-supported projects. Funding is on a concessional loan basis not exceeding $50,000. In all cases, project sponsors must contribute at least 25 percent of the cost. For nonprofit entities such as voluntary organizations and foundations, grants and loans are available from OPIC to initiate programs for assisting in the transfer of technology to developing countries or to facilitate U.S. investments. Generally, they are multi-year undertakings of approximately $100,000 annually.

Agency for International Development (AID)

In some countries (currently 10), AID has provided loans or grant assistance in the form of Commodity Import Programs (CIPs), which finance the procurement of a wide variety of basic commodity imports. Funds are allocated by the foreign government to its various ministries and to the private sector to provide the foreign exchange needed to purchase such things. AID publishes lists of importers to assist suppliers. AID commodity eligibility lists include certain kinds of books and exclude others. They also include categories of magazines.

AID also provides project loans or grants to finance specific facilities and undertakings. Commodities purchased under these undertakings are called project procurements. As in CIPs, AID does almost no buying. There is no foreign country private sector involvement in the project. Procurement grants are made to foreign governments and ministries.

Small Business Administration

The focus of the Small Business Administration (SBA) is exclusively on assistance to small and middle-sized businesses of the kind that, numerically at least, make up the largest segment of the book industry. However, the SBA "opinion molder policy," codified in Section 120.2 of SBA's regulations, precludes SBA from granting financial assistance or other support to any opinion molder, defined as a concern that is "engaged in the creation, origination, expression, dissemination, propagation, or distribution of ideas, values, thoughts, opinions, or similar intellectual property, regardless of medium, form, or content."[9] S2084, 1984, sought to repeal this policy, retaining it only in cases where financial assistance would be adverse or detrimental to a legitimate public interest; and where the loan proceeds would be used primarily to promote or criticize political or religious ideas.

In his statement before the Committee on Small Business of the U.S. Senate on May 17, 1984, SBA administrator James C. Sanders noted that the rule is not new, having been adopted in 1953 from SBA's predecessor, the Reconstruction Finance Corporation. Over the years, SBA has promulgated seven regulatory exceptions, from job printing firms to general book or music (record) stores and merchandise stores that may sell books, newspapers, etc. The exceptions generally focus on the fact that such excepted companies do not advocate any particular viewpoint or idea. Mr. Sanders indicated that eight regulatory changes in the opinion molder policy have been proposed since 1980 alone, and none has been made final despite a plethora of comments received in response.

---

[9] James C. Sanders, "Statement . . . Before the Committee on Small Business, United States Senate, May 17, 1984" (Washington, D.C.: SBA Press Release).

Mr. Sanders indicated that the SBA was open to change such as proposed in S2084. SBA would have this apply to both direct and guaranteed loans. Furthermore, any determination by Congress with respect to alternatives must include in the legislation or accompanying legislative history language that further identifies the nature of the proscribed matter. A clear congressional finding as to the types of businesses ineligible for SBA assistance would be welcomed. Finally, SBA objected to the bill's requirement for a hearing with respect to determinations by SBA of proscribed activities. The agency favored further clarification of proposed exceptions, which would permit easier administration by financial assistance personnel and obviate the need for such hearings. This legislation has not moved forward since that time, but may be reintroduced. It is suggested that experiences with this problem in connection with government export oriented book programs in the past (chapter 5 and chapter 15) might contribute to resolution of the SBA problem, insofar as the SBA opinion molder rule affects assistance to small publishers and exporters. This rule is called to the attention of the U.S. Books Abroad Task Force in the context of its mandate, since SBA and the Eximbank signed agreements in 1984 that would provide export loans to small businesses.

The foregoing discussion of government programs and activities speaks volumes concerning the need for book industry education on international business discussed in chapter 10. The eight agencies charged with export expansion developed the guide edited by William A. Delphos and published by John Wiley & Sons, parallelling a joint multi-media effort by them to educate American businessmen directly on export program assistance. A teleconference was held among 50 cities, and 5,000 to 6,000 company representatives participated. The eight agencies presented their programs and were questioned by 11 businessmen on a panel who had actual experience with government programs and could focus on problematic areas, as well as relate their own experience with government programs. The private sector in each of the cities picked up part of the costs; the teleconference has since been made available in film form to public television. That approach touched only the surface and involved very few, if any, publishers. It should be considered by the Task Force in deciding how the programs discussed in this study can be communicated to the publishing industry in relevant terms that will evoke response. Perhaps the matter of an extended educational conference(s) should be referred to whatever institutions or committees are developed pursuant to chapter 13 of this study.

5

Currency Convertibility as a Barrier to Book Exports

Donald E. McNeil

The United States is the world's largest commercial book exporter, or at least it was in 1980, the most recent year for which firm market share data are available.[1] The American share of the total international book trade that year was 21.8 percent; the second largest exporter was the United Kingdom, with a 20.5 percent share. France and Germany followed, in that order.[2] Unfortunately, the data from which the Department of Commerce makes its comparisons is primarily collected and maintained by the United Nations in New York, and is obviously and seriously out of date because of varying reporting lags among UN members. (The Soviet Union does not report at all, and is not included.) Commerce expects to produce a 1981–82 report in 1985, which will give some insight into the trend at the beginning of this decade. What we know for certain at this writing is that the U.S. market share declined from 26 percent in 1975 to the 21.8 percent share posted in 1980. Hence, although U.S. exports increased in value and in quantity each year over the 1973–83 decade, total world demand for book imports increased at a more rapid pace. The price of U.S. books and the shortage of dollars available with which to import books or buy reprint and translation rights at any price are credited by international professionals as the root causes of the book gap. The strong

[1] Market Share Reports Commodity Series, SITC, No. 892.11, "Printed Books and Pamphlets 1978–80" (National Technical Information Service, Department of Commerce).

[2] "Market share" is a country's share of total exports from 14 largest supplier countries to the world, including to each other. See SITC No. 892.11.

exchange value of the dollar against other currencies compounded the pricing problem for both books and rights.

The impact of prices on the ability of the consumer to buy U.S. books presents a special challenge for those concerned about access in this study—access, that is, by the individual scholar, intellectual, opinion leader, professional, or student. Thus, while price is intimately intertwined with currency problems and costs, the Reid Foundation Study Group treats unit retail prices as a separate problem in chapter 6. Suffice it here to note from Commerce Department statistics that, while the value of U.S. book export sales increased 400 percent in the 1973–83 decade, units sold increased by only 25 percent in the same period. In addition, while foreign buyers spent $641.3 million to acquire American books in 1982, and $642.8 million in 1984, they received 45 million *fewer copies* in the latter year for their money.[3] Not all of that unit decline in 1984 is due to pricing, of course. Selection plays a part, as those who allocate dollars for imports where scarce hard currencies are controlled determine the categories of books to be imported based on need. Thus, the sale of U.S. professional, scholarly, scientific, technical, and medical books, and university textbooks in the natural sciences continues to increase, even though those categories are not only the highest priced books to begin with, but categories on which unit retail prices are seen as rising more rapidly. (The lowest priced hardcover books in these categories in 1983 according to industry statistics were medical books, at an average of $33.02. In trade paperback, medical books were also the lowest, averaging $14.32).[4]

Department of Commerce data showing book exports valued at $641.3 million in 1982 and $642.8 million in 1984 suggest relatively stable allocations of currency for book purchases on a global basis. However, assuming that demand remained constant, while the units purchasable with the allocations dropped by 45 million, there were insufficient dollars available to meet needs. Analysis of the Commerce Department's export data geographically reveals that the currency shortages of the developing countries are as profound as has been reported and growing. Almost $500 million of U.S. book exports in 1982, or 77 percent, were absorbed by just 17 markets: the English-speaking countries of Canada, the United Kingdom, Australia, New Zealand, South Africa, and Ireland bought 63 percent; Japan, the Philippines, and nine countries of Western Europe purchased 14 percent. In 1984, sales to those same countries totalled almost $540 million or 84 percent of what was exported. The most startling fact represented by these numbers is that the

---

[3] Except where otherwise noted, all export statistics are those of the Bureau of the Census, Department of Commerce, in the annual FT 446, Schedule B reports, "Commodity by Country" (see chapter 11).

[4] Chandler B. Grannis, "U.S. Book Title Output and Average Prices, Final Figures for 1983," *Publishers Weekly,* September 7, 1984.

other 131 countries, both developing and developed, on which Commerce has data were able to spend only $102.8 million to buy books from the U.S. in 1984—only 16 percent of total book exports. The book gap in the developing world is indeed as large as professionals have been stating for many years, and in a brief three years has grown substantially under the impact of current dollar gap problems.

Some specific observations on the movement of U.S. books into various developing areas in 1984 extracted from the Commerce data can further clarify the picture.

1. U.S. sales to Mexico, our largest Latin American customer, plunged 67 percent between 1982 and 1983 (15,753,584 copies to 5,024,753) then recovered slightly in 1984, with purchases rising to 6,117,132 books. Only Panama in Central America has not recovered from a 1983 dollar crisis, however. Except for Nicaragua, U.S. aid is thought to have had an impact on the situation in that area, with 1984 increases over 1982 of 350 percent (El Salvador), 80 percent (Costa Rica), and 40 percent (Guatemala). Even Nicaragua managed to allow enough dollars to increase purchases from 113, 690 in 1982 to 151,719 in 1984. But the Panama decline was from 960,437 units in 1982 to 670,049 in 1984.
2. In South America as a region, sales were off 18 percent between 1982 and 1983, and fell further in 1984 to 26 percent off 1982's 11,226,337 books. Argentine purchases from the U.S. have decreased 35 percent over the three-year 1982–84 span; sales to Peru were off 48 percent for the same time period; Chile's were down a similar 48 percent. But while Paraguay dropped by 66 percent, Uruguay almost disappeared from the market—100,844 in 1982 down to 16,007 in 1983, and then to 3,012 in 1984. Venezuela was off from 2,984,864 to 2,216,559 over the three years; Brazil was down to 2,133,406 in 1984 from 2,976,666 in 1982.
3. Africa south of the Sahara (except South Africa) has been a bleak market for American books, as for other commodities, for many years. Sales to the region fell from a modest enough 16,443,278 books in 1982 to 8,463,341 in 1983, not quite a 50 percent decline. Sales in only 10 countries exceeded 100,000 books in 1984. Nigeria, the country with the largest English literacy on the continent, most clearly demonstrated the worldwide dollar problem. Dependent on oil revenues for foreign currency, Nigerian book imports from the U.S. reflected the decline in oil prices. Nigerian book purchases from the U.S. were 13,745,609 copies in 1982, 5,463,048 in 1983, and 1,418,662 in 1984—a drop of almost 90 percent!

In our discussion of copyright law (chapter 3), it was reported that the lack of American dollars for imports, the strong value of the dollar, and the high retail price of American books have combined to stimulate the growth of book piracy, Third World demands for compulsory licensing, and declining legitimate translation and reprint rights sales for world or regional languages. As those political and economic stress signals convey, the impact of the dollar on the foreign book trade is pervasive. The U.S. cannot export to countries that do not have American dollars, and cannot sell reprint or translation rights to countries lacking them. Countries that do have American currency and can buy rights are unable to sell their editions, in the case of world languages (American or otherwise), to the many countries that do not have dollars. Dollars are thus the most important concern to be addressed by this U.S. Books Abroad study. America's cultural influence will decline, its voice in foreign and international intellectual debate will be diminished, publishing industry growth will be stunted, and piracy will flourish as long as foreign countries lack sufficient American currency for trade.

There are two basic ways for the U.S. government to approach the currency barrier: make dollars available, to countries of special concern to the U.S., with which to buy American books or rights; or convert local currencies received by U.S. book exporters into dollars. The only current examples of the former tactic identified in researching this study are several AID programs. In connection with specific technical assistance or development programs, AID provides project loans or grants in dollars to foreign governments, for the purchase of necessary project-related materials from the U.S. In some countries (currently a total of 10), AID also provides loans or grant assistance with which to finance procurement of a wide variety of basic imports. This assistance approach, the Commodity Import Programs (CIPS), involves the allocation of CIP dollars by the foreign government to its various ministries and to private sector importers as needed to purchase such basic commodities. In either CIPs or project procurement, AID itself does almost no buying. However, under the terms of the grants and/or loans, the participating foreign government agrees that purchasing will be governed by AID Commodity Eligibility Listings.

Available from AID to U.S. exporters on request, the Commodity Eligibility Listings discuss books in Schedule 2, Part 5, "Books, Pamphlets, and Other Printed and Manuscript Material." To wit: "Religious books, dictionaries, encyclopedias, textbooks, and similar books" are eligible, as are newspapers and periodicals. Ineligible for these import programs are "Rare books, prints, collectors' items, material primarily of prurient appeal, comic books, fashion, and sport magazines." Egypt ($300 million) and Sudan ($120 million) are currently the only sizeable CIP programs, but all 10 country CIPs provide experience for AID and USIA on which to base a currency program for foreign customers for books in which funds are provided to an importer, institutions, etc. Although an AID description of Egypt's 1983 grant allocation expenditures did not identify any books among the commodities purchased with these funds, it is noted that Egypt imported $2.5 million in books from the U.S. in 1984 at least partially as a product of its grants or from other dollar holdings freed up by the CIP. AID accepts the names of any U.S. exporters requesting inclusion on AID lists for foreign buyers.

Some Reid Foundation Study Group discussants state that for effective results, any foreign loans or grants intended to enhance book imports from the U.S. should (in consultation with foreign governments) be made directly to the libraries or institutions for which the book import enhancement is intended. It has been suggested that, if grants are made to a government, or to institutions with a government's agreement, the recipient might be required to deposit an equivalent amount in local currencies into a U.S. government account in the country from which expenditures would be made for the local enhancement of America's book trade. For example, assistance for the production of reprints or translations provided by local currencies generated by dollar transactions involving these accounts would be a logical step. Retail prices could be adjusted to the purchasing power of students and/or sales promotion could be encouraged. Alternatively, the provision of discount coupons to the students, similar to the UNESCO coupon of earlier years, is proposed by several Task Force members to reduce retail prices. Reid Foundation Study Group discussants also thought that increased allocations of dollars for books from the dollars held by foreign governments should be pursued, on some matching basis with the dollars made available by the U.S.

The alternative mechanism for coping with foreign dollar shortages, authorizing American exporters to accept local currencies and then converting those currencies into dollars, is by no means an unprecedented governmental approach. Reid Foundation Study Group members and discussants did not, however, find any such approach presently in operation. As reported in chapter 4, current export assistance programs provide insurance against loss due to arbitrary blockage of currency exchange or artificially fixed exchange rates, but do not presently provide a fluid exchange system. The Informational Media Guarantee Program (IMG), a convertibility program in operation between 1948 and 1968, could be an informative model for any current program. Discussants and Task Force members stated that the successes and problems of that program should be studied to develop approaches to dollar shortages that will be effective in responding to the current problems.

CURRENCY CONVERTIBILITY FOR MEDIA (1948–1968)

Origin, Legislative History, and Purpose[5]

Ideological and economic conditions in the Third World today to which this U.S. Books Abroad study is a response echo those of post-war Europe, besieged at that time by the economic ravages of World War II and the political

[5] *A History of the Informational Media Guarantee Program* (unpublished report, USIA) is the principal source for this segment of the study.

threat posed by the Soviet Union. Section 111(b)(3), Title 1, of the Foreign Assistance Act of 1948 (Title 1 was cited as the "Economic Cooperation Act of 1948") as passed by the Senate provided for an investment guarantee program designed to enlist American business in Europe's recovery by assuring foreign currency proceeds could be transferred into dollars. A House amendment by Representative Karl Mundt identified media as industries specifically included in the legislation for coverage by a guarantee program. This amendment, accepted by the Senate, included a directive to "promote through private channels that have been prevented from operating heretofore, a true understanding of American institutions and policy among the nations."

The Informational Media Guarantee Program (IMG), as the Mundt amendment came to be called, enabled media producers to sell their materials in European countries with dollar shortages by accepting local currency in payment. Such local funds were then given guaranteed convertibility into U.S. dollars by the U.S. Treasury. (All other business risks, such as failure of the buyer to pay in any currency, were assumed by the entrepreneur.) The Mutual Security Act of 1951 (Section 520) extended IMG to countries outside Europe, while the Mutual Security Act of 1952 (Section 536) transferred administration of the program from the Mutual Security Agency to the Department of State. (This transfer was actually accomplished by Executive Order 10638; the legislation left to the president the decision as to the administering agency.) From January, 1952, to August, 1953, the Department of State's semi-autonomous International Information Administration (IIA) ran the IMG program. In August, 1953, President Eisenhower created USIA out of what had been IIA programs by Executive Order 10476, and USIA was to administer IMG until its termination in 1968.

IMG was established to eliminate the foreign exchange barrier as an impediment to the free flow of ideas. Although IMG's implicit relationship to economic and technical assistance efforts and its obvious contribution to the stimulation of foreign trade and an improved balance of payments were also considered important, the program's stated purpose, as identified in the 1948 ECA Act and in many congressional documents thereafter, was to serve as an adjunct to the government's international information activities. Its relocation to the State Department in 1952 and to USIA in 1953 was logical in light of this stated purpose. Had its purpose been only trade stimulation or technical assistance, IMG would properly have remained with other investment guarantee programs in a developing-country-oriented agency. The other convertibility programs of 1948 were administered by AID and its successors until 1971, when the Overseas Private Investment Corporation (OPIC) was formed, and took charge of AID's private investment incentive programs. Meanwhile, the Mutual Security Act of 1956 (Section 11) completed the separation of IMG from other guarantee programs by amending Section 1011 of the United States Information and Educational Exchange Act of 1948 to authorize the director of USIA to assume the obligations related to media guarantees provided for in the 1948 Economic Cooperation Act.

How IMG Operated

An IMG program was initiated by a bilateral agreement between the U.S. government and that of a participating country. The agreement was an exchange of diplomatic notes that became the legal basis for the program and also described the terms of operation. Implementing details were determined each year at the working level of the two governments. Based on the agreement and implementing arrangements, USIA made guarantees to U.S. exporters whose petitions to make sales in a participating country had received that government's approval.

The currency guarantees were provided by contract between USIA and the exporter. Such a contract established among other things the level of USIA's liability to the exporter, the time limits of the guarantee, and the types of materials covered by the guarantee. Thereafter, the exporter did business with importers in the participating country in a normal fashion, protected only against the hazard of accepting blocked currency for sales. Upon receipt of payment in blocked currency, the exporter applied to the USIA for conversion and presented a draft for the currency. The agency in turn entitled the exporter to receive from the Treasury a dollar payment equivalent in value to the blocked or non-convertible foreign currency proceeds of the sale. The Treasury Department then deposited the foreign currency proceeds in an account where they were available for use (in exchange for U.S. dollars appropriated by the Congress) by the U.S. government to pay regular in-country embassy operating expenses in the participating country, subject to any limitations contained in the bilateral agreement.

USIA screened materials proposed for export under currency convertibility guarantee contracts, and selected for coverage only those that came within the statutory guidelines and the more specific criteria established in 1961. Exporters were encouraged to submit their materials for screening prior to making shipments, to avoid having requests for conversion of foreign currency proceeds rejected.

Media Exports Eligible for IMG

Originally (in 1948), eligible information media included "books, pamphlets, magazines, prints, play scripts, motion pictures, film scripts, projection slides, musical scores, musical and other acoustical recordings, news services, the rights to make, use, or perform any of the foregoing, and other generally used instruments or means for conveying information, insofar as the content of such media is in fact intended to convey knowledge or is expressive of the life or culture of the United States." Fairly liberal interpretation of the guidelines in the earliest years of the program, including the test that constructive criticism is a hallmark of democracy, allowed almost any item not directly prejudicial to U.S. interests to receive coverage.

Ineligible materials were those that were "patently lewd or salacious, *conveyed political propaganda inimical to the best interests of the U.S.*, or were of a too specialized or trivial interest" (emphasis added). Examples of the latter categories were "scientific abstracts, rare books or collector's items, fads and novelty publications, and miscellaneous publications such as dream books, coin albums, comic books, yoga, etc."

Censorship controversies are probably latent in any American program or activity in which the federal government is involved in the selection and rejection of media materials. As noted in chapter 4, the assumption of latency produced a Small Business Administration (SBA) policy that avoids the problem altogether, by totally excluding media enterprises from SBA assistance programs. Such a solution is not possible for agencies such as USIA and AID whose fundamental objectives require the distribution of media materials abroad. In the case of IMG, the charge of censorship was a persistent one, balanced only be criticism of USIA in the Congress for not being sufficiently selective.

None of the efforts to define materials eligible for IMG assistance was entirely satisfactory to all parties involved. Hence, a history of these efforts is not essential to this study. The criteria in effect when the program was terminated in 1968 were those prepared at the request of USIA Director Edward R. Murrow in 1961. Presumably accommodating all the conflicting interests considered possible at that time, those criteria read as follows:

> The term "informational media" includes books, periodicals, motion pictures, TV films, music scores, phonograph records, news services, film strips, publication rights, maps, and any other generally used medium for conveying information. Not all types of informational media are covered in every country of IMG operations. IMG does not provide coverage for equipment (e.g., projectors, recorders, play-back machines, duplicating devices, laboratory models) and supplies (e.g., paper, film stock, tapes, record blanks), or for other unprocessed merchandise used to produce informational materials.
>
> With few exceptions, eligibility is limited to materials of American origin and predominantly American subject matter. Among those works generally found eligible for IMG support are American publications (i.e., books, pamphlets, and periodicals) in the fields of pure and applied sciences; engineering and technology; social sciences and education; law and public administration; business, economics, and finance; American history and geography; American literary works (except fiction); materials for teaching English as a foreign language; philosophy; biographies of Americans; fine arts, architecture, and applied arts; general reference works.
>
> Other publications, including American fiction and periodicals of general circulation, as found eligible by the agency on a title-by-title basis may be covered under IMG contracts.
>
> Publications generally ineligible for IMG support are: (1) reprints, transla-

tions, and revisions of works originally published outside the U.S.; (2) materials of foreign manufacture or materials published in the U.S. by a foreign-owned company including publications of international organizations, public or private; (3) abstracts, annotated indexes, bibliographies, and digests of international literature; (4) merchandise sales catalogs, or adaptations thereof; (5) rare books, limited editions, deluxe editions, and other expensive publications prized as collectors items; (6) materials for teaching languages other than English; (7) art and architecture publications dealing largely with the works of non-American artists and architects; (8) musicology and music publications, unless a substantial portion of the content is devoted to works of American composers; (9) travel guides, entertainment guides, and similar publications, unless a substantial portion of the content relates to the United States; (10) fashion publications which do not have significant instructional value including substantial text of a serious nature; (11) hobby and how-to publications, including but not limited to cookbooks, flower arranging, beauty culture, yachting, hunting, pet care, etc., unless found eligible by the agency on a title-by-title basis; (12) all other publications which do not make a positive contribution in support of U.S. policy objectives and reflect favorably on the United States. This would include but would not be limited to publications concerning the following: astrology, comics, cartoons, jokes, puzzles, hypnotism, palmistry, judo, coin albums, etc.

Financial Problems Arise

IMG was funded via public debt financing rather than annual appropriations. Since publishers paid a fee of 1½ percent of sales to participate in the program, and since the object of the program was mere currency convertibility, IMG theoretically should have been self-sustaining. However, due to fluctuations in exchange rates for the currencies involved, the Treasury Department absorbed great losses on the subsequent sale of IMG foreign currency proceeds for dollars, and charged those losses to USIA. At the program's termination, the agency's assumed "indebtedness" to Treasury totaled $31,620,170. USIA had paid back $9,509,170 provided by Congress in appropriated funds, leaving a net borrowing of $22,114,000 still on the Treasury Department books. For many in Congress, after-the-fact appropriation requests by USIA to repay the Treasury constituted a serious infraction of the historic rule that Congress controls the purse strings and must appropriate all executive branch funds in advance of use. Legislative branch feelings on this matter were so strong that USIA's indebtedness was not cleared from the Treasury books by the Congress until 1983.

Payments to publishers in the nineteen years of IMG's operation totalled $83,325,033 which, when divided by USIA's total indebtedness, translated to a taxpayer cost of 38 cents for each dollar of media material sold by publishers, exclusive of USIA administrative expenses. This created a second fiscally related problem for IMG, in that Congress charged it with providing subsidies, an accusation strenuously denied by the publishing industry. Although only normal dollar profits accrued to publishers—USIA's role being theoretically that of a facilitator of currency exchange—the fact that the federal government incurred expenses and unintended losses for private business transactions could logically if not legally be considered, if not a subsidy, at least a "subvention." The crux of this argument lay in the fact that subsidy or subvention made the case for government determination of material eligibility stronger.

A third problem related to finance was how the acquired foreign currency was used by the U.S. government. Some countries felt that without restrictions on use of the funds they were losing control of a portion of their foreign currency receipts. If they lost, for example, the dollar payments for local expenses of U.S. diplomatic missions and received instead IMG-converted local currency, the U.S. was, in effect, paying its local expenses in merchandise, i.e., books instead of dollars. Put another way, in effect the U.S. was usurping a foreign government's financial role in the discretionary use of dollars for foreign purchases. Some observers saw justification for foreign governments placing restrictions on the U.S. use of local IMG currency, but strong congressional objection to foreign veto of the free use of funds owned by the U.S. led USIA to finally refrain from entering into agreements where currenty use would be restricted.

Substantive Problems Arise

Publishers had indicated concerns about censorship in their earliest responses to congressional charges of USIA subsidy. In 1957 congressional hearings, a publishers' representative stated, "We have sought no subsidies and would no more accept any than we would accept restrictions on our editorial freedom." As we have seen, it was the position of the industry that all an exporter received from an IMG transaction was the same amount in dollars that would have been received had the buyer been able to pay in dollars. In addition, the exporter paid a fee of 1½ percent to the government and, as noted, assumed all normal business risks. Hence, the industry argued that no subsidy was given and that selection by USIA of materials to be covered under IMG was inappropriate.

Cries of "censorship" predictably intensified when the 1961 list of included and excluded categories of books cited above was issued. The American Book Publishers Council (predecessor organization to the AAP) wrote to USIA Director Murrow asking for clarification of the list, pointing to the fact that publishers received no profit from sales that they would not have received had buyers themselves paid the dollar cost. USIA Director Murrow's response, in noting that the government was incurring real costs in the operation of IMG, stated "Any publisher is free to sell . . . any publication he wishes as long as he does not look to the United States Treasury for subvention of the transaction," but emphasized that USIA had a responsibility to ensure that the results of IMG transactions supported U.S. interests.

Termination of IMG—1968

As this brief history suggests, there developed sharply conflicting and articulated opinions about IMG. Its eligibility standards were considered too liberal by some, too restrictive by others. To some it was a government propaganda device, to others it was a subsidy to exporters, and to still others it was censorship. To some, the revolving fund was the only feasible way to relate government funding to normal commercial operations; to many in Congress it was "back-door financing" that evaded the appropriation process.

It was the method of financing that finally precipitated termination of the program. The Senate Appropriations Committee had constantly voiced its displeasure that USIA was able to secure funds from the Treasury Department without regular appropriation. This displeasure was compounded when the agency sought appropriations to pay the Treasury Department for currency losses. IMG was finally liquidated by cutting off funds for administering it. In the USIA appropriation of 1967, the agency was expressly prohibited from using any of its funds for salary and operations of the IMG. The Senate Appropriations Committee directed that the cost of liquidating IMG be absorbed within that year's regular appropriation. Liquidation was accomplished by October 31, 1968.

A convertibility program at the present time would not involve new program authorization by the Congress. Section 111 (b)(3), Title 1, of the Foreign Assistance Act of 1948 (cited as the Economic Recovery Act of 1948 and providing for IMG) was never rescinded. Similarly, the Mutual Security Act of 1956 (Section 11) amending Section 1011 of the United States Information and Educational Exchange Act of 1948 to authorize the director of USIA to assume the obligations related to media guarantee provided for in the 1948 Economic Recovery Act is still in effect. It is the conclusion of the Reid Foundation Study Group that all that is required to restore a currency convertibility program is inclusion of new funding for it in a USIA appropriation act. Presumably that act, the congressional appropriation committee reports on it, and/or USIA regulations pursuant to the act could provide for steps that eliminate the problems of the earlier IMG that led to its demise.

Some discussants with intimate recollections of the earlier program believe that it would be most useful if the legislation or the House and Senate committee reports spelled out somewhat more precisely the intent of the Congress as to categories of books that would be covered by a new program, and those that would not. Realism dictates that agency responsibility, congressional pressure, and taxpayer interests would demand some pre-selection system. Wise, judicious selection undoubtedly, but pre-selection nevertheless.

Hence, the more clearly the Congress states its intent, the fewer problems there will be for those who must administer the program.

Present Day Currency Convertibility Needs and the IMG Experience

As the export data cited at the beginning of this chapter clearly show, termination of IMG did not mean that developing countries with few dollars to spend on American books in 1968 resolved their problem by other means. Perhaps the most startling data are these: in 1973, the U.S. exported books valued at $160 million; in 1983, the value of U.S. exports was $607 million, an increase of almost 400 percent. However, the number of books exported in 1973 totaled 194.5 million copies, while 1983 exports totaled 242.7 million copies, an increase of just under 25 percent. In view of the tremendous expansion in literacy in the developing world in those 10 years, and the fact reported earlier that 84 percent of our 1984 export sales went to 16 developed countries and the Philippines, it seems clear that the gap between book supply and demand is enormous in the Third World. A considerable part of the shortfall is perhaps due to insufficient development of U.S. export experience and promotional efforts discussed in other chapters of this study, underlined by currency problems. The problem becomes even more crucial, industry professionals have emphasized, when the growth in Soviet foreign language publication production over that same 20 years is noted—a priority distribution effort from which no bookseller or student in the developing world is turned away due to lack of currency.

During the last three years of IMG's existence several attempts were made to substantially alter it so as to satisfy critics in both houses of Congress. A final attempt to save the program was Senate S1030, introduced in the first session of the 90th Congress in 1967. Senator William Fulbright sponsored the legislation, and hearings were held in March and April, 1967, by the Senate Committee on Foreign Relations. The bill addressed many of the criticisms IMG had encountered in 20 years, but the principal proposed change was in the method of funding, which was the root of congressional dissatisfaction. However, there was still too much distaste for the IMG in Congress, and the U.S. was entering a period when, while President Lyndon Johnson was seeking a broad new U.S. International Books and Libraries Program, congressional disagreement on Vietnam was being translated into reduced funding for all U.S. overseas commitments. The Fulbright IMG revision died in committee, as had others.

In 1978, a currency convertibility program proposal was prepared and submitted to the Commission on Security and Cooperation in Europe by Leo N. Albert, then chairman of Prentice Hall International, Inc.[6] The proposal

[6] Leo N. Albert, "In Response to Helsinki: A Proposal to the Commission on Security and Cooperation by the Association of American Publishers" (New York: AAP, 1978). photocopy.

was focused on Eastern Europe, where a lack of dollars had reduced the flow of American publications to a trickle, according to Commerce Department annual export statistics. Because of the lack of response to the Helsinki accords by the Soviet Union and Eastern Europe, the Albert approach to currency convertibility also received little U.S. government response. The Albert proposal was then and still remains, however, the most serious effort to analyze objections to the IMG program and provide an approach that meets those objections. In outline, the proposal was as follows:

1. Financing of a new program would be subject to congressional authorization and appropriation procedures. Legislation would set an overall authorized dollar ceiling for IMG conversion, or it would set categorical limits for each participating nation (that is, specify countries and the amount for each per year). This addressed the "program's basic weakness and the ultimate, but not sole, cause of its demise," i.e., the bypass of normal congressional appropriation processes.
2. Foreign currencies received from a U.S. exporter would be converted at a rate of exchange determined by the U.S. and the participating country, and the exchange rate would be reviewed as often as necessary to provide for the closest possible response to currency fluctuations. Foreign currencies received by the U.S. would, by authorization and appropriation, be used in the participating country for programs designed to implement the goals of the U.S. Books Abroad project, and would not be used to fund ongoing U.S. programs and expenses.
3. The U.S. and those governments of importing countries would mutually establish criteria for the types of media materials eligible for coverage in the program, and the U.S. agency involved would also monitor shipments to make sure that they were within statutory guidelines. All transactions would be subject to audit by the responsible agency before conversion payments for shipments would be made.
4. Procedures for administering the program would be essentially the same as for the IMG.

As Mr. Albert observed, the financing approach should meet Congress's most critical objections to the program. Step 2 eliminates the second currency conversion from foreign currency back into dollars that created losses for the Treasury and, hence, the cries of "subsidy." Step 2 is doubly effective in that appropriated currency would be used to move American books into the participating country in the form of exports and copyright licenses; then, in the form of foreign currency, the same appropriation would be applied to the U.S. Books Abroad programs in the participating country, e.g., book translations, book fair exhibits, book promotion programs, or a reduction in the price of U.S. books to the consumer discussed in chapter 6.

Step 3 addresses concerns about censorship that plagued IMG. Although as an element of overall U.S. Books Abroad policy criteria would need to be specific, the Albert proposal follows the precedent set up by the AID

Commodity Import Program discussed at the outset of this chapter, in which AID and the participating foreign governments agree on a Commodity Eligibility List to be used by the latter. The Albert proposal does not differ much from the IMG eligibility listing, albeit that was set by USIA acting alone, with general direction from Congress. The experience of the IMG program leads to the question of whether or not selection of materials can be amicably handled to the satisfaction of all parties in any government program. One solution is to have the administering U.S. agency and the participating foreign government make those decisions prior to publisher involvement.

The content question would be more limited if the general response to a currency convertibility program now found in governmental circles were the basis for enactment. There is no clear support in concerned government agencies for any broad-gauged convertibility program for books at this time. As discussants in several agencies observed, currency convertibility is a problem for many U.S. industries, all of whom would welcome a government convertibility program for their products. For those government observers, only a program specifically related to books and scholarly journals in the interest of national security is sufficiently distinguishable from general export trade needs to be justifiable. Those governmental discussants suggest a program administered by USIA covering books closely related to USIA objectives as one more likely to receive a favorable executive branch and congressional response.

Some discussants suggested that there might possibly be two such programs, the second being a technological transfer effort funded by AID consisting of development-related titles in science, technology, medicine, education, etc. A 1982 AID policy paper, "Basic Education and Technical Training," and a Policy Determination paper (PD-10, February 17, 1984), on "Development Communications," reflect current general policies to which books relate. There is precedent for separately funded programs administered by one agency in the USIA/AID P.L. 480 textbook programs (chapter 16). AID funds for a scientific and technical textbook program in India, and USIA funds for a general textbook program in economics, international relations, the social sciences, and the arts, were administered by a single USIA Book Program Office in New Delhi in the late 1960s. USIA assumed responsibility because, as is true today, that agency had the necessary Washington bibliographic and publishing support services.

In sum, there are two feasible approaches to alleviating dollar shortages in the Third World for which there are precedents; dollar funding through and in concert with foreign governments, or dollar funding through agreements with American publishers. Both approaches allow a second use of the dollars, in the form of foreign currency applied to other projects. In either situation, the executive branch and Congress would determine countries eligible for participation, and ceilings on dollars available for conversion, as well as ceilings on programs to be funded with foreign currency that work toward eliminating the barriers to U.S. book exports identified in other chapters of this study. Also, neither approach is exclusive of the other, and combination possibilities are many.

Whether convertibility dollars are made available through the foreign government involved or through U.S. publishers, many discussants believe that bilateral convertibility agreements should ensure that these dollars are used for additional purchases of American books, and not substituted for dollars now earmarked for book imports from foreign dollar holdings. Several Task Force members have proposed that allocation of dollars for imports be increased by such governments concomitantly with American-owned dollars, as a recognition of the priority placed on books by those governments. Books, while without the immediate impact on development of many imports, are no less important to a nation's health.

What effective currency convertibility for books would cost today is difficult to estimate. The earlier program distributed materials valued at $83,325,033 over a period of 19 years, for an average of $4.4 million per year. That was, however, many years ago, and while the amount may seem small, it probably represents a program of perhaps $20 to $25 million in current dollars per year. Literacy rates have increased, populations have increased, indeed the number of countries in existence has probably doubled. (Only 21 countries were involved in the earlier IMG program.) The amounts needed at the outset depend on whether or not concerned book people want to initiate a small pilot program in priority countries or a large multinational one. The latter seems ideal, the former more realistic. But it can be reasonably expected that to have a meaningful impact on the book gap the funding involved should be estimated at eventually being in the $50 million per annum range. Since the foreign book world has developed immensely over the 17 years since IMG was terminated, more mature publishing industries can now be more effectively helped by facilitating greater access to reprint and translation rights. We are estimating a total U.S. book program would cost $50 million if the government seeks double service from the convertibility funding, by authorizing expenditure of foreign currencies generated for overseas costs of the various programs needing funding discussed in other chapters.

6

Low-Priced Books for the Developing World

William M. Childs

The Florence Agreement, sometimes called the "free flow of books" treaty, of which the United States is a signatory, is aimed at the elimination of tariffs and other barriers to the flow of books and other scientific, educational, and cultural materials. The Helsinki Treaty calls for the free east-west flow of information, including books and other publications. Sponsors of these agreements were motivated by the belief that if economic sanctions such as tariffs (which apply even to publishers' catalogs and other promotional materials, in some cases), exchange controls, and quotas, as well as political and moral censorship (often idiosyncratic), could be eased, if not eliminated, then information and knowledge could be made freely available throughout the developing as well as the developed world. While there can be no serious quarrel that such barriers are inherently undesirable and do, in fact, interfere with the availability of books in many countries, neither treaty addresses one of the fundamental impediments to getting more American books (and those of other developed countries as well) into bookstores, libraries, and universities around the world. Once we remove tariffs and political barriers, we have still to address the underlying barrier to the purchase of American books in the developing world—their high prices (as well as, of course, the critical shortages of dollars in most of the developing world).

Of all the barriers to the export of American books examined in this Reid Foundation study, one stands out as being most insurmountable: for the low income population that is the majority of would-be buyers in the developing world, American books are very high priced. They are now among the most expensive books in the world, even for students in the U.S. who pay in dollars. Once these books enter the international marketplace, they become even more costly. At transshipment points, prices are marked up by the U.S. publisher's branch offices through which the order is fulfilled, since the branch must pay for incoming freight, storage, and order fulfillment. While this is a logical and cost-effective procedure intended to speed up delivery time, it is a step that also means an incremental price increase for the eventual buyer.

In any circumstances, the foreign importer is also a factor in price escalation. Importers must take into account fluctuations in the value of their country's currency in setting prices. Due to current economic realities, between the time an importer receives a book and the time payment in dollars is due, the exchange rate will probably have decreased to the importer's disadvantage, e.g., a sale in pesos based on an exchange rate of 150 to the dollar, followed by the need to make payment at 200 pesos to the dollar, can mean a loss. Similarly, both importers and the booksellers through whom they distribute books work on borrowed capital: in Argentina, for example, that borrowing is done at an interest rate of 140%. The foreign student examining an American book at the local bookseller will often times find prices equivalent to double or more the original retail dollar price in the U.S. The result: purchase of only a few copies by a university library, for reserve shelf use by an entire class, or the selection of another text—often enough an English-language text from the Soviet Union.

American books are priced beyond the reach of most overseas students and general readers in many cases even when the dollars to cover import costs are available. English is widely used in university courses, not just in former English-speaking British colonies but in most of the developed world as well. Textbooks are in great demand and for many courses American books are considered the best. If that demand cannot be legitimately satisfied, at reasonable prices, then piracy will satisfy it—or "compulsory licensing" will. (This alternative form of piracy advocated by many Third World governments is now permissible under the Berne Convention and UCC, the international copyright conventions discussed in chapter 3.) There is no doubt that getting legitimate editions of the most popular textbooks into developing country markets at affordable prices is the most effective response to the pirates. Most established booksellers would prefer handling an authorized edition to selling a pirated facsimile.

USIA's book publishing program can make a direct contribution to price reductions as it did during the 1950s and 1960s (as will be explained in greater detail in chapter 14). However, it will take USIA several years to gear up its low-priced book publishing activity—and the first major infusion of added funding for USIA is not expected until 1986. Attention should, therefore, be focused on what private sector U.S. publishers are already doing to meet the market price challenge, those activities that the federal government might facilitate to fulfill immediate needs. In addition, it is important to understand those private sector initiatives in order to supplement or build upon rather than replace them. One veteran observer expressed concern, based on his experience over the past 30 years with government programs, that government support programs have at times led publishers into avenues of trade development that, once government assistance is no longer available, cannot be supported by the private sector alone.

U.S. publishers are, of course, well aware of the problem of high prices. Today, many multinational publishers (as discussed in chapter 2) are producing "International Student Editions (ISE)" or "Export Editions" at lower prices. Exporters report that they are addressing the problem with the publishers they represent abroad, and their response has also been reduced-price editions in the export market for certain texts. (It is worth noting that a strong dollar in 1985 means non-competitive American prices in Europe, as well as in the countries of the Third World, and failure to reduce the dollar price of certain books simply means turning over the European market to British and German textbooks in English.)

The Birth of the International Student Edition

In the early post-war years, major American textbook publishers (McGraw-Hill, Prentice-Hall, John Wiley & Sons, etc.) sensed a developing overseas market for textbooks in English. They recognized that their prices would have to be lowered if they were to penetrate this burgeoning market and wrest some of it away from their British competitors. To accomplish this, they initially developed specially produced international student editions—known in some cases as "Asian Editions," since the intended market at that stage was primarily Asian countries such as Japan. Manufacturing cost advantages were soon discovered in Japan, which offered acceptable production quality and better-than-average efficiencies of production. By the early 1960s, American publishers were able to introduce well-produced paperback editions of their standard texts at prices about one-third to one-half their U.S. list price.

As Japan's economy developed and its currency strengthened, in-country publication costs rose, and earlier production cost advantages were gradually eroded. Some ISE publishers shifted production to Hong Kong, and then Singapore. Others began producing their ISEs domestically as overruns (print runs added to a fixed print order, sometimes using lower quality paper and/or binding methods, to help lower prices and take advantage of the economy of numbers) in the 1970s, when the dollar weakened in value. For a time, it was more cost-efficient to buy paper and print and bind in the U.S. International student editions produced in the U.S. were most often labeled "Export Editions." Today, many textbook publishers, probably including the majority of the larger houses, continue to look to student or export editions to shore up sagging export sales. Hence, the production of low-priced international editions is still a major activity of the international divisions of the largest American textbook houses. However, because of inflation and rising paper and production costs, these publishers are now forced to price such editions at about two-thirds the price of their domestic editions.

If U.S. books are to reach a wide audience overseas today, clearly it must be in the form of low-priced international or export editions. American publishers and/or collaborating foreign houses must produce specially priced versions of selected books attuned to the special needs and pocketbook of the overseas buyer. As was mentioned in chapter 2, the major American textbook publishers have established subsidiary publishing and distributing firms in many countries around the world for just that purpose. These subsidiaries' original function may have been providing more efficient and economical fulfillment of foreign orders for domestic U.S. editions (through the warehousing of books in geographically strategic locations around the world), but their main purpose today is producing inexpensive overseas editions of parent firm U.S. editions in reprint, translated, and/or adapted forms to meet the needs of overseas audiences.

Not all American multinational publishers agree that ISEs or special export editions are cost effective, and perhaps not enough is known about how successful these international student and export editions have been over their 25-year life span. On the surface, at least, it would seem unquestionable that more American textbooks have been sold abroad than would have been the case without ISEs. One informed analysis, accepted by a minority to be sure, holds that while more copies of some books have very likely been sold, ISEs have not been profit-making ventures for publishers. A good textbook will sell at almost any price, in the view of a number of seasoned international marketing directors, but a mediocre one cannot be made very profitable even in a low-priced edition.

One publisher's experience with setting a special low price for one of its best-selling medical textbooks is worth recounting here. Williams & Wilkins, a major medical textbook and reference publisher and a relative newcomer to export editions, created a low-priced version of one of its classic anatomy texts, primarily for Egypt's medical schools. There had been strong demand in Egypt for the book over many years and in the mid-1970s Williams & Wilkins decided to produce a low-priced edition as an overrun to their regular printing (using the same quality paper and binding). It was possible to lower the $32 list price (now $40) by roughly 40%, to $20 (now $25). Lowering the price actually required a revised cost accounting formula for use with the overrun portion of the total copies printed. Today, almost a decade (and several printings) later, the publisher has found it to be no better than a break-even venture from the profit and loss standpoint: however, the company considers this project a worthwhile and highly desirable one. It has opened the door to other Williams & Wilkins books in Egypt and the Middle East, enhanced the company's stature in the international textbook market, and probably discouraged piracy of a valuable property.

It is worth mentioning that the pioneer American publishers on the international scene were the several joint Indo-U.S. publishing ventures established in the 1960s in India to support the newly launched P.L. 480 Textbook Program (see chapter 14). These early international ventures were implemented by such U.S. textbook publishers as Prentice-Hall, McGraw-Hill, Van Nostrand, and John Wiley & Sons. Their partnership agreements have all outlasted that particular program and even today produce inexpensive Indian reprints, translations, and/or adapted editions from the American home office list. These companies have moved successfully into purely indigenous publishing as well, and all these American multinational activities are carried on without benefit of any U.S. or Indian government subsidy. (The government of India has aided its publishers with specially priced text paper.)

At this point, neither industry nor government has any statistically clear idea of the magnitude of ISE or export edition publishing. How many titles are thus produced? Which American books are available in these low-priced editions? In which countries are they available? This is an important deficiency, for both industry and government. The publishing industry, its principal bibliographer, R.R. Bowker, and involved government agencies (USIA, AID, and the Commerce Department, principally) should give serious consideration to compiling a list of American books in print published abroad (it could and should include as well those special low-priced export editions published in the U.S. for export only). Such a list would be enormously useful, overseas and in the U.S., to publishers, booksellers, analysts, and governments. AID and USIA in particular could look to it as a potentially rich source of relatively inexpensive books supportive of their missions overseas and, therefore, worth promoting and using. Such a list could also demonstrate to foreign governments looking for chances to award compulsory licenses to their publishers that reasonably priced American books are in fact available for their students and other readers.

The Role of the Government

American publishers alone cannot meet the market pricing challenge. American government agencies have an obligation to help provide American books to overseas readers at prices they can afford that is fundamental to U.S. foreign policy and America's relations with the developing world, in the view of the Reid Foundation Study Group. Past U.S. government (USIA and AID) programs, as explained in chapters 13 and 14, have indeed made this their goal, in part. However, some collaborative public-private efforts toward getting more U.S. books into the classrooms, libraries, and bookstores of the developing world at affordable and competitive prices are currently needed. USIA and AID, in particular, should explore, with publishers, ways of supporting special overrun low-priced export editions of selected books related to the interests of both U.S. agencies. The rich experience of many American publishers producing and marketing ISEs and export editions offers excellent opportunities for a realistic public-private approach to the market pricing challenge.

The United Kingdom leads other Western governments in promoting sales of its industry's books abroad at low prices, providing direct assistance through the English Language Book Society (ELBS) of the British Council. The ELBS supports overrun editions of textbooks and other works concerning British society and government policies, which it then helps the publishers promote through an active exhibits program in nearly 80 developing countries. Each publisher produces a low priced edition, as an adjunct of regular editions, and binds the book in a cover that is uniform for all books in the specially priced series regardless of publisher. In 1984, some 1.5 million low-priced ELBS textbooks were sold.

The Reid Foundation Study Group recommends borrowing from the ELBS concept, and believes American publishers would cooperate. However, it is doubtful that, given the realities of the federal budget, either USIA or AID would give serious consideration to requesting the funds required for any large-scale ELBS-type publishing project. Nevertheless, it would be feasible, and desirable, for USIA and AID to develop such an arrangement with American publishers at least on a book-by-book basis. Toward this end, USIA should consult with the British Council on the mechanics of the ELBS program over its 25-year life. There is a precedent for such an arrangement: in 1959, the British Council consulted USIA for help in setting up its ELBS program, based on agency experience with its now defunct Student Edition Program (chapter 14).

A revitalized USIA overseas book publishing program (discussed in chapter 14) should give strong emphasis to restoration of the P. L. 480 Textbook Program in some form, a program which turned out almost 12 million low-priced textbooks in its nearly 20-year history. Under P. L. 480, surplus American agricultural commodities are sold to certain developing countries, including some Eastern European nations, for which payment is accepted in local currencies. Congress then authorizes the expenditure of local currencies accumulated in this fashion to fund American embassies and assistance programs, subject to agreement with the foreign government concerned. One such assistance program so authorized in the past was the production of American university textbooks, usually in English language reprint editions but with a few in translations as well (e.g., Arabic, Serbo-Croatian, and Spanish), in the country where the currency was accumulated. American publishers cooperated, making rights available and facilitating the production process in many cases. USIA administered P.L. 480 programs in most instances (with funding from AID) for books related to assistance activities in the case of the program in India). In the course of de-emphasizing books in the 1970s, USIA also reduced the size of the P.L. Textbook Program: only 2,000 textbooks were turned out in fiscal year 1984, in contrast with 1.6 million in India alone in fiscal year 1970.

Educational development in many countries was helped greatly through the low-priced American textbooks made available by P.L. 480, especially in India, which was the recipient of two-thirds of all textbooks produced by this program.[1] Not only were American textbooks selected by the education ministries of those countries involved made available through P.L. 480, they were sold at affordable prices. In India, for example, P.L. 480 reprints for students were one-fifth the price of original U.S. editions. Educators and publishers with continuing experience in foreign markets believe that this reprinting activity or something akin to it is of prime importance in the formulation of any in-country book program, second only to relieving the problem of currency convertibility.

In view of the geographical expansion of book needs that has occurred since the demise of the P.L. 480 program, any new program should consider exporting books produced in one developing country to similarly situated neighbors. Perhaps American publishers could take the lead by preparing a few case studies on the status of American textbook usage today in colleges and universities of key developing countries such as India and Egypt. These studies could be presented to USIA and AID to initiate a dialogue and a public-private cooperative effort. The Reid Foundation Study Group concludes that the U.S. government must play a role in ensuring that textbooks and other books related to America's foreign policy interests are available overseas at prices that reading audiences can afford. However, two cautions should be considered. USIA and AID, the two agencies primarily concerned, should be aware of the potential impact of excessively low prices on the existing market. If American publishers are having some success introducing books into a given country at U.S. prices (or at the price of their international editions), then a large-scale infusion of books at much lower prices will disrupt market pricing and development. Such an observation seems obvious, but book program history mandates its restatement. The goal in such situations should be to promote the available editions and reduce cost where appropriate by subsidizing the student buyer.

In cases where a country is impoverished, short of foreign exchange, and/or has an inadequate book distribution and selling infrastructure in place, as is true of many African countries, then the introduction of such low-priced

[1] *U.S. Books Abroad.*

books even on a large scale would be appropriate and desirable. To introduce large quantities of low-priced books in such cases would not be disruptive, as no American publishers are currently attempting to establish markets in these countries. The following issues must also be taken into account: what is the impact of especially low prices on a given market over the long run? What happens when USIA and/or AID after a period of time stop providing low-priced books? Does the market become so conditioned to low prices that it cannot adjust to world prices? Can a student suddenly afford to pay $25 for a textbook that has been available for $5? These are probably unanswerable questions at this time: nevertheless, they should be considered in planning and implementing low-priced book programs.

Finally, as USIA is the U.S. government agency most concerned with American books abroad, it is the view of the Reid Foundation Study Group that that agency should take the lead in initiating a dialogue to help induce public-private cooperation in the production of greater numbers of low-priced American books for overseas markets. USIA book program directors should learn which publishers are bringing out which American books, for which markets, in low-priced international student or export editions. They will want to offer collaborative aid for the greater promotion of selected low-priced books that especially support USIA—and AID—objectives. Such information will also be helpful in producing additional low-priced titles to meet both agencies' special needs. A final note: publishers might anticipate such a collaborative initiative on the part of USIA and help by making available to both agencies lists of books that are currently available in low-priced international editions.

PART III

INTRODUCING BOOKS TO THEIR MARKETS

7

Dissemination of Information on the Content of American Books

William M. Childs

American publishers are struggling to maintain export sales at 8 percent of the total annual book sales of the industry. Factors affecting export sales such as high prices, economic problems, literacy, and inadequate distribution and bookselling infrastructures need to be examined when considering America's weakening overseas distribution. However, an equally important question is: If readers and prospective book buyers in other countries have no more access to information about American books than appears to be the case, then how can most publishers hope to do very well in overseas markets? Publishers and other discussants whom the Reid Foundation Study Group consulted, as well as many Task Force members themselves, agree that a major obstacle to improving book exports is the current lack of information about American books abroad. This information gap on the content of American books impedes the strengthening of American book exports as much as do economic barriers. It hampers foreign importers, booksellers, librarians, professionals, and educational institutions in deciding *what* to order.

As Dan Lacy has noted in chapter 2, the largest U. S. publishers maintain branches in major markets and, hence, have an opportunity to inform those markets about their product. They send salesmen to visit booksellers, wholesalers, libraries, etc., distribute catalogs, exhibit at book fairs, and otherwise acquaint buyers with the content of their books. However, the information devices upon which most American publishers must depend to promote their books in both foreign and domestic markets are the standard bibliographic tools such as *Books in Print* and *Publishers' Weekly*. Book review journals, such as *Booklist, Choice, Library Journal*, The *New York Review of Books*, and the book review sections of major American newspapers, including the *New York Times Book Review*, the *Washington Post Book World*, the *Chicago Tribune Book World*, the *Los Angeles Herald Examiner Book World*, etc., are equally essential to buyer knowledge about books. In the case of serious, scholarly writings, the journals of major American learned and professional societies and associations are often the only reviews of professional works.

Collectively, such publications represent the main sources of information on American books for the American librarian and bookseller as well as for professionals, scholars, students, and general readers. Because of their high cost, unfortunately, they are largely beyond the reach of the overseas market. In addition, a general disinterest in international promotion on the part of professional journal marketing staffs, due to the complexities and costs of promotion abroad, makes these publications an unknown quantity in many countries especially in those of the developing world.

In the past, through much more active and better financed programs presenting books and publications to libraries, universities, and other institutions abroad as well as to selected individuals, USIA and private and non-profit groups included bibliographic publications and journals in their foreign librarian training seminars and workshops. In addition the American libraries abroad under USIA and AID sponsorship sought to familiarize librarians in other countries with American bibliographic publications—and how to use them. However, in the case of USIA book and library programs, when funding was reduced, priority had to be shifted to promotion of specific books of substantive program value. Few books and journals valuable as bibliographic resources are distributed beyond USIA's own collections. In fact, as USIA posts have been forced to cut back on the number and kind of books and publications they can purchase, even for their own libraries, their selection criteria have narrowed to those titles which most directly and intrinsically relate to specific USIA programs. While most USIA libraries still contain basic bibliographic resources, serious journals and newspapers with book review coverage were severely reduced in number. Unquestionably, one urgent need, and one which the U. S. Books Abroad Task Force will want to consider in any recommendations aimed at improving knowledge of U.S. books abroad, is access to adequate bibliographic tools and review materials.

While book fairs and thematic exhibits that bring academics and book professionals together to examine books are valuable, if not essential, they are only once-a-year or sporadic opportunities to physically study books. Continuity of communication is essential in bringing information to readers located far from regular distribution centers. That continuity is best ensured through regular access to the kind of bibliographic materials cited above. Consequently, USIA should consider renewing major book review journals and bibliographic publications in the collections of all of its libraries. One Task Force member went so far as to recommend that "USIA libraries should be liberally supplied with publishers' catalogs and with bibliographic tools which they (American publishers) would make available." And, especially important, USIA should ensure that recipients of "Operations Outreach," which informs audiences of new additions to USIA library collections, include local librarians, booksellers, and publishers. Availability is only a first step. Education in the use of such materials is equally important. USIA library staff can expect that solid, current information on new books and on the process of acquiring them will attract new library users with professional needs and technical questions.

While there is general agreement in the U.S. Books Abroad Task Force on the desirability of also providing such bibliographic materials directly to individual users, one member reminds us that the process of identifying suitable recipient institutions is hardly a mechanical one. Not all organizations will benefit from having current information on American books; many libraries do not serve a clientele that reads American books, either because of language or because the books are not relevant to particular interests. Not all organizations have funding with which to purchase expensive American books once they learn about them. Moreover, these bibliographic resources themselves are becoming increasingly expensive (a principal reason they have not been more widely used abroad) and it will not be possible to provide them to all the indigenous libraries and other institutions abroad that could benefit from them. Hence, careful thought needs to be given to identifying those institutions and organizations that should receive books and gift subscriptions. American publishers' representatives who regularly call on overseas libraries and booksellers can help book-oriented institutions such as USIA, AID, and local Asia Foundation offices in evaluating and helping qualify local libraries, bookstores, etc., as recipients of such materials.

While USIA posts maintain audience lists that undoubtedly include at least the most important libraries and book trade-related institutions abroad, a relatively new American firm, IBIS Information Services, maintains international mailing lists extensively covering all categories of worldwide book use. IBIS is formerly a British organization, and is now established as an American list rental service as well. IBIS lists include libraries, booksellers, universities, and schools, as well as individual professors and teachers by discipline. IBIS is well known to major American publishers, and should become known to smaller ones who are newcomers or who are about to try the international sales field as well as to managers of government book program staffs, as a potential resource for selecting recipients for the bibliographic publications under discussion. Individual U.S. publishers now selling abroad, as well as export representatives, maintain their own lists, albeit often as well-guarded trade secrets, and may be willing to help identify promising recipients of bibliographic materials from USIA's overseas libraries, USAID missions abroad, and private groups such as the Asia Foundation.

Once recipients have been selected and begin to receive gift publications, follow-up by donors is necessary. These are costly publications, and there will be more libraries, booksellers, and educational institutions with demonstrated need and interest than USIA, for one, will be able to supply, even with enhanced funding for such purposes. Do recipients know how to use the publications provided? Do they use them or promote them to clients, or are they merely shelved or stored for possible reference? The continued provision of book review and bibliographic information should be justified by USIA field posts, following regular monitoring of their use or the lack thereof.

The role of U.S. publishers is central here in terms of the availability of titles that may not reach review or bibliographic media for some time. Clearly, it is the primary responsibility of each individual publisher to disseminate his catalogs to potential overseas buyers. The larger publishers, with foreign subsidiaries and multinational infrastructure, do an effective job of getting their catalogs and other promotional materials into the hands of librarians and booksellers abroad. So, too, do export representatives and, to a lesser extent, the largest U.S. wholesalers. However, publishers and export representatives are selective and must limit standard distribution to countries where there appears to be a reasonable chance of selling their books. Catalogs are always costly to produce, and even more expensive to distribute internationally; hence, those promoting internationally carefully consider cost-effectiveness in distribution. This means, unfortunately, that librarians and booksellers in the developing world may never see an American publisher's catalog and will know little about the impressive range and breadth of American book publishing. Economic short-cuts such as bulk shipment of catalogs to a single client for distribution within a country are forestalled in many cases by high customs fees and taxes on the import of "advertising" in bulk.

Although there has traditionally been a reluctance by some U.S. embassies to become too directly involved in trade activities, overseas posts and missions of involved U.S. agencies—USIA, AID, and the Commerce Department particularly—can play an important role in facilitating wider familiarity with and access to American publishers' catalogs. This is not to suggest that U.S. embassies take over the job of promoting and selling a given publisher's books. Rather, it is appropriate to the functions of the three named agencies to have a representative collection of publishers' catalogs in their libraries and on display in other appropriate locations. AID, for example, might find it beneficial to its various development projects to have catalogs listing and describing American books in development fields (e.g., agriculture, education, engineering, family planning, public health, etc.) available on reference shelves at project sites. The Commerce Department maintains libraries in connection with commercial attaché offices in most American embassies around the world, for the purpose of providing reference materials for host country businessmen interested in doing business with American firms. Local publishers, booksellers, and importers visit these libraries from time to time, and would do so more often if American catalogs were available.

Then, too, local businessmen looking for references on doing business with the Americans would find references to American books in their fields that are otherwise not likely to be known in their country to be especially valuable. This is not a new recommendation for the Commerce Department, whose overseas libraries do contain catalogs of major export industries; rather, it is a recommendation that the book industry be given special consideration in the context of its importance to this national security study. USIA librarians are already on the promotional mailing lists of many publishers, but whether catalogs and promotional materials are maintained for their patrons or for themselves is discretionary.

As important as book review journals and other bibliographic tools and publisher materials are, we must keep in mind that they are, for the most part, designed and produced with American users in mind. They do not necessarily highlight books of special interest to USIA foreign audiences. That agency needs to alert local opinion leaders to American books which are relevant to USIA's mission and purpose, and give them information on the content of such books. The publications so far discussed undoubtedly have value in serving USIA's special purpose. However, many serious professional and educational works are simply not reviewed in the general media, and scholarly journals have space limitations resulting in reviews long after publication that leave any real promotion to word-of-mouth discussion among colleagues at conferences, seminars, and association meetings. Other governments face a similar problem, i.e., how to provide information about books that especially promote their national interests. For those with major book industries, one answer has been to produce special listings and appraisals of such books in an attractive publications format—review journals that are made available on a regular basis to international book constituencies. The British Council produces the most informative and popular monthly journal, *British Book News,* which lists and at least briefly reviews most important British books. Editorially prepared by a staff that calls on the academic and professional communities for substantive judgements and appraisals of what is useful, *British Book News* is printed and distributed for the council by the prominent British publisher and book export firm, B.H. Blackwell's. *British Book News* has become in part self-sufficient, through paid subscriptions, which Blackwell's promotes, and advertising by British publishers. France, Spain, and Germany are among those countries with similar publications, either in English or in their native languages. The Soviets, with their aggressive export distribution policy, produce *Books and Art in the USSR,* a quarterly publication listing and reviewing books, and featuring articles on cultural subjects as well as reprinted speeches of party and governmental leaders.

USIA also produces journals and magazines in support of its various programs that include book reviews or book lists, *Problems of Communism* and *English Teaching Forum* being the most well known. In the mid 1960s, the agency initiated a short-lived *American Book Review*, consisting largely of reprinted reviews from the domestic media rather than original news as in the British publication. Faced with a shrinking budget and staff, USIA decided that it was necessary to rely on regular book review publications (*Booklist, Library Journal,* etc.) and forego a review journal specifically directed at the foreign reader. Ironically, the British Council editors note that when *British Book News* was initiated, *American Book Review* was a major source of ideas for its development.

More recently, the USIA library in Tokyo launched its own book promotion publication in Japanese on an experimental basis. *U.S. Book News* contained reviews of books excerpted from the USIA "Book Announcements" and informed local publishers that the books were available at the library for examination as translation candidates. In terms of the number of bids offered to acquire rights, the results were encouraging and the *News* found that even in a media-rich country like Japan bibliographic needs were not being met from traditional commercial services. Unexpectedly, book importers began asking to be included on the *News* mailing list, and the USIA library was able to report that commercial imports were an unplanned result of its translation promotion.

As we have reported, Task Force members and other discussants consulted by the Reid Foundation Study Group agree without reservation that a principal barrier to the buying of American books and translation rights around the world is the lack of these bibliographic materials and reviews. The Task Force should consider the most effective roles for the principal U.S. government agencies concerned with promoting U.S. books or trade abroad and ensure a steady flow of information on the content of American books to academic and scholarly communities, journalists, publishers, booksellers, librarians, etc. Among the options that the Reid Foundation Study Group believes merit the Task Force's special attention are those listed below.

1. Announcements through the AAP, *Publishers' Weekly,* and other media, of the government's interest in having publisher catalogs available in its overseas installations.
2. Adding of major book review publications to USIA library collections, as well as providing complimentary subscriptions to them and to the book review sections of major American newspapers for selected host country libraries and, in developing countries, to local publishers and booksellers.

3. Adding scholarly and professional journals to USIA libraries, and providing complimentary subscriptions for leading foreign members of these disciplines and professions. This would give them a greater sense of collegiality with their American counterparts and inform them of the status of American research in their disciplines, as well as provide them with information about current books through review essays and regular book reviews. The Task Force will also want to consider the possibility of public and private sector grants to American learned societies and associations that would enable them to establish complimentary memberships and offer gratis subscriptions to foreign leaders in the disciplines.
4. Provision of *Books in Print* for any institution or organization needing American books regularly. This publication is very expensive and scarcely used abroad, except by the most affluent organizations in developed countries. The Task Force will want to consider the feasibility of providing relatively new back copies to selected booksellers, publishers, and libraries. (The Asia Foundation already does this for its client institutions by soliciting from U.S. booksellers donations of their prior editions as they purchase the latest ones available.)

Methods of identifying appropriate recipient institutions and organizations, as well as ways to provide subscriptions for the above-mentioned publications, include:

1. USIA overseas posts can determine recipients and make direct presentations;
2. USIA can make grants to American nonprofit institutions such as the Asia Foundation, AMIDEAST, and the Inter-American Foundation to help identify accredited recipients, purchase subscriptions, and handle mailings.
3. USIA can provide direct funding to the ALA, R.R. Bowker, and other publishers of academic, scholarly, and professional journals, allowing them to provide complimentary subscriptions.

A specially tailored book review journal listing books directly relevant to USIA interests can be considered, one to be distributed by USIA overseas posts to booksellers, librarians, professors, journalists, writers, other intellectual leaders, and general readers with an interest in the United States. It could be similar to *British Book News,* featuring brief reviews prepared in the scholarly community. ALA Executive Director and Task Force member Robert Wedgeworth urges pre-existing reviews that appear in existing media should be used for content of the American journal, to the extent this is possible.

8

International Book Fairs and Book Exhibits

William M. Childs

The need to inform overseas institutions and individuals on the content of American books by providing them with a continuing flow of book review and bibliographic publications was addressed in the preceding chapter; the technical question of how to order American books will be reviewed in chapter 12. This chapter examines international exhibits, an equally important informational and promotional tool giving buyers the chance to become familiar with book content and, *at the same time,* with ordering and payment procedures, far from an automatic process. Principal opportunities for exhibiting books overseas are offered by international book fairs. These are essentially events for professionals of the international book world where publishers, booksellers, and rights brokers from many countries conduct business with each other. Only a few can claim to be truly international: Frankfurt, Barcelona-Madrid, perhaps Cairo, and the Indian World Book Fair in New Delhi. (Both Cairo and New Delhi, however, open their doors to the general public.) International fairs, best described as national fairs with an international flavor, however, abound, providing opportunities for displaying and selling books throughout the world. International book fairs are held annually in such developing countries as Algeria, Argentina, Bahrain, Brazil, Egypt, India, Iraq, Kuwait, the Philippines, Saudi Arabia, Senegal, and Zimbabwe, and in developed countries such as Belgium, France, Germany, Italy, Japan, Spain, and the United Kingdom. Socialist countries with such fairs include Bulgaria, Hungary, Poland, the Peoples Republic of China, the U.S.S.R. (biennial), and Yugoslavia.

Do American publishers take full advantage of these opportunities? The Reid Foundation Study Group has established that few do, and even fewer explore the growing opportunities to display books presented by international scholarly and professional association meetings that move annually from country to country. Task Force members were nearly unanimous in rating participation in international book fairs and exhibits as high in importance as any of the other forms of promotion, i.e., book reviews, bibliographic publications, advertising, direct mail, etc. Many discussants pointed to the rising costs of more direct, targeted international promotion making exhibiting a more attractive and necessary option. (Even the larger publishers are forced to curtail calls by their overseas sales representatives on bookstores, libraries, and universities, and limit the numbers of sample copies they provide and the catalogs and promotional mailings they send, etc.) Book fairs are trade events, that bring together under one roof (several in the case of giants such as Frankfurt) virtually all of the world's major importers, distributors, and booksellers—from developed as well as developing countries. These essentially trade events offer opportunities far beyond taking orders. Relationships can be established and cemented with booksellers from every corner of the earth, as can enduring friendships. Newcomers and even old hands to international book fairs should look for and expect to find such well-established importers and booksellers as Argentina's Isay Klasse (Tres Americas), Australia's James Bennet (John E. Bennet Co.), Egypt's Ahmed Amin (Academic Bookshop) or Sayed E. Gabri (Al Ahram), Israel's Eri Steimatzky (Steimatzky's Agency), Japan's Tommy Nao (Kinokunia Co.), Hiroyuki Watanabe (Toppan Co.), or Charles Tuttle (Charles E. Tuttle Co.), Lebanon's Marco Hazan or Jihad Naufal (Levant Distributors Co.), to name only a handful of members of the world's widely known international bookselling community.

Trade fairs also provide marketing opportunities that extend well beyond selling books. The larger ones beginning with Frankfurt have become brokering exchanges for subsidiary rights transactions as the book world is very well aware. Frankfurt especially has also become the meeting ground of the publishing conglomerates, the multinationals—the board room away from home. Here, acquisitions, mergers, takeovers, etc., are negotiated and, sometimes, consummated. This level of doing business at the major trade fairs is not likely to concern the larger part of the U.S. publishing world. But, there is something for everyone. To see and be seen is all part of the international publishing and bookselling world. Reid Foundation Study Group members, with the confirmation of Task Force members and many discussants, believe that American publishers large and small planning to expand their already established international operations, as well as those planning to sell books beyond the water's edge, would be well advised to give serious thought and consideration to displaying their books at international book fairs and exhibits.

A distinction is made here between book fairs and book exhibits. The one brings together book world professionals, publishers, and booksellers, to buy and sell books, of course, but also to buy and sell rights as well as to prospect for imprints and publishing firms to merge into one's multinational complex. The other, much more modest in impact on the industry, brings together people interested in books to buy and to read. These are usually academic or professional members of associations attending an international conference, convention, or meeting of their association. Here, a publisher can find an audience he might not otherwise ever reach. Most major academic disciplines on the university level have formed a professional association. Many of these have joined an international federation with their counterparts in other countries, which holds annual meetings rotating among member association countries.

There is, of course, an impressive American presence at the largest international book fair—Frankfurt. One collective exhibit organizer consulted by a Reid Foundation Study Group member said that if the Frankfurt International Book Fair were the only gauge by which to measure the American involvement on the international book trade scene, there would be no reason to be concerned. His group's American cooperative stand at Frankfurt has always been well received and usually has as many publishers represented as can be accommodated. He attributes this success at Frankfurt to the widely held belief among American publishers that the Frankfurt fair is a critical one for a number of reasons, most having to do with developing prestige at home as well as abroad. Some 6,500 publishers from 78 countries showed more than 350,000 titles in the international halls at Frankfurt this year, making absence almost more noticeable than presence for a book publisher on the rise.

However, that is not that exhibitor's experience with other book fairs, nor does it hold true with respect to meetings of scholarly and professional associations and international congresses where book exhibiting opportunities are increasing. He mails out invitations for a number of varied exhibits each year, to large and small commercial publishers as well as to associations and research institutes. The rate of response is mostly disappointing. Of significance to the subject of international book fairs and exhibits—and to the U.S. Books Abroad study—is the typical reason given when he makes follow-up phone calls: in nine out of ten cases, publishers inform him that they are not interested in book exports.

As we point out in other chapters in this study, our research has revealed that many American publishers are awed and even intimidated by the complexities of selling books abroad: customs and shipping requirements, exchange rates, pro forma invoices, and the many other requirements and formalities of doing business in far off markets. They also tend to doubt that the expense of promoting to overseas markets, at least in Third World countries, can be proven cost-effective when measured against the results—nor worth the risk and bother.

Experienced observers on the international book scene believe, too, that many of the smaller commercial houses and nonprofit sector publishers carrying on important research and producing valuable studies relevant to the needs and interests of overseas readers ignore opportunities to display their publications abroad, due to the complexities of participation, the mounting costs of exhibiting overseas, and doubts that exhibiting so far from home is worth the trouble and cost. Many hope that simply sending catalogs and promotional brochures, or just encouraging word-of-mouth publicity, will bring in as many foreign orders as could reasonably be expected anyway.

It seems, therefore, that while "everybody" shows up at Frankfurt, only the larger U.S. textbook houses are represented at other book fairs, especially those in developing countries. Feffer & Simons, a U.S. publishers' export representative firm, is the most consistent collective exhibitor, and neither that firm nor the largest publishers currently extend their displays to professional, disciplinary, and association meetings.

A public-private effort toward developing awareness of exhibit opportunities around the world and toward making the cost of participation more attractive is, in the view of Reid Foundation Study Group members, very much in the national interest, and will eventually result in self-supporting exhibit displays becoming part of publisher overseas promotion programs. We have found that some smaller commercial publishers and most, if not all, association publishers lack confidence that they are sufficiently sophisticated even in marketing and promoting their books at home, and tend to doubt they could find their way through the maze of overseas bookselling. Some nonprofit publishers are only just beginning to show up at exhibits in the U.S. and believe they are simply not yet ready to venture into the unknown business of international book fairs or even into the international meetings of their counterpart associations held abroad, which their own scholars often attend. With public-private involvement, we believe participation of this increasingly significant sector of American publishing in international efforts could be increased.

The U.S. Information Agency and the Department of Commerce should take the lead in coordinating U.S. participation in international book fairs and exhibits, including organizing American national stands at those events where that is the more appropriate approach. Either or both agencies should consider providing support for the private sector presence at national stands it may organize.

Book exhibit activities that USIA, AID and the Commerce Department have successfully supported in the past include:

1. *American National Stands*. A U.S. national stand organized jointly by USIA and the Association of American Publishers and the Association of American University Presses (AAUP) appeared each year at Frankfurt until 1972. It would be desirable to reestablish that cooperative arrange-

ment with the industry, which could also provide a model to be replicated at other international fairs, especially those in developing countries. The exhibit would include books related to USIA interests as well as other serious American books in all fields. It should include books published in other countries under USIA aegis as well, and serve as a base for informing foreign publishers about USIA's publishing and library programs in their countries. USIA has taken the first steps toward such participation with a stand at Frankfurt in 1983 and 1984 that displayed prize-winning American books (an exhibit which the Reid Foundation Study Group hopes will expand next year to include the *Choice* "best scholarly books of the year" selections), a collection of bibliographic reference materials for attendee use, and a computer terminal that provided access to book trade software programs. Duplicate sets were shown at Liber '84 in Barcelona (Spain, October, 1984) and the January, 1985, Cairo International Book Fair with good results.

2. *USIA Participation in Other International Book Fairs and Other Book Exhibits*. Selected smaller book fairs, especially those in developing countries and those organized in connection with meetings of academic and professional associations, can be readily identified and evaluated as to their suitability for American book exhibits by either the public or private sector—or both. While American publishers may not be interested in having their own exhibits or in sending representatives, it would be in their interest to provide complimentary display copies of books, catalogs, and other promotional materials for one or more collective stands or a U.S. national display organized by USIA. Such gatherings provide excellent opportunities for expanding the involvement of smaller commercial publishers and nonprofit organizations, and for introducing them into the international book fairs and exhibits beyond Frankfurt. Whether a U.S. stand appears alone, or is supplemented or displaced by collective or individual private stands, can remain an open question, answered in the context of each event and the likely market served by it.
3. *USIA Thematic Exhibits*. USIA is to be commended for continuing, albeit on a very modest scale, its thematic book exhibits, and should be encouraged to step up this activity in terms of collection sizes, number of sets of each collection, and the number of exhibit events. In 1983, USIA displayed such thematic exhibits on some 60 occasions, compared with an average of some 200 or more events annually in the 1960s. In consultation with American publishers, USIA determines the themes of collections shown by its overseas posts at seminars, professional gatherings, and at national book events. For example, thematic exhibits currently circulating among USIA posts include "America's Best Prize-Winning Books, 1983–1984," "Women in the Contemporary World," and "Electronic Age." Publishers donate the books to be shown, and

USIA handles shipping and display costs. More American publishers and nonprofit groups should be involved, and local booksellers should be encouraged to sell books or at least take orders at these exhibits. Such events present an opportunity to develop ties between local book trade firms and American exporters. USIA staff in charge of such exhibits should take every opportunity also to involve the USAID missions, which should see these exhibits as a chance to display books on development-related themes, for the benefit of their constituents.

4. *U.S. Trade Shows*. The Department of Commerce Commercial Attachés organize several kinds of book exhibits through their Overseas Trade Centers. The stimulus for Overseas Trade Centers' exhibits is trade-related, of course, with emphasis on such technical topics as engineering, computer science, medicine, and business administration. Books are welcome as a component of appropriate thematic shows, as well as being the focus of separate shows at certain centers from time to time (most recent 1984 book shows were held in Sao Paulo, Brazil, and Milan). Discussants from industry as well as government believe that Commerce Trade Centers, Commercial Sections, and USIA offices at U.S. embassies could make book trade shows more effective by joining forces and expanding categories of books displayed to include additional, but related themes, such as U.S. economic history, free market economics, U.S. trade policy, etc.
5. *Permanent Display Centers*. Apart from book fairs and other exhibit events, USIA, AID, and Commerce offices in publishing or trade centers around the world have in the past set up semi-permanent or permanent displays of American books in their respective interest fields, usually in either Commerce or USIA facilities. The USAID mission in Cairo, for example, in the late 1970s set up a textbook display center with the cooperation of the USIA American Library to show Egyptian professors the range of American textbooks in development-related fields. American publishers provided complimentary display copies and fulfilled requests for examination copies. Such permanent displays give sponsoring USIA posts and other embassy offices the chance to put books supporting their objectives in front of their respective audiences, and allow these organizations to receive constituent feedback on books of interest.

In a survey probing USIA overseas posts' reactions to reinvigorated book program plans, nearly 60 indicated a desire to participate in local book events and indicated interest in holding independent exhibitions under their sponsorship. In response, USIA has already included specific enhancement funding for "Book Exhibits and Fairs" in its proposed fiscal year 1986 American Books Abroad budget. Funding is earmarked for shipping, space rental, production of catalogs and brochures, and additional personnel at home as well as at exhibition events.

While funding is being sought for enhanced efforts, USIA has enough of a foundation of experience to allow a significant presence at several major international book fairs, and to launch some new exhibits independent of such fairs (including restoration of its thematic book exhibit program). What is lacking at the present time, however, is a trained exhibit staff. The need for rebuilding book promotion and publishing expertise is recognized in the agency's 1986 budget, and addressed as well in chapters 10 and 14. However, many publishers and others believe USIA should move quickly into exhibit activities to maintain the momentum created in 1983–84 with modest stands at the major fairs. The current lack of experienced and knowledgeable staff need not interfere with this progress and does not preclude quick action. Experienced specialists can be made available, from groups such as those listed below.

1. American and foreign publishing associations, publishing firms, and book trade organizations.
2. Cooperative exhibit firms with experience in the collective exhibition of books from many publishers on a fee basis, such as Academia Book Exhibits.
3. Export representative firms that mount cooperative exhibits with their client publishers at Frankfurt and other international book fairs, such as Feffer & Simons, Kaiman & Polon, et al.
4. Wholesalers such as Baker & Taylor and Key Books International that buy and sell books from most U.S. publishers and have been increasing their international book fair exposure, as well as related firms such as U.S.A. Book Expo, which expects soon to be established as an export trading company (see chapter 4). The latter combines features of a wholesaling organization with collective displays. Baker and Taylor is also venturing onto new ground, with a collective stand announced for the September, 1985, Moscow International Book Fair in which 191 publishers have agreed to display books.
5. Other specialists experienced in international book exhibiting and knowledgeable in guiding booksellers, librarians, professors, students, and general book readers around the world on how to order American books.

Some skeptics question whether international book fairs and exhibits can provide the continuing communication between U.S. and foreign publishers or booksellers on new and forthcoming books that catalogs, mailings, and periodic sales visits can provide. After all, they observe, book fairs are only once-a-year events, and some (the Jerusalem International Book Fair, India's World Book Fair, and the Moscow International Book Fair) are held only every other year. Still, most U.S. Books Abroad Task Force members and discussants who have participated in such events are convinced that book fairs and exhibits are fundamentally important. They provide the only opportunities available for the overseas book world to see and handle a large number of new

American books at one place and time. And, when American representatives are present, prospective buyers or publishers can learn not just about the books themselves but also about how to order them or acquire English language reprint or translations rights. In addition, the Reid Foundation Study Group considers book fairs to be essential for building the personal relationships between American and foreign book people that are the most consistent and lasting means of international book development. Exhibits at association congresses and professional meetings tie authors and readers, scholars and disciplines together in ways that have impact well beyond the immediate events.

There seems to be little disagreement with the idea that USIA should take the lead in organizing American national stands at international book fairs and at other events with book exhibit possibilities, and in coordinating the activities of American publishers, collective exhibitors, and local publishers and booksellers. Increasing participation at these events by the numerous smaller commercial presses, as well as by the nonprofit, scholarly publishers whose books and journals are so little known abroad, should be a goal for USIA, which should also involve other government agencies with responsibilities for economic development and promoting U.S. commercial interests. Other governments (British, French, Italian, Spanish, and Soviet, for example) facilitate the participation of their domestic publishers at fairs with free transportation of books and exhibit materials, subsidized travel costs for publisher representatives, reimbursement for exhibit space rental, etc. The French government's office of promotion of French publishing provided exhibits of its country's books at 60 events in 1984; the British Council at over 750; and the Soviet Union exhibited at over 1,500!

More information is needed on opportunities to exhibit American books around the world. Reid Foundation Study Group members were unable to identify any comprehensive listing or source of information on the great number of book trade, academic, and professional meetings at which these other governments help their publishers exhibit. The AAP International Division publishes an annual listing for members titled "Profiles of Major International Book Fairs" that covers 20 fairs, but no other events. The AAP planned at one stage to compile information on more book fairs but that effort was dropped some time ago. Once each year, *Publishers' Weekly* publishes a calendar of book fairs, but it and a similar listing in *Literary Market Place* (both the American and international editions) are briefer than that of the AAP. Neither USIA nor the Department of Commerce now attempts to assemble such information in any organized fashion.

As an initial step, then, toward encouraging greater U.S. participation in international book fairs and book exhibiting events, Reid Foundation Study Group members believe that a central file on such exhibits is needed, one that would include all essential information needed by interested exhibitors. It should contain information on sponsoring organizations, purpose, names and addresses of organizers, dates, costs, application requirements, opportunities to sell books, involvement of the local book trade, customs formalities, numbers and kinds of exhibitors, and any other pertinent information. It should include as well evaluations of strengths and weaknesses, exhibit by exhibit, by past U.S. and other exhibitors, as the AAP study does for the fairs it includes in its "Profile."

The Reid Foundation Study Group has suggested the following options for consideration by the U.S. Books Abroad Task Force in making its recommendations to USIA:

1. The Department of Commerce and USIA should take the lead in the establishment and maintenance of a central file on international and national book fairs as well as on other events offering exhibit opportunities, and promote the list in the publishing community generally. The contents of the file could be maintained and developed by either the public or the private sector, the main concerns being accuracy and access to the private and nonprofit publishing sectors.
2. The federal government should participate directly in all international book fairs, mounting American stands as cooperative ventures with the industry as well as facilitating individual and collective publisher exhibits where they are appropriate and likely to be effective. A smaller U.S. presence could be arranged for national and local book fairs where American publishers would probably not find it feasible to exhibit individually.
3. USIA, as the agency with the most closely related cultural objectives, should work to ensure that there are American book exhibits at international gatherings of professionals and scholars focused on the disciplines related to those events. If appropriate, USIA could facilitate displays in cooperation with the U.S. organization involved or with other non-profit institutions.
4. USIA should reinvigorate its thematic exhibit program, with the cooperation of individual American publishers, and every opportunity should be taken to involve local booksellers to ensure the availability of books for sale or, at the least, the presence of someone to take orders. These collections have in the past made it possible for USIA posts to sustain the interest of special groups in American books when few other opportunities were available.
5. Government agencies such as USIA, the Department of State, AID, and the Department of Commerce should join in establishing permanent display centers to house American books in educational and development-related fields, business, and management, and on American

culture, society, and policies. Such centers would be located either in U.S. embassies abroad, in USIA libraries or Commerce Trade Centers, or in private institutions.

In chapter 16 this study points to activities of foreign governments that directly support their publishers in a great many international book fairs and book exhibits. The Reid Foundation Study Group is not necessarily suggesting that U.S. national policy requires direct support of American publishers at all events. However, the national interest—from a commercial, cultural, and informational standpoint—would seem to call for governmental leadership in a public-private cooperative endeavor to ensure greater U.S. presence in book exhibits overseas. In almost all cases the public sector should be present at fairs to provide access to information, especially on publishers not represented, albeit the nature of each event will determine the relative size of public and/or private stands.

9

Seeding the Marketplace: Presentations and Donated Books

Donald E. McNeil

Presentation is an immediately apparent response to the shortage of American books abroad, bypassing many problems that handicap commercial distribution. In addition, books distributed by non-governmental institutions appeal to and at the same time demonstrate U.S. philanthropic traditions. Between 1950 and 1985 some 85 million American books were distributed abroad by nonprofit institutions and businesses, according to professionals in the field, books that went primarily to developing countries of Africa, Asia, and Latin America. At various times, at least part of the cost for distributing those books was provided by AID, USIA, the Library of Congress, or other governmental bodies with specialized international interests. In addition, it is estimated that government agencies themselves distributed as many as 35 million donated and purchased presentation books over that same time span.

While the 120 million books distributed in the developing world represent an impressive demonstration of American philanthropy—with an annualized distribution rate of 3.4 million books—only a dent has been made in the book gap via donations. Also, the greater percentage of the books was distributed prior to 1970, for tax reasons that are explained below. USIA, for example, distributed as many books in one year in the 1960s as it did during the entire decade of the 1970s. In the ensuing years, developing world populations have expanded, literacy has grown sharply, and several new generations of students have reached the book market age. Even though books considered here are those written in English, it must be remembered that English has become the global language of many professions; it is a national language in countries formerly colonized by the British, and, as observed in previous chapters, it is the language of instruction in many university disciplines.

At a rate of 3.5 million donated books per year (or even at the 5 million level that nonprofit distribution organizations believe they could readily handle) observers conclude that donations can be made without negative impact on commercial exports. In fact, seeding the marketplace is an important byproduct of donations. Donated books create and maintain familiarity for needy readers who will some day be buying American books; they aid and improve the learning of English in countries where English teaching might well falter without them.

Obviously, for the recipients, all book donations are without cost. For the intermediary agencies, there are costs for all presentations, which are sometimes shared by the recipients: however, most often delivery costs must be funded by the distributor. It is necessary to distinguish between books purchased by the intermediary groups and books that they receive without charge from individual, institutional, and corporate donors. In the latter case, to the extent that there is a cost to the original donor (e.g., production cost for a publisher), such cost can be recouped through a tax deduction for a charitable contribution.

Government agencies such as AID and USIA are the major providers of purchased presentations. In the nonprofit sector one significant book buyer is the Asia Foundation, which spends about $500,000 annually on books for its Asian constituency. Freedom House purchases most of the titles selected for its bookshelves. Since these presentation books are purchased by the distributing agency, they can be titles related to specific programs of that particular agency. Recipients of purchased presentations from USIA are usually individuals whose in-depth understanding of a subject is important for diplomatic reasons. More broadly directed USIA presentations focus on building American studies and literature collections at universities, as well as ensuring that important U.S. texts are available at educational institutions where comparative literature, government, economics, etc., are studied. Books are also purchased to support the work of exchange scholars, such as those abroad in the Fulbright program. AID has no book program as such at this time, but books related to specific needs that arise in developmental programs are purchased with AID funds. Such books are selected and purchased by the foreign institution involved in the project, with no direct AID procurement role.

Selection is a factor in purchased presentations that gives that category a notable advantage over donated books, although whether that advantage was emphasized by discussants to this study was determined primarily by their perspective and prior experience. Essentially, those who prefer selected purchase are concerned that the attraction of donated books—they are free and involve many volunteers—has in the past led to higher budgetary priorities for such books than for those purchased by the federal government, an emphasis not in keeping with the substantive usefulness of the donations to the recipients. These professionals stress that necessary preparation such as sorting, examination and discard of unusables, repair, and repacking narrows the apparent cost effectiveness edge of donations when these services are performed by salaried personnel. Cutting manpower costs in the U.S. by shipping to recipient countries for sorting is sometimes effective: however this occurs mostly when there is an explicit understanding between private donors here and the intended recipients that the latter will sort, and when books can be shipped free through space-available programs such as the Department of the Navy's Operation Handclasp.

During the 1960s, USIA funding for distribution of unsorted used-book collections was discontinued due to Congressional doubts about spending for books of which the content was unknown. Problems also arose at USIA posts when shipments arrived unsorted. Recipients were disappointed too; they had not expected anything less than current, mint-condition texts from American embassies. The policy of leaving such used book donations entirely to private and nonprofit channels is still in effect, and no discussants involved with this study suggested a change. Recipients abroad have also learned from experience and a policy of not accepting used or miscellaneous collections has been adopted in some countries.

The distribution of donated books funded by government agencies is not ruled out, however, by earlier experiences. At least 70 percent of the 120 million books donated over 35 years is estimated to have come from mint condition stocks of U.S. publishers, as charitable donations for which the donors took a tax write-off. Until 1969, the Internal Revenue Code allowed a write-off for charitable donations of inventory property by a corporation at the "fair market value," which was translated in most industries as the retail value of the donation. Books eligible for such a deduction were made available to charitable institutions and government agencies from overstocks, unsold remainders, and dated editions soon to be replaced, in quantities sometimes limited only by the ability of the distributor to effectively place them abroad and to finance the cost of handling, shipping, and delivery.

Current stock donations by publishers were particularly attractive to USIA because bibliographic information was readily available in catalogs, allowing informed, program-related selection; such books were also available in multiple copies, allowing both cost-effective service to a number of U.S. embassies at the same time and multiple copy donations for use as classroom texts. While selection was limited to what was offered, informed selection was nevertheless possible from within the offered lists. During its peak donated book year, 1966, USIA distributed some 4.5 million texts. Financial assistance to nonprofit organizations supplemented that direct effort. The Asia

Foundation, the Darien (Connecticut) Book Project, Project HOPE, the Brothers Brothers Foundation, Freedom House, and the Pan American Development Foundation are among the donated book organizations that USIA, AID, and the U.S. Navy's Operation Handclasp assisted in the 1960s, and which still distribute books in the 1980s.

The 1969 revision of the Internal Revenue Code reduced the corporate charitable deduction for a donation of inventory property to the manufacturing cost. The effect on international donated book activities was dramatic and immediate. At USIA, where donations dropped from the millions to a low of less than 100,000 in the 1970s and 1980s, a separate donated book office and budget item were abolished. In the private sector, the tax change had an impact on nonprofit distribution efforts. In an article for the *Encyclopedia of Library Information Science* not yet published, Leonard R. Sussman of Freedom House reports that "eight U.S. book donation programs that were operating in the early 1970s are no longer functioning."[1] In 1980 and 1981, the Asia Foundation reported publisher donations to be 409,000 and 327,000, respectively.[2]

In 1981, private sector mobilization in support of public diplomacy was reaffirmed by USIA Director Charles Z. Wick as being critical to USIA's success. Donated books supporting agency objectives were given top priority on the agenda of a USIA Book and Library Advisory Committee Wick created that year. Committee members were surprised to find on their agenda small donation requests from abroad that were clearly justifiable, (e.g., some 400 titles for the American studies collection of a Scandinavian library) for which procurement funding was not available in USIA. Agency resource staff members for the committee explained that a budget was set for each USIA office abroad to cover all program costs for a fiscal year. However, country budgets had shrunk during the 1970s because of inflation as well as additional nonbibliographic program requirements created without comparable funding increases. In 1981, Director Wick asked the committee not only to study provision of donated books to needy overseas institutions but to USIA's own shrunken library collections as well. Until the present time, USIA has fulfilled the terms of agreements, worked out with publishers in the 1950s, that no donated books would be added to its own library collections. The book industry wants to make sure that donations are not substituted for USIA purchases, and that precedents will not be set for donated book requests from other governmental institutions that traditionally purchase their books. This concern that donations not replace purchases is recognized by nonprofit

---

[1] Leonard R. Sussman, "International Book Donation Programs," *Encyclopedia of Library Information Science* (in press, 1985).

[2] Books For Asia, *Program Report, 1981* (San Francisco: Asia Foundation, 1982).

groups such as the Asia Foundation,[3] whose donated book distribution is carefully structured to meet pressing book needs of specific institutions unable to afford them. Some few developing countries are excluded entirely as donated book recipients because of market potential identified by publishers. In others, foundation offices screen book requests carefully in terms of the content of the request and the need status of the institution. Publishers can and do proscribe distribution in certain countries; what they cannot do under tax rules is specify the country or recipients that *will* receive their donation. Foreign country proscription on donated book use applies equally to government distributor organizations such as USIA that receive donations from the industry.

In late 1983, USIA's Book and Library Advisory Committee concluded that only a change in the deduction given publishers for donations on their tax returns would, in the current economic situation, increase the number of books donated to USIA in any meaningful way. (Total book donations to USIA in 1983 numbered 57,000.) Limited to manufacturing cost for a charitable deduction, publishers have turned to an expanding remainder market providing at least minimal return. Books that publishers do not wish to see on the U.S. remainder market because of continuing or replacement sales can be sold abroad or, alternatively, destroyed. In several instances during the 1970 energy crisis years, burning books to heat warehouses combined a manufacturing cost deduction with energy cost savings.

A suggestion that funds be allocated by USIA to pay the shipping cost from publishers' warehouses to USIA warehouses was not considered to be a useful idea. The agency already had a modest budget for this purpose, but found that when publishers did decide to donate books, in most cases they did not consider such assistance necessary. The USIA Book and Library Advisory Committee proposed to Director Wick that an increase in the tax deduction to twice the manufacturing cost be sought through legislation. The U.S. Advisory Commission on Public Diplomacy independently recommended an increase in the tax deduction to the president and the Congress as necessary not only to USIA's public diplomacy mission, but to that of the many nonprofit groups that in the past had made important contributions to filling the book needs of the Third World.[4]

On March 22, 1984, Director Wick presented the advisory committee's proposal for a tax deduction increase to the Department of the Treasury for

---

[3] The Asia Foundation, Paper prepared for the Helen Dwight Reid Educational Foundation on "Books for Asia" (San Francisco: Asia Foundation, 1984.)

[4] U.S. Advisory Commission on Public Diplomacy, *Annual Report to the Congress and the President, 1983* (Washington, D.C.: USIA, 1984).

comment.[5] Mr. Wick observed that the advisory committee was aware that the overall federal economic situation in 1984 meant that it was not the best time to propose an increase in any tax deduction. The committee had pursued the matter because of the fact, that in 1981 and again in 1982, Congress had enacted two exceptions to the manufacturing cost limitation on corporate charitable deductions, and might favorably receive a third proposal for books to be distributed in developing countries to meet critical needs there. In response, the Treasury Department's position was explained as follows:

> In the case of a charitable contribution of appreciated property, the correct result from a tax policy perspective is to require the realization of gain upon the donation and to allow a deduction equal to the property's fair market value. The donor would thus be treated as if he had sold the property and contributed the proceeds to charity. Indeed, the Treasury Department in 1968 proposed such a provision where ordinary income property, including inventory, was donated to charity. In order to achieve substantially the same result, Congress in 1969 enacted the existing provision that limits the charitable contribution deduction allowed for inventory to the cost of producing the property.
>
> The proposal that has been suggested to you with respect to certain contributions of books would limit the effect of the provision enacted in 1969 and would depart from the correct tax policy result. Moreover, an increase in the allowable deduction to twice the manufacturing cost would in most cases shift the cost of the contributed property almost entirely to the Treasury, thereby effectively relieving the donor of most of the cost of the donation. Therefore, although we understand the tremendous importance of making American books available abroad, the Treasury Department would be opposed to any further exception to the rule that the donor of inventory property is entitled to deduct only the cost of producing the property."[6]

By the time the Treasury letter was received at USIA, the tax proposal had been overtaken by events: the National Security Council had dispatched its memorandum to USIA concerning the initiation of the current U.S. Books Abroad study. The independent pursuit of a tax law change has been pursued no further, as the question of donated book needs was merged into the broader national security focus on books of the Reid Foundation study and the Task Force recommendations. In reporting on the Wick/McNamar exchange, however, *Taxation and Accounting* (Bureau of National Affairs, No. 114, June 13, 1984) stated "A Treasury spokesman said department representatives (in response to an invitation from Mr. Wick) will attend the (Task Force) meeting, but added that Treasury still opposes an across-the-board liberalization of tax deductions for donated books."

Meanwhile, an examination of the special rules relative to tax deductions

---

[5] Letter, USIA Director Charles Z. Wick to Deputy Secretary of the Treasury R. T. McNamar, March 23, 1984.

[6] Letter, Deputy Secretary of the Treasury R.T. McNamar to USIA Director Charles Z. Wick, May 1, 1984.

for donations enacted by Congress in 1981 and 1982 was being made in philanthropic and corporate tax circles, to determine what book donations might qualify. The Special Rule of 1982 (Internal Revenue Code, Section 170[e][4]) is applicable only to "contributions of scientific property used for research," and has been cited in donated books discussions only as evidence of the possible receptivity of Congress to further change in justifiable circumstances. Also, the charitable deduction for such donations was set at twice the manufacturing cost. The Special Rule of 1981, however, (Internal Revenue Code, Section 170[e][3]) concerns "certain contributions of inventory and other property," and reads essentially as follows:

> Qualified contributions—for purposes of this paragraph, a qualified contribution shall mean a charitable contribution of (inventory) property . . . by a corporation . . . to an organization which is described in Section 501[c][3] as exempt under Section 501[a] (other than a private foundation as defined in Section 509[a] which is not an operating foundation, as defined in Section 4942[j][3]), but only if—
> (i) the use of the property by the donee is related to the purpose or function constituting the basis for its exemption under Section 501 and the property is to be used by the donee solely for the care of the ill, the needy, or infants;
> (ii) the property is not transferred by the donee in exchange for money, other property, or services;
> (iii) the taxpayer receives from the donee a written statement representing that its use and disposition of the property will be in accordance with the provisions of clauses (i) and (ii). . . .

Analysis of the requirements of this special rule by publishers, intermediaries, and 501[c][3] organizations and the development of procedures for handling, transfer, and certification that will meet those requirements have resulted in a substantial increase in books made available by publishers.

In its 1984 annual report, the Asia Foundation recorded that the number of new books and journals it donated rose to 800,000 in 1983, and that volume was expected to increase in 1984 (total 1983 book and journal distribution was 1.175 million).[7] The Brothers Brothers Foundation reports its annual distribution in 1983 to have been 1.5 million books. The Foundation for Books to China expects to distribute 250,000 books in each of the next two years. Most of these increases in donations are credited to implementation by charities and publishers of the "ill, the needy, or infants" provision of the 1981 Special Rule. The total of 4 million donated books distributed by private charities in 1983 is expected to increase to 5 million in 1985, assuming that the requirements of the Special Rule can continue to be interpreted as they are.[8] But the Asia Foundation notes that "if the law were to be amended to give a greater

[7] The Asia Foundation, *Annual Report,* 1984 (San Francisco: Asia Foundation, 1984).

[8] Luke Hingson, "Private Efforts to Provide Book Donations Overseas" (memorandum, July 29, 1984, to Donald E. McNeil, Reid Foundation). Brothers Brothers Foundation, Pittsburgh.

incentive for giving donated books, this would be to the foundation's advantage. Of greater importance would be a broader definition of to whom the donated books could be given. If narrowly confined to the "ill, the needy, or infants," many if not most of the foundation's current recipients could be ruled out."[9]

Compliance requirements for the Special Rule donations are admittedly awkward, and indeed costly. "Regulations on completing documentation, stamping books, and maintaining logs are costly in terms of staff time, and will become more costly if donations increase," the Asia Foundation reports. The foundation notes that the additional record keeping on titles sent abroad and individual title lists detailing local distribution in each country have been determined by the publisher donors as necessary for their tax records if they are to receive the tax deduction of twice their production costs. Assuming a continuation of these Special Rule procedures, the alternative to cutting costs through compliance simplification is to secure additional public and private funding for the increased cost.

USIA is not a 501[c][3] institution, of course, and is not eligible as a recipient organization under the 1981 Special Rule. As we have seen, donations to USIA are deductible only at the manufacturing cost level. In 1984, working with 25-year veteran donated books specialist Max Celnick, the agency conducted an experiment in Tanzania designed to see how the Special Rule might economically serve its purposes. A nonprofit organization in the U.S. received books from publishers, based on its 501[c][3] status, and complied with all state-side requirements described above by the Asia Foundation prior to delivering the books to USIA for transport to a private organization in Tanzania. The latter group provided lists of in-country recipients to the American embassy to be transmitted back to the nonprofit organization in the U.S. for publisher audit purposes certifying that the recipients had been needy. The process proved cumbersome, but the agency believes the experiment was successful and can work in other situations. In addition, the USIA General Counsel ruled that the process met the requirements of the tax code Special Rule.[10]

As noted by the Asia Foundation, requirements of the Special Rule add to the cost of handling donated books. We have referred several times in this chapter to the already existing cost of donated books, e.g., the costs of receiving, sorting, storage, packing, handling, shipping and delivery. Such costs are particularly and frequently emphasized by skeptics who are more comfortable with selected purchased books. Handling costs are not over-

[9] Asia Foundation paper for the Reid Foundation.

[10] Letter, USIA Director Charles Z. Wick to Deputy Secretary of the Treasury R.T. McNamar, May 22, 1984.

looked, indeed cannot be, by advocates of donated book programs. In the past two years, there has been a notable increase in the requests of nonprofit institutions for assistance from the public sector to cover such costs. In 1983 and 1984, USIA gave modest ad hoc grants to the Asia Foundation, the Foundation for Books to China, and the Brothers Brothers Foundation. AID provided modest 1984 grants to the Brothers Brothers Foundation from its Ocean Freight Reimbursement Program for shipments to the English-speaking Caribbean and Africa. In 1985 and beyond, if an expanded donated book effort by such groups is to be encouraged, substantial new funding will be required.

The cost of handling book donations varies with the organization, its method of operation, and its customers. All of the nonprofit organizations observed by Reid Foundation researchers have imaginatively tapped American shipping lines, foreign shipping lines, and airlines, for free or reduced-cost space. Many publishers, as was noted earlier, willingly deliver books to U.S. warehouses of donee organizations without charge. Volunteers sort and pack wherever possible. In the recipient-country, off-loading, sorting, and actual distributions are funded in many instances by the recipient organization, the government of that country, or a charitable institution in the country. Even with these low-cost procedures the Asia Foundation estimates costs averaging 75¢ per book for all expenses from publisher to final recipient. To fund donations, USIA has proposed an initial 1986 budget of $400,000 to be used for direct distribution of books by the agency as well as for assistance to private institutions. That is considered only a beginning, by professional discussants like Max Celnick and Brothers Brothers Foundation president Luke Hingson, if the potential book donations identified are to be transferred to needy users. For example, the Asia Foundation has proposed that with a $1 million funding increase it can distribute to already identified institutions some 2.35 million books and journals, 1.25 million more than the total shipped in 1984.[11] There is no doubt that other institutions will propose similar expansion, if the described interpretation of the 1981 Special Rule for corporate donations is accepted by the IRS and makes possible the availability of more books from publishers. Aside from what government can provide, charities will need to enhance their efforts to increase funding from private sources.

The fact that USIA is the government agency with a specific book mission has focused attention on that agency in connection with donated book funding. While USIA concerns are broad in terms of relevant book subjects,

---

[11] The Asia Foundation, "Preliminary Proposal to the United States Information Agency on Expansion of the Asia Foundation Books for Asia Programs in FY 1986" (San Francisco: Asia Foundation, 1984).

the national interest as defined in this study addresses topics equally related to trade, economic, and technical assistance programs. Other agencies in the public sector ought to join ranks to fund additional donated books related to their objectives, especially AID. That agency presently has a modest program to finance the shipping costs of voluntary aid agencies (the Ocean Freight Reimbursement Program). AID officers note that not only is it a modest fund, but the great number of applicants for such funding make it of minimum value to the concerns of this study. The U.S. Books Abroad Task Force will likely want to suggest an increase for donated book funding in the budgets of AID and various governmental libraries, recognizing that USIA's budget cannot begin to meet the need for scientific, technical, and medical books while meeting USIA's own cultural and social science objectives.

In general, there seems little doubt in this study that there is a major role for donated books, a role needing new emphasis. The fact that donations have limitations, beyond which funding for the purchase of specific books is the only option, has also been emphasized. In fact, the need for a sizeable increase in government funding to buy books for libraries and presentation is not diminished by donations. In addition, donors and donees must be made to understand that donations will not preempt any future commercial activity for American books, and certainly will not dilute the present market. Title selection of donations needs to be studied by all parties on a continuing basis. According to Max Celnick, of the 4 million books distributed abroad in 1983 by nonprofit institutions, some 60 percent were scholarly works representing areas of governmental interest. Content concerns will therefore persist, relative to the question of which donations will be funded by USIA or AID. While discussants urge that as many donations as possible be channeled through nonprofit groups rather than government, to preserve the charitable nature of this activity, it is primarily scholarly and technical books that will justify government funding of donation efforts. (Some Task Force members do believe donations should include children's books.) In any event, Max Celnick agrees that increased selectivity can and should be part of donated book enhancements financed by government.

SELECTED CURRENT GOVERNMENT BOOK PRESENTATION ACTIVITIES

Agency for International Development (AID)

"Project Procurement" and "Commodity Import Program" funding to finance purchases related to AID projects is available to governments of countries where there are assistance programs, for book purchases. The AID Ocean Freight Reimbursement Program finances distribution of donated commodities, including books, to AID-assisted countries.

Department of Agriculture

The National Agricultural Library (NAL) distributes U.S. books, serials, and reports abroad in exchange for foreign publications. The Worldwide Network of Agricultural Libraries of the NAL provides interlibrary loan service, photocopy services, and bibliographic information to individuals and organizations through member libraries.

Department of Health and Human Services

The National Library of Medicine (NLM), part of the National Institutes of Health, has some 400 exchange partners in 72 countries to which NLM sends copies of its bibliographic publications in exchange for foreign materials.

Government Printing Office (GPO)

Under the International Exchange Program, the GPO distributes governmental publications to designated foreign libraries and is reimbursed for the distribution costs by the Smithsonian Institution. Since the GPO is required by law to be self-sustaining, USIA and other government agencies operating abroad must purchase government publications from the GPO for donation purposes as well as for their own libraries.

Library of Congress (LC)

The primary Library of Congress presentation program involves the distribution of American books abroad in exchange for publications of the recipient library's country. The LC exchanges publications with some 13,500 foreign and international libraries. In addition, the library participates in the mutual exchange of official publications with 92 other governments, in accordance with treaties, stipulations, conventions, and other formal agreements. About 1.4 million publications are distributed abroad by the Library of Congress annually.

Operation Handclasp

This Department of the Navy program is a space-available shipping activity using Navy ships. Space on board is available to nonprofit organizations, depending on destination, without charge. Donors are responsible for the delivery cost to the port of embarkation.

Smithsonian Institution

The Smithsonian International Exchange Service is a system through which learned societies in the United States exchange their publications for those of similar institutions in foreign countries. The service has, since 1886, also been the bureau through which U.S. government publications are provided to foreign governments in exchange for their official publications.

U.S. Information Agency (USIA)

Limited funds are available for special presentation purchases, as part of the country budget for each USIA post. Originally required by Congress, and now set by the USIA in Washington, D.C., a ceiling is placed on the funds each post can spend for presentations. In the case of donated books received from publishers, the individual USIA post pays shipping costs from its country budget. The Fulbright and other exchange grantees receive small dollar amounts, as part of their grants, for the purchase of books and materials. The Educational Specialist Grantee Program provides Fulbright grantees with single copies of perhaps 10 titles related to their projects, provided by publishers as promotional copies through the USIA Book Programs Division. Book translation programs provide posts with multiple copies of U.S. titles translated abroad, for presentation to institutions and libraries, and to be used also as promotional samples for textbook committees, educators, book reviewers, and booksellers.

SELECTED CURRENT PRIVATE DONATED BOOK ACTIVITIES

The Adventist Development & Relief Agency International

ADRA is an arm of the Seventh Day Adventists Charities, and books are but one element of its activities. However, ADRA distributes between 100,000 and 150,000 books annually, primarily in developing countries.

Books for Asia Program, Asia Foundation

The Asia Foundation's presentation activity, the largest of that foundation's programs, distributed 1.1 million donated books and journals in 1984 and expects to distribute as many again in 1985. The foundation would like to increase that volume by 1.25 million books in 1986 (new total: 2.35 million), sending books to 10 Asian countries where the foundation has offices which screen and match books and recipients carefully, and through other channels to 14 additional Asian and Pacific countries. Purchased presentations at the $500,000 annual level are made in addition to the donations, and are for special collections in high priority fields. The recipients in those instances are identified before purchases are made.

Brothers Brothers Foundation

Established as a medical assistance charity in 1958, the Brothers Brothers Foundation has gradually expanded its efforts to include the provision of commodities other than medicine that meet developing country needs. Since 1980, the foundation has made book donations that reached an annual level of 1.5 million books in 1983. A special area of involvement for this organization has been the Caribbean, where one major effort has been extensively stocking libraries in English-speaking countries in which the foundation is active. President Luke Hingson reports that the foundation's activities in Africa are expanding, most immediately in the food and medical assistance fields in response to the famine. However, more books will also be sent.

Darien (Connecticut) Book Project

In existence since the 1950s, the Darien project collects books, repairs them as needed, and distributes them abroad at a rate of between 50,000 and 100,000 annually at the present time, using private funds and volunteers.

Freedom House

The Freedom House Bookshelf, initiated some 25 years ago, consisted of 10 titles in American history, culture, literature, and science, chosen by scholars and distributed to potential leaders in Third World countries. In 1969, USIA's "Books USA" program was absorbed by Freedom House to become "Freedom House/Books USA," now consisting of some 90 to 120 titles on each shelf. Since 1959, some 3 million books have been purchased with specially solicited funds and distributed directly or through various U.S. offices abroad. Freedom House has proposed to USIA that the project be continued and expanded in the context of this current book program study.

Foundation for Books for China, San Francisco

Established in 1980, this foundation has already distributed some 700,000 books in the People's Republic of China, with ocean freight assistance from the American President Line. Executive Director Bradford P. Smith reports that the foundation expects to have distributed 250,000 books per year in 1984 and 1985. Distribution is handled currently by various government agencies and educational institutions in China. The foundation also operates a cooperative book program with UNICEF.

International Book Project (IBP), Lexington, Kentucky

This organization acts as a clearing house for donations by individuals and groups throughout the country, matching donors with donees who also contact them for information. In addition, the IBP itself distributes between 50,000 and 100,000 books per year using local volunteers and funding collected in the private sector.

Project HOPE

Project HOPE has been in existence for more than 20 years, providing medical care and medical training in the developing world. One little-known aspect of its program is the presentation of medical books to institutions in the Third World. Providing up to 70,000 books per year, this organization is the largest distributor of donated medical books in the world.

Universal Serials and Book Exchange Inc. (USBE)

Beginning in 1948 as the U.S. Book Exchange, this institution has served as a clearing house in accepting and redistributing publications for libraries around the world. The name was changed in 1975 to emphasize the importance of serials in its distribution program. Libraries join the USBE program as members and pledge to deposit what publications they can in the central clearing house, pay an annual membership fee, and pay a handling fee for each publication they order and receive from USBE stocks. Reflecting the name change, more than 90 percent of the publications that the USBE distributes are journals. Between 1948 and 1981, USBE total distribution reached 14 million items.

Max Celnick, Inc., Publishing Consultants

Max Celnick, Inc., does not itself distribute donated books abroad. Rather, the company acts as a link between charitable organizations and would-be donor publishers. Thus, although some large publishers may wish to deal directly with charities, a great number use the Celnick organization to handle the documentation required by the 1981 Special Rule on deductions. Conversely, charities are able to receive lists of books from a greater number of publishers and in a greater variety of fields from which to select titles. Mr. Celnick is himself a librarian who has worked with donated books since 1960.

Providing information about these various programs to American embassies can lessen the book gap simply by making possible direct people-to-people communication on foreign book needs. Programs of both AID and USIA could benefit, with minimal cost, and it is recommended that the Washington offices of each agency coordinate dissemination of such information abroad, i.e., through AID's Office of Private and Voluntary Cooperation and USIA's Book Program Division. This approach is also in keeping with the view of most Task Force members that donations should, as much as possible, be left to the private sector.

PART IV

INTERNATIONAL EDUCATION AND MARKET INFORMATION

10

Education for Publishing: At Home and Abroad

William M. Childs, Lois Spice Haig,
and *Kenneth Thurston Hurst*

Introduction

American technical assistance programs over the years since World War II have tended to view the aid process as one of technology *transfer to*, rather than an *exchange* of knowledge and know-how *with*, the developing countries they are designed to help. This approach suggests to many discussants consulted by the Reid Foundation Study Group an underlying lack of understanding of and empathy for Third World countries which has often guided U.S. aid programs. In a major study of modernization and development in the Third World, Howard J. Wiarda, a resident scholar and director of the Center for Hemispheric Studies at the American Enterprise Institute for Public Policy Research, challenges the premises and handling of technical assistance programs of the past 30 years. In the initial volume[1] of that study, Professor Wirarda observes that "at the root of our foreign policy dilemmas in these areas is a deeply ingrained American ethnocentrism, an inability to understand the Third World on its own terms, an insistence on viewing it through the lenses of our own Western experience, and the condescending and patronizing attitudes that such ethnocentrism implies." He brings a certain pragmatism to his argument for greater understanding of and appreciation for Third World culture and people, reminding us that "the Third World has

[1] Howard J. Wiarda, *Ethnocentrism in Foreign Policy: Can We Understand the Third World?* (Washington, D.C.: American Enterprise Institute for Public Policy Research, 1985).

become increasingly important to us economically. We now trade more with the Third World, including the Middle East and Latin America, than with Western Europe and Japan *combined*."

Educational Exchange

For purposes of this discussion, the authors view education for international publishing as a form of technical assistance, one clearly involving *educational exchange*. In their view, American publishers have as much to learn from their overseas trading partners as they have to learn from their American counterparts—an educational process "at home and abroad." And, the authors' experiences in international marketing lead them to believe that American publishers can learn a great deal about foreign commercial practices as well as foreign government requirements directly from publishers and booksellers of countries to which they hope to export their books. Task Force members and discussants consulted on this point accept the premise that basically everything an American publisher needs to know about how to export his books can be learned through exchanges of information and know-how with the overseas book world.

Each side brings a different cultural perspective and set of needs to the trading process, of course. And this presents a challenge to American publishers. The authors believe that unless and until the American publishing industry overall can develop more understanding of their trading partners' institutions, cultures, and societies, it is unlikely that they can significantly improve sagging book exports to Third World countries—even if they master the mechanics and techniques of the export process.[2] Without more understanding of foreign cultures, American publishers are not very likely to develop much, if any, appreciation of the fact that each overseas market has its own peculiarities, not only legal differences but nuances of expression, the first essential in the learning process in education for international publishing. The successful American book exporter needs to know them all. Thus, the authors approach the subject of education for publishing as a two-way affair, having as much to do with the needs of American publishers as it does with those of foreign publishers. For the overseas publisher and bookseller, the acquisition of knowledge from American publishers can only add to professional growth at various levels of management in publishing and bookselling firms. On the American side, lack of knowledge of how other countries' book trade industries work clearly hampers America's international market development and trade expansion. An exchange of information and know-how be-

---

[2] They feel also that this cultural understanding should include learning—and using—the languages of countries to which the industry hopes to export American books.

tween American publishers and their overseas trading partners, especially those in developing countries, can be of mutual benefit.

Participants

Two groups, then, that will be of specific interest here are:

1. *American publishers currently engaged in export marketing* (or those planning to enter the foreign market). Task Force members and other professional observers agree that the almost total lack of knowledge of overseas markets and how to approach them on the part of so many American publishers is one of the major impediments to American book exports. If so many publishers know so little about how to export their books in the first place, as seems to be the case, how can many individual publishing houses ever expect to enter the book export field? How can the industry as a whole hope to see its book exports rise above a minimal 6–8 percent of overall book sales? Indoctrination of marketing and sales personnel into the intricacies and complexities of the book export business would seem to be a priority of some immediacy, therefore. Otherwise, there seems little point in addressing the rest of the barriers to book exports or in pursuing recommendations and options explored in other chapters of this book. Many Americans publishers (see chapter 12), in turn, are unsure about the equally complex process of selling books abroad, and many are too intimidated to even start. There is little doubt that individual firms and the industry overall would benefit from knowing more about how foreign publishers operate and how importing and bookselling take place in countries around the world. What is the purpose of letters of credit issued to book importers in many Third World countries? Can Americans deal directly with private sector book importers in Egypt? What is the function of public sector importers there? What is the current situation in India on import licenses, University Grants Commission funds for libraries, etc.? Which countries exercise exchange controls, quotas, etc.? What about mark-ups? Are official prices really inflated, often as much as two times? If so, why?

   The authors believe that with exposure to the process and to prospective overseas trading partners in the various educational programs under discussion here, that inexperienced American publishers export-wise can overcome their reluctance to deal with foreign markets. While larger firms may know and have already explored at least some of these practicalities, there are many smaller companies who have yet to export their first book. As a result, thousands of American books do not travel beyond these shores and the messages they contain never reach foreign readers.

2. *Foreign importers and booksellers handling American books* (as well as buying translation and reprint right), those either already dealing with

American publishers and export representative firms, or those planning to import American books and needing to learn how to work with American publishers. Foreign publishers and booksellers often find ordering and paying for American books a bewilderingly complex process—which it admittedly is.

Much of the rest of the chapter will be devoted to educational and training opportunities, either already available or proposed, concerning book import and export practices. Before proceeding, however, two other groups whose needs should be included in this discussion of education for publishing are: (3) *overseas publishers* and (4) *U.S. government personnel*. While it may be assumed that American publishers are all masters of all aspects of publishing and marketing—other than *export* practices and procedures as discussed above—the same may not be assumed in the case of overseas publishers, in the developing world. Hence, *education and training in actual book publishing practices* is a need the authors identify for publishers from developing countries and incorporate in the scope of the following review of approaches to education for publishing. While learning the basic skills of the publishing process is essential (editorial, design, production, and marketing and promotion), not be be overlooked for owners and managers of overseas publishing houses is a solid introduction to *management and business*. Opportunities present in such courses for exposure to senior level managers of American publishing houses can be invaluable for overseas publishers seeking information and guidance on how to successfully and profitably run their own publishing enterprises. *U.S. government personnel*, the fourth group with a urgent need for education in all phases of the publishing process, and managers' from book-oriented agencies who may be assigned to reinvigorated or newly established overseas book publishing and promotion programs at USIA, AID, and the Department of Commerce. More than one Task Force member[3] and discussant stressed that it is essential that only "publishing-wise" personnel be assigned to manage such programs. Included among USIA and Commerce staff who the authors believe should be introduced to the world of book publishing are regional and country librarians who are in a position to promote American books to readers in countries in which they supervise overseas libraries (see also chapter 14).

Thus, in the following review of programs for education for publishing that the authors urge be explored to help meet educational and informational

---

[3] In particular, Datus C. Smith, Jr., a founder and long-term president of Franklin Book Programs, worked closely with U.S. government book programs and knows their operations intimately. He served as rapporteur for the Reid Foundation paper on USIA book programs (chapter 14 in this study) during its development and insisted that agency personnel in charge of book programs must be "publishing-wise."

needs under discussion in this chapter, participants will be those in the following four categories:

1. American publishers wanting to enter the export market and/or needing more information and knowledge about export procedures and how overseas importers and booksellers function;
2. foreign importers and booksellers, especially those from developing countries, interested in importing American books and/or needing more information on how to order, how to work with American publishers and export representative firms, how to handle international payments, etc.;
3. overseas publishers needing up-to-date information concerning all aspects of book publishing, including editorial, acquisitions, design, production, printing and binding, promotion, management and finance, and marketing and sales; and
4. personnel of U.S. government agencies, including librarians, assigned to manage overseas book publishing and promotion programs, and/or American overseas libraries.

Before proceeding further, the authors think this an appropriate point to insert a caution for those involved in the participant selection process. In most developing countries, the chief executive will understandably insist upon being his firm's representative for foreign travel, but he may not necessarily be the person best suited to benefit from the training proposed here. The most suitable person would most likely be a top lieutenant or some other specialist department head. In such cases, it might be advisable to invite both.

Another caution. It is important also that the top management of overseas firms from which younger managers are selected for training in the U.S. give their fullest support. One source, with many years experience in publishing education whom the authors consulted on this point, has noted instances where this was not the case and a new intern/trainee returned to his or her firm finding no established plan to provide meaningful assignments and opportunities for advancement—a wasted opportunity. This discussant went on to comment that "The commitment on the part of the overseas company must be total—and that is often difficult to achieve."[4] Also, members of the Reid Foundation Study Group themselves have observed situations in more than one Third World country where the enhanced qualifications of returning middle-level managers in publishing and book import houses were unwelcome. Senior managers felt threatened by the upgraded qualifications of their younger collegues. Moreover, salary structures and policies ruled out adequate compensation for younger, better trained, upwardly mobile managers

[4] Letter dated September 20, 1984, from Elizabeth A. Geiser, director of the University of Denver Publishing Institute (and senior vice president for business development of the Gale Research Company) to William M. Childs, Reid Foundation Study Group.

and executives. All of this must be considered in the selection of participants for training programs.

Government Educational Exchange Programs

It is encouraging to note that USIA already envisions its exchange programs as appropriate vehicles for bringing foreign professionals to the U.S. for education in publishing, as well as for sending American publishing and bookselling specialists abroad to participate in educational programs such as professional meetings, seminars, and workshops. In its 1986 budget request for an enhanced overseas book program, USIA has delineated twin objectives for such exchanges:

1. "To increase American knowledge about overseas publishing, selling, buying, and reading habits";
2. "To increase the knowledge of overseas book-related individuals and institutions about American publishing and distribution, with emphasis on the most effective ways to obtain American books."

This is a welcome step. The authors believe that AID should be encouraged also to include book world people in its participant training programs to be scheduled into the educational programs discussed in this chapter. They suggest also that government efforts in educational exchange could and should be supported and even supplemented through some involvement by a coalition of private and independent organizations.

Education for Book Exporting

Unfortunately, there currently exists no ongoing educational program that covers the needs of neophyte American export managers in depth, or as its sole purpose. The Association of American Publishers (AAP) International Division has held seminars in the past with panels of professionals tackling these topics, and these were well attended. But the only continuing book export seminars today are sponsored by *Folio* magazine—"Pubmart" in the spring and "Face to Face" in the fall. However, they are set up as only one- or two-day courses and offer a broad curriculum on the overall publishing process. Sessions on exporting must compete with simultaneous classes on other aspects of book publishing. Thus, the authors see a need for a specially organized two- or three-day seminar, perhaps several times each year, devoted solely to the basic mechanics of book exporting. Such seminars should be aimed at educating present and prospective export managers in the hands-on, practical, nuts-and-bolts of book exporting—what to do and how to do it. They need to know how book importers in other countries function (hence the importance of including overseas publishers, importers, and booksellers). It is not enough for an American publisher to be handed a list of importers by country—a "walk through the yellow pages" approach. To become effective, he needs to know how to supply that importer, what documents are involved, how he can safeguard his title in shipment, when he can realistic expect to be paid, what recourse he has if he is not paid, when to request a letter of credit, and when to supply an open account. Perhaps, most important, how can he generate demand for his titles in the first place? How can he secure orders at reasonable cost? These are just a few of the questions that arise to perplex the neophyte exporter.

The program should be designed and presented by experienced executives from the international division of major American publishing firms who can bring to it experience in exporting and managing overseas subsidiaries. Every effort—and this is of critical importance—should be made by sponsors and organizers of such seminars to involve experienced foreign book importers, distributors, and booksellers, both as faculty and students. Their input and the perspective that they could bring to the seminars would be invaluable.

Overseas-Based Educational Opportunities: Book Fairs

Much of the exchange of knowledge proposed in this chapter can be best accomplished at seminars, workshops, conferences, and other siminar meetings, which the authors suggest could be readily organized, in many cases, in connection with *international book fairs*. Public-private efforts toward bringing American publishers and export representative firms together with foreign publishers and booksellers in such gatherings could be explored with good results, the authors believe, perhaps under leadership of USIA and the Department of Commerce, seizing those opportunities for the collaboration of private and independent sector organizations and institutions mentioned earlier (see also chapter 13). Such training programs can be relatively inexpensive and are not difficult to organize. An example was the four-day seminar in New Delhi in 1980 that the AAP International Division held under USIA sponsorship as a feature of the Fourth India World Book Fair. It covered the main areas of editorial work, production, sales and marketing, finance, and management. The seminar was judged to be highly successful by participants, the nearly two hundred delegates who attended from all over India, and USIA participants. Since that event and as a direct result of it, one-day mini-seminars, sponsored by the AAP and the Federation of Indian Publishers have been a feature of subsequent India book fairs.

In the authors' opinion, such overseas seminars have a reciprocal advantage. They involve the American publishers in the market problems of local publishers and thereby provide opportunities for them to develop a keener grasp of the local market. Unfortunately, such programs are held only sporadically—and, moreover, only the more internationally seasoned American publishers are involved. But, several professional sources share the view that more American publishers could be encouraged to attend and could be enlisted to give short courses overseas in the various aspects of book and journal publishing, at these fairs and at specially convened educational programs. Many travel frequently and have assured the authors of their interest and willingness to participate.

Here again, the authors think that a leadership role for USIA in helping organize and sponsor similar events at other international book fairs is called for. Opportunities are present at all of the major international book fairs—Frankfurt, Mexico, New Delhi, Sao Paulo, Jerusalem, Cairo, London, Singapore—and the authors and Task Force members urge USIA to take the initiative in exploiting those opportunities. These fairs are all attended by American publishers, and would provide convenient forums for organized exchanges of half or full day duration (longer in some cases). Little has been attempted along these lines and such exchanges should prove useful to both sides. As an important feature of stepped-up book programs, it is hoped that USIA would accept a leadership and organizational role and to do everything possible to involve other agencies, especially AID and the Department of Commerce. At the same time, no one connected with the U.S. Books Abroad project intends that sponsorship of such seminars and conferences at international book fairs by U.S. government agencies rules out or discourages involvement of other organizations and institutions. It has been the contention of the Reid Foundation Study Group, one shared by many Task Force members and other professional observers (including USIA officials), that private and independent sector organizations have a role in the education for publishing process under discussion here—and indeed in the overall U.S. Books Abroad project, as discussed in greater detail in chapter 13.

The authors want to stress at this point that publishing education courses that will be covered below can at best give only a basic grounding in the function and practice of book exporting. To be successful, an international marketing manager needs periodic briefing updates on a continuing basis, since conditions and climates are constantly changing, and political and economic factors can transform a market overnight. One ideal opportunity to stay in touch with the overseas book market is presented by the American Booksellers Associations' (ABA) annual conference which is becoming—unofficially, to be sure—the American international book fair. It is attended not only by a great many American publishers, large and small, who produce perhaps as many as 70% of our books, but also by an increasing number of foreign booksellers and publishers. According to John F. Baker, Editor-in-Chief of *Publishers Weekly*, the number of foreign visitors attending the 1985 ABA convention and exhibit "was greater than ever."[5] With so many American publishers in attendance and a large part of the international book trade on hand, the ABA would seem to offer conveniences and cost advantages for holding one-day workshops annually, for the purpose of sharing information

[5] John F. Baker, "ABA 1985: On the International Side," *Publishers Weekly*, June 21, 1985.

and updating both sides on changing conditions and climates. One foreign visitor to the 1985 ABA sought to link the ABA and the ALA annual meetings (the ABA convention is held in late May; the ALA meeting is usually in mid-July), suggesting that "it would be good to have the two big American conventions, the ABA and the American Library Association closer together, so we could do them both in one trip."[6] There is a suggestion here as well for organizers (AAP, AAUP, ABA, SSP, and government agencies) of the suggested workshops that both events, particularly if they were held nearer together, offer good opportunities for training foreign publishers and booksellers. Just as the ABA brings together in one place at the same time the largest conclave of U.S. publishers and booksellers, the ALA brings the largest number of U.S. publishers and librarians together under one roof. And, the ALA also attracts a growing number of foreign publishers and booksellers.

As ideal as the U.S.-based ABA clearly is in so many respects for American publishers, there are also excellent opportunities at the overseas fairs. They may be even more ideally suited (although they are less well attended by the Americans, especially the smaller houses). Many more representatives of the overseas book trade are present and, moreover, being abroad can bring a dimension of reality to the fact of being engaged in international trade for the U.S. publisher, an impression not so easily obtained in a domestic setting. Added travel costs would be more than repaid by enhanced understanding of overseas markets. The overseas international book fairs, especially Frankfurt, which attracts more American publishers large and small than any other overseas book event, offer ideal and suitable opportunities for such one-day workshops.

Again, a major role should be played by leading overseas booksellers and librarians (many of whom seek to import books directly from American publishers, in many cases at the cost of considerable trial, error, and frustration) to help determine coverage and present material. Obviously the knowledge and perspective they would bring to suggested training programs would add a dimension and enrichment to those meetings that only their involvement could provide. Moreover, their participation as lecturers and instructors could be enormously helpful to the overseas participants themselves, giving them opportunities to learn more about conditions and practices of the American book export process in a meaningful exchange of information and know-how with their American trading partners. While the formal part of such programs would be obviously of great benefit to them, equally important would be that opportunity always present during off hours for informal exchanges of information, experiences, and viewpoints—as well as for establishing business

---

[6] Ibid.

relationships and friendships, an invaluable but difficult to obtain asset in international business ventures.

In addition to arranging for lectures and discussions on the technical aspects of book exports, organizers should give serious consideration to the participation of economic and political analysts from the departments of State and Commerce. They would supplement the professional curriculum by giving lectures and briefings on investment and trade climates in regions and individual countries around the world. Both agencies share concerns over declining American book exports and should, therefore, be willing to participate, sharing their special knowledge and current information and enhancing their own information bank at the same time.

Institutions/Organizations

How could such seminars be organized? One obvious approach would be the AAP International Division. But arrangements would have to be made to ensure that the sessions were open to personnel of non-AAP members. (Many of the smaller commercial and nonprofit publishers who would especially benefit are not members.) The Association of American University Presses (AAUP) with its member presses operating on university campuses, should be encouraged to organize and host publishing courses. Then, the Association of American Booksellers (ABA) should be enlisted not just to provide lecturers and instructors for bookselling courses but to actually organize and conduct them. Above in the section on international book fairs, the authors discuss proposed seminars with American and foreign participants attending the annual ABA convention; certainly the ABA itself would have to be involved in these meetings as sponsors and organizers. The authors believe that booksellers have hands-on experience with U.S. publishers and their methods to share with foreign counterparts—both problems and solutions. Clearly, there is a role here also for the American Library Association (ALA). Libraries are essential to book and journal publishing not just as major institutional consumers (which they are) but as institutions which are just as important and influential in encouraging reading as are schools. And librarians—and their association—relate to publishers on a daily basis. They should all be involved in any education for overseas publishers and booksellers on how U.S. publishing works.

Not to be overlooked, of course, are existing publishing education programs at universities, institutes, and independent organizations. (See Appendix 4 for a list of U.S. institutions with courses for the book trade.) Such organizations have the experience, organizational know-how, staffs, access to specialists, etc., already in place. These facilities and experience could be employed for special courses for foreign publishers and booksellers which would be conducted either independently or as part of regular courses presented at these institutions. Once the purpose and goals of such special courses on export practices and procedures have been outlined—and its financial viability established—these institutions should be able to quickly structure and set up whatever training programs may be desired.

Education in Publishing Skills and Practices

This discussion of educational and training needs and opportunities up to this point has dealt with those concerning the first two groups of prospective trainees or interns: i.e., American publishers planning to enter the book export field and overseas book importers needing more information on American book export practices—the actual trading partners. Now consideration will be given to the needs of Third World publishers for education in the *basic skills of book publishing*, editorial, design, and production, including marketing, promotion, and sales. Again, the authors stress the importance also of sessions in publishing management and business especially for owners and managing directors of overseas houses. Before examining available publishing education courses, mention should be made of a rarely acknowledged ongoing overseas-based educational process already taking place in several countries. American publishers' subsidiary firms (discussed in chapter 2) recruit and train promising young foreign national university graduates for responsible positions in editing, design, production, marketing, and sales. Many become managers and directors (for examples, see names of managing directors of U.S. overseas publishing subsidiaries listed in "International Literary Marketplace"). A number of U.S. publishers had already established overseas branches or subsidiaries by the early 1950s, employing host country nationals and training them where necessary. By 1982, according to Curtis Benjamin's study,[7] some 32 American publishers reported having set up 82 foreign subsidiaries. These overseas subsidiaries provide training in all aspects of the publishing process for employees who, if they follow tradition of publishing personnel in the U.S., rotate their employment into and out of U.S. subsidiaries and indigenous firms, bringing skills and experience benefitting lesser trained and experienced employees.

Opportunities for educating personnel of overseas publishing houses in the basics of book and journal publishing are readily available in the U.S. *Literary Market Place* (1985 edition) lists some 37 American universities and organizations offering "Courses for the Book Trade." While, according to information supplied to R.R. Bowker, only about half of those institutions and organizations sponsor formal courses in major aspects of book, journal, and magazine publishing (the rest teach exclusively writing and editing), Lois Spice Haig, one of the authors of this chapter, has developed a more compre-

[7] *U.S. Books Abroad*

hensive listing of courses in professional publishing available in the U.S. (Appendix 4). For more ready reference, entries of several major university publishing education programs are elaborated here (in alphabetical order):

1. *Howard University Press Book Publishing Institute* (2900 Van Ness Street, N.W., Washington, D.C. 20008). A five-week intensive course provides a basic overview of the book publishing industry. The curriculum explores the editorial process, book and jacket design, marketing, and financial management.
2. *New York University, School of Continuing Education* (2 University Place, New York, N.Y. 10003). A comprehensive two-week seminar covering all aspects of book publishing.
3. *Northwestern University, College of Continuing Professional Education, Chicago Book Clinic, Professional Publishing Program* (339 East Chicago Avenue, Chicago, Illinois 60611). The Chicago Book Clinic, the major association of publishing professionals in the Midwest for the past 50 years, founded the Professional Publishing Program's continuing education courses and seminars in all aspects of book and journal publishing, taught by experienced, qualified professionals.
4. *Radcliffe College/Harvard University, Radcliffe Publishing Procedures Course* (6 Ash Street, Cambridge, Massachusetts 02138). A six-week, full-time course covering all aspects of book and magazine publishing, with half the time spent in lectures and the other half in workshops. Formal lectures are supplemented with field trips to Boston-area publishing houses and printing plants.
5. *Stanford University, Stanford Publishing Course* (Stanford Alumni Association, Stanford, California 94305). A two-week program for publishing professionals, which through workshops and lectures gives an overview of book and magazine publishing. The course is taught by heads of houses, experts in the field as well as the Stanford faculty.
6. *University of Chicago, Publishing Program* (5835 Kimbark Avenue, Chicago, Illinois 60637). Courses in book editing, design, production, marketing and management for beginners and professionals.
7. *University of Denver Publishing Institute* (Graduate School of Librarianship, Denver, Colorado 80208). A four-week, full-time summer institute on all phases of book publishing combining workshops in editing, production, and marketing with lectures by professionals.

In addition to programming visiting foreign publishers into these existing courses, the authors and several other publishing discussants see merit in custom tailoring special one- or two-week courses (or possibly longer for some special needs) at one or more of the institutions mentioned above, courses integrated into the international visitors' attendance at the ABA convention. But the authors do not suggest that attendance be tied strictly to the ABA. Consideration should be given to bringing groups of prospective trainees/interns at other times, under a coordinated U.S. government-industry approach. Such courses could provide an overview of American publishing operations specifically slanted toward special foreign concerns. This could prove much more useful for them than classes intended essentially for domestic publishing personnel. Workshops could be arranged utilizing American specialists in international publishing familiar with overseas conditions and the needs of publishing staffs from abroad. A full range of subjects of special interest to participants could be covered: selling to the American market, how to export to developed/developing countries, book clubs and how they operate, financial planning in publishing, manuscript acquisition and evaluation methods, licensing foreign translations, preparing the manuscript for publication, production management, effective book design, how to increase profitability, book marketing, managing the sales force, selling books by direct mail, etc. A feature of such specially organized courses might be special briefings in Washington, D.C., at the host agency (i.e., USIA, AID, and the Department of Commerce) as well as meetings at other agencies such as the Department of State, Library of Congress, the Government Printing Office, and so forth.

Another training option for overseas participants, especially those new to a publishing career, would be internship programs in American publishing houses. The authors believe that there would be considerable merit in such internships and that the American publishing industry should seriously consider establishing several as an industry undertaking. Such industry-sponsored internships might rotate trainees from house to house and should include some time with export representative firms. Alun Davies, vice president and director of Bantam Books' International Division, spoke on this subject in an interview at the first (1985) Shanghai International Book Fair, as reported by *Publishers Weekly*.[8] The fair was organized and hosted by the Shanghai Publishers Association and was under the direction of the association's vice president, Chang Ruizhi, who had earlier served a one-year publishing internship at Bantam. Mr. Davies explained that Mr. Chang had "worked in every division of Bantam, from the editorial department to the warehouse, and concentrated on distribution." He went on to observe that he "would like to see a dozen Mr. Changs come to the United States to learn about our book trade. It would pay enormous dividends for us."

As mentioned earlier, personnel of U.S. government agencies assigned to book and library programs are a fourth category of prospective interns or trainees who need a similar education in publishing. Their needs are not

---

[8] Marianne Yen, "American Books in China," *Publishers Weekly*, May 31, 1985.

markedly different from those of the other three groups. Hence, the authors suggest that those U.S. government agencies with personnel likely to be assigned to book programs should immediately begin to schedule employees into regular publishing courses offered at the universities listed above. Their training should also include participation in the special programs discussed above in connection with the ABA and the overseas international book fairs.

Reid Foundation Study Group members recall that in the early 1960s under the newly launched USIA Latin American Book Program, that agency rapidly expanded the size of its book officer corps. Edward R. Murrow, the director, ordered a training program for USIA officers assigned to manage the expanding programs. With the cooperation of the American Book Publishers Council (forerunner of the AAP) and the New York University Graduate School of Publishing (now the New York University School of Continuing Education), a six-week course was quickly set up for some 20 USIA officers in the fall of 1961. No former evaluation was ever undertaken but most participants judged it successful. Unfortunately for USIA's longer-range needs, the agency did not continue with that course or other training for newly assigned book program officers. And, with the benefit of hindsight, Reid Foundation Study Group members believe it was unfortunate also that agency librarians were not included. The authors believe that the 1961 experience can serve as a model for a contemporary version, with the potential for an introduction to the world of book and journal publishing for all U.S. government professionals who could benefit from a general indoctrination.

Research/Surveys of Needs

To launch the activities discussed above, more information is needed than appears to be currently available, in the view of the authors. For purposes of planning and organizing the programs suggested above, they see a need for a data base of information on publishers, booksellers, librarians, authors, and translators around the world. This would include information on the size, structure, personnel, and functions of as many publishing-related firms and organizations as possible. (See also chapter 12). The project data base would attempt to include also information on in-country and overseas training given to their staffs. Such information is not currently available in various publications such as the *International Literary Market Place, Who Distributes What and Where,* or in any industry reports and data the authors have been able to obtain. Reid Foundation Study Group and Task Force members were in agreement that USIA should again take the lead here, as well as seeking collaboration of AID and the Department of Commerce in providing such a data base in the government or supporting one outside of the government. Private sector input would in any event be essential, as would continuing liaison with the AAP International Division, the AAUP, and the Society for Scholarly Publishing.

Little is currently known either of international events that could provide opportunities for the educational programs discussed above. The Reid Foundation Study Group believes that a clear need exists here for a study, one with the purpose of presenting USIA, other agencies, the publishing industry, and other private and independent sector organizations with a 1-year or 18-month program of proposed overseas publishing seminars and workshops in conjunction with international book fairs and book exhibits including schedules, costs, etc. Discussants consulted on this point have suggested that a study group comprised of former publishing executives as well as other independent international producers could be recruited and organized for this purpose, possibly as a joint USIA-industry effort. Again, the authors believe it entirely appropriate and desirable for a private and independent sector collaboration to arrange for, fund, and undertake such a study.

Funding

The authors have not directly addressed the matter of funding in the discussion of educational programs, including the suggested studies and data base. Overall, it seems clear that there are shared public-private interests that make facilitation of the proposed exchange of information programs a U.S. national objective. Throughout this study, Reid Foundation Study Group members, in agreement with Task Force members and discussants, have urged public-private sector approaches to dealing with barriers to American book exports. Clearly, the education and training under discussion here for managers and staffs of overseas publishing and bookselling firms is no exception. Thus, the authors urge that USIA (with coordinated support of AID and the Department of Commerce), enlist the support of private and independent sector organizations as well as book world commercial firms in helping organize, structure, and fund courses for foreign publishers and booksellers at these institutions. Presumably, tuition and participation costs for American publishers and U.S. government persosnnel would be borne by their firms and agencies.

Conclusions

"Education for Publishing" is a critically important need, and in the context of the foregoing discussion it should have the following objectives: (a) to increase American publishers' knowledge of overseas publishing, bookselling, buying, and reading habits; (b) to increase knowledge of executives and managers of all levels in overseas publishing houses, book trade firms, libraries, and institutions concerning American publishing and bookselling, with emphasis on the most effective ways to obtain American books; and (c) to provide U.S. government personnel managing overseas book and library activities with basic knowledge of the functioning of book and scholarly journal publishing, both at home and abroad and to inform them of what American publishers are doing to promote American books abroad.

All appropriate types of private and public sector efforts should be considered to help achieve these ends. The authors have at several junctions suggested that USIA should be asked to take the lead in this mission. There is a role, of course, for other U.S. government agencies as well, including AID and the Department of Commerce under guidance of a SIG, senior inter-agency book committee. (See chapter 13). Such an inter-agency committee could address such matters as jurisdictions and responsibilities and generally establish roles for each involved agency.

There is a call here for a concerted effort to help increase American book exports by expanding our knowledge of foreign markets and opportunities. That concerted effort, as the authors define it, involves U.S. government agencies, of course, but it requires serious involvement of private and non-profit independent sector organizations as well. The American publishing industry, other industries, and many foundations, research institutes, universities, and other institutions that comprise the independent sector all share concerns over the state of our knowledge of American book exports and need to be included in the formulation of an international training policy. The options discussed in this chapter on education are aimed at helping to achieve that goal.

11

Statistics and Data for International Trade

William S. Lofquist and *Donald E. McNeil*

The goal of the U.S. Books Abroad Task Force is to enhance the presence of American books overseas. Since enhancement implies a basis from which development will take place, it is important to determine the degree to which the commercial flow of American books is or is not now meeting foreign demand, in both quantitative and qualitative terms. The fundamental questions become, as posited by one Task Force member at an early meeting of the group, "What do we know about what they really *want* from us? What are they buying? What are other major powers doing?"

Early in the study's progress on this chapter, it was established that statistics sufficient to objectively compare our exports to those of other world powers and to affirm the nature of the book gap were available. Such data are reported in the various chapters of the study to which they are applicable. However, what also became apparent from that initial research was the real lack of data sufficient for the development of effective commercial strategies and the pinpointing of substantive or geographic problem areas—in sum, the kind of data required for measurement of need, development, and results. As one discussant expressed it: "There are enough data for the policy makers to determine that there is a problem, and decide to do something about it. There are not enough data for the program managers, the export managers, and the salesmen who must do the job."

CURRENT STATUS OF EXPORTS

Analysis of available export data revealed several overall situation trends. The U.S. is the world's largest book exporter, and has been since the 1950s, but its share of the total international market is declining proportionally. America's share of total 1980 book exports ($2.7 billion) from the world's 14 major exporting countries[1] came to $583 million, or 21.8 percent of the total. The United States' share of this group's exports was over 26 percent only five years earlier. Thus, although America's dollar volume and number of copies shipped have increased each year for the past decade, total international purchases from the 14 countries have increased at a faster rate. The United Kingdom exported books valued at $553 million in 1980, while West Germany exported $404 million worth. (The third-place showing of West Germany combines efficient export promotion with a rapidly expanding production of scientific and technical works in English.) France was in fourth place, with 1980 sales of $303 million. The U.S.S.R. is not included in international reports, and is not among the 14 nations analyzed, since it is not Soviet policy to report such statistics: however, as we have seen, the 1984 USIA study, "Soviet Book Exports, 1973–82," shows that exports in all languages have more than doubled in ruble value during that period. The report suggests at the same time that commercial export is probably not the main avenue for dissemination of Soviet literature in languages other than those of the U.S.S.R.

U.S. book exports increased considerably over the past decade, with dollar volume growth averaging 12.1 percent annually and gains in unit shipments averaging 4.2 percent per annum. However, while annual dollar value increased 400 percent in the 1973–83 decade, unit shipments increased only 25 percent, highlighting the importance of affordability. (The average price of an American hardcover book rose from $17.32 in 1977 to $25.15 in 1983; trade paperbacks rose from $5.93 to $11.79 in the same period.) The fact that total sales have continued to rise, in a time of hard currency shortages, can only reflect the popularity of American books. A crisis point will surely be reached in the Third World, however, as the strong dollar (worsening already depressed exchange rates, for the developing world especially) pushes U.S. book prices further beyond the reach of these foreign readers.

U.S. 1983 book exports totaled 242.7 million copies valued at $607 million, off 5.3 percent from 1982. However, 12 countries of the developed world (Australia, Canada, Japan, and 9 countries in Western Europe), and the Philippines (a traditional U.S. market), absorbed 78 percent of American sales

---

[1] Data provided by the Department of Commerce, based primarily on material maintained by the United Nations Office in New York. Statistics for 1981–82 will be available in 1985.

in 1983 and actually increased their dollar share of U.S. exports by $5 million over 1982, reflecting dramatically how underdeveloped American trade with the Third World and Eastern Europe actually is. In 1984, reflecting both inflation and the dollar shortage, U.S. worldwide export sales were valued at $643 million, a recovery of the 1983 losses and a $1 million increase over 1982. With that dollar increase, buyers purchased 249.8 million copies, or 45 million less than in 1982.

There has been a considerable shift in the types of U. S. books sold abroad during the 1973–83 period, with exports of general trade books increasing and those of U. S. educational books declining. Some discussants suggest that this in part results from changing publisher and educator definitions of what constitutes a text, a collateral work, or a trade book. These figures also suggest an increased demand for trade paperbacks, reflecting the rising price of hardback books noted above and the current trend toward first publication of many trade works in paperback rather than in hardcover, e.g., first novels, poetry.

The average weight of books exported declined by 15 percent over the 1973–83 period, also reflecting gains in the number of paperback books sold.

American publishers are shipping increasing quantities of books by air rather than surface transportation, reflecting market demands for faster service that British publishers have been meeting with consolidated containerized air shipments. To India and Pakistan, British costs for air shipment in this manner are comparable to vessel rates.

Despite their high prices, America's technical, scientific, and professional books represent the single fastest-growing book export category.

Sources of U. S. Books Abroad Statistics

The private sector depends primarily on the Commerce Department for its basic data on the U. S. export trade. The Association of American Publishers (AAP) *Industry Statistical Report* is an annual publication in which all publishers, whether members of the association or not, are invited to participate. While the largest publishers are almost all members of the association and are included in the annual report, many smaller publishers are not; export figures appear only briefly in one table in each Standard International Trade Classification (SITC) section of the report (see SITC categories below), with focuses only on Canada, Australia, New Zealand, and the United Kingdom. "Latin America," "Asia," "Continental Europe," and "Africa, Near and Middle East," are the four broad regional categories used. The Book Industry Study Group (BISG) produces *Book Industry Trends*, an annual publication which presents data for the current year in the context of the past five years and a five-year future projection. It is supplemented by *Monthly Book Industry Trends*. However, both the monthly and the annual BISG reports are derived from AAP and Commerce Department statistics, and, as in the case of the

AAP report, place little emphasis on exports. The International Division of the AAP has twice attempted its own reporting on exports, but this is not a regular activity. AAP *International Division Sales Reports* were published for 1977 and 1978, with 67 publishers participating in 1977 and 56 publishers participating in 1978. However, as is true of the larger AAP annual report, these publishers constitute the "giants" of the industry. The only other private sector study Reid Foundation Study Group researchers were able to identify was an AAP International Division study on English-teaching literature covering only the 1982–83 period.

International Trade Administration, Department of Commerce

The Office of Trade Data and Analysis of the International Trade Administration (ITA) publishes market share reports on an annual and biennial basis, compiled from source material maintained either by the United Nations offices in New York City or through official national import documents of other countries. Coding of the data follows the SITC system, and international trade in books appears under one of the following classifications:

SITC Number	Description
892.1	Books, pamphlets, maps, globes
892.11	Books and pamphlets
892.12	Children's picture and painting books
892.85	Music, in books and sheets

These statistical compilations have been published for over a decade. The most recent year covered was 1980; statistics for the period 1981–82 will be available early in 1985.

The ITA reports are available in two formats, a commodity series and a country series:

Commodity series. Exports of books and pamphlets from the 14 principal book exporting countries to the world, the United States, and to 97 major trading nations appear in the Market Share Report, Commodity Series SITC No. 892.11. The statistics are supplied on a current dollar basis; no data are available on weight, method of transportation, or number of copies shipped. The 14 exporting countries covered are: the United States, Austria, Belgium-Luxembourg, Canada, Denmark, France, the Federal Republic of Germany, Italy, Japan, the Netherlands, Norway, Sweden, Switzerland, and the United Kingdom.

Although the statistics provide an accurate description of direct sales from the principal exporting countries listed, the result omits such important producers as Spain, Mexico, Argentina, Singapore, Taiwan, and Hong Kong. This omission hinders substantive analyses of many areas; for example, the entire Spanish-speaking world.

Country series. Export figures of books and pamphlets (SITC No. 892.11) to a given country in this series are those reported from the 14 major trading nations or those taken from official national import statistics of the particular country. Only current dollar values are shown, and when the published data show exports from only 14 major countries, a significant weakness in coverage is presented. In the case of a country such as India, for example, failure to show book imports from Singapore significantly understates the extent of international book trade in English engaged in by Indian booksellers. Official national import statistics are used wherever they are available, e.g., in the case of Brazil.

Bureau of the Census

The Foreign Trade Division, Bureau of the Census, compiles data supplied by the U.S. Customs Service on nine U.S. book export classifications: religious books; dictionaries and thesauruses; encyclopedias and other reference works; textbooks; technical, scientific, and professional books; mass market paperback books; music books; children's picture and coloring books; and all other books.

The data are published on a monthly or annual basis in five Census foreign trade publications. These are listed below, along with their frequency.

1. FT-410—"U. S. Exports: Schedule E, Commodity by Country" (monthly).
2. FT-446—"U. S. Exports: Schedule B, Commodity by Country" (annual).
3. FT-450—"U. S. Exports: Schedule E, Commodity Groupings by World, Area, and Country" (monthly) shows statistics by weight and dollar value, and by method of shipment (vessel or air) except rail or truck, i.e. to Canada and Mexico.
4. FT-455—"U. S. Exports: World, Area, and Country, by Schedule E Commodity Groupings" (monthly): similar to 450. Statistics arranged in more abbreviated system under area or country headings.
5. FT-610—"U. S. Exports: Domestic Merchandise, SITC-Based Products by World Area" (annual).

In addition, a special monthly book export tabulation is supplied by the Census Bureau to ITA's Printing and Publishing Program.

The source of these data are customs declarations required of any exported book shipments valued at $500 or more ($2,000 in the case of Canada). The country of destination is provided on the declaration by the exporter, who must also identify the content of the shipment according to the nine book classifications previously listed. These Census Bureau statistics are comprehensive and highly reliable, but subject to a number of qualifications and limitations relative to the needs of this study.

1. Census reports do not include book shipments to individual countries where the average dollar volume is less than $5,000 per month. Hence, some countries might not appear in the data at all, and others only sporadically.
2. Since no data are collected on shipments valued under $500 or shipments to Canada valued under $2,000, publishing analysts feel that the statistics could understate actual American export volume by 15 to 50 percent, particularly in the case of Canada. Many small U. S. publishers, especially scholarly publishers and university presses, regularly export books in quantities valued at less than $500, as do many export representatives, wholesalers and jobbers, and organizations providing institutional services (i.e., to foreign libraries). Even larger publishers observe that small orders are very characteristic of the publishing business, in which many if not most bookseller-buyers in Third World countries are cottage industries with limited capital for inventory investments. Several exporters argue that exports to those countries may be underestimated by as much as 100 percent and the subject has been debated for many years. Although the Census Bureau has not conducted studies to determine the estimated value of book shipments under $500, it has found that shipments of less than $500 represent only 1 percent of total U.S. exports of all merchandise.
3. No provision is made for distinguishing between hardcover and trade paperback books. Trade paperback book production and sales have grown significantly in the U.S., yet no statistical mechanism exists to track their growth abroad. The trade paperback will take on even greater significance in years to come, as more originals such as first novels and poetry are produced in this form to hold down prices. This category of paperback already contains the least expensive editions of a substantial majority of the kind of book of interest to the public policy community.
4. Some of the largest U. S. publishers have distribution centers located abroad, from which U.S. books are transshipped to final destinations. To the extent that transshipping occurs (in places such as Singapore, Hong Kong, Japan, the United Kingdom, the Netherlands, and West Germany), U.S. export data record only the value of shipments to distribution centers and do not track transshipments to final purchasers. Reported shipments to Singapore and the Netherlands, for example, are well out of proportion to the likely English language readership in those countries. Since all books to Korea are direct shipments, while those to Indonesia are both direct and indirect (unrecorded) shipments from Singapore, there is currently no accurate way to compare the two markets.

The recorded export value of U. S. books shipped will not reflect their correct value if a country's importing officials indicate the need for placement of a lower valuation to facilitate entry.

Critical Gaps in Export Data

Not all additional data that might be useful to an analytical study of this subject would be financially practical to compile, but certain categories are of great importance to planning, publication, and promotion as described in other chapters. The most notable gaps are in the areas mentioned below.

Translation rights sales and books published abroad in translation represent categories of book export activity that would seem of greatest interest to planners. Yet, the only available information in these areas is AAP's *Industry Statistical Reports*—fragmentary data on revenues from subsidiary rights provided by those publishers who voluntarily respond on AAP annual survey forms. In economic terms, one observer estimates the contribution to America's balance of payments from the sale of trade book rights alone to be $70 to $80 million. Perhaps as many as 125 million copies of translated and reprinted American books were produced under this $80 million in rights sales. (The definition of trade books used here includes the bestseller novels and nonfiction that are found in mass market paperback racks in the U.S. Their appeal is universal.)

Of special interest here is the matter of content, i.e., what American books are being produced abroad in translation. This is a critical question for USIA when contemplating translations with agency support and for authors, literary agents, and publishers determining responses to the question posed at the outset of this chapter: "What do they want from us?" Assuming that adequate dissemination of information on the content of American books has taken place, there is a need for better ways to determine what copyright licenses to promote in which countries.

English language reprinting and English language book production abroad are categories of information essential to an understanding of export figures provided by the Department of Commerce, from which they are lacking. Some decrease in exports to the Third World may be due to the fact that these countries are obtaining American books in English through production abroad rather than imports from the U.S. In 1984, 32 U.S. publishers reported ownership of 82 foreign subsidiaries. Eight firms have five or more, and three listed 10 or more. The largest company had 14 subsidiaries, of which 6 publish books in English. Where English-language reprint rights have been sold to foreign producers, the questions become: where have they been sold, and which titles have been printed?

It is known, for example, that the United Kingdom is the largest buyer of English language reprint rights from the U.S., and that British publishers request and often receive reprint rights for developing countries that are former British colonies. Countries such as India are asking for, and receiving in some cases, Indian English reprint rights from the British publishers. India's activities in this area, as the third largest English-speaking books producer, are likely to increase.

Export figures from other major publishing countries, particularly for works in English, are also needed for market analysis. Some data are available in the market share reports prepared by the Census Bureau, but the language of the exported works is unidentified. National import statistics already used in the case of market share reports could improve analyses of what America's friends and competitors are exporting in English. It is safe to say that any country desiring a real share of the world book market will need to be publishing in English by the year 2000.

Book piracy has been dealt with previously in chapter 3 (on copyright). Until now, there have been no concrete data on piracy available, on which to base formal government action. Trade monitoring by Commerce and USIA offices abroad suggested in chapter 3 should be coordinated with a central office for reporting, which could also receive the new International Committee for the Protection of Intellectual Property Rights (ICPIPR) reports. The group of international publishers which constitute the ICPIPR has been developing a uniform piracy reporting form among themselves, which might also be used by U.S. governmental monitors.

Transmission of shipments through regional distribution centers is a critical concern for those seeking to determine which countries need the most attention when program priorities are set. As long as there is a lack of information on the reshipment of books out of the United Kingdom, the Netherlands, West Germany, Singapore, and Japan, the U.S. will be unable to address that concern.

The Search for Better Data

The Book Industry Study Group (BISG) mentioned earlier in this chapter has been identified as an institution that prepares reports on book publishing; with contracts from publishers, it subcontracts research and publishes the results itself. Similarly, the Center for Book Research, of the University of Scranton, is a new nonprofit organization that contemplates research projects under grants in addition to publishing a quarterly journal on book research. The director of the center, John Dessauer, has indicated that the center has the resources to handle at least ad hoc studies, such as research on the percentages of books shipped in quantities under $500.

Considering statistical needs in terms of their substantive importance, the Reid Foundation Study Group identified four areas of action as those that should be considered by the U.S. Books Abroad Task Force and by others concerned about the statistical base of U.S. book trade expansion efforts.

1. The Commerce Department should convene a meeting, of publishing professionals and those in the private sector generally concerned with U. S. books abroad and government agencies such as USIA and AID, to revise the content categories on customs forms for export and import reporting so as to include more useful substantive areas such as social sciences, literature, and

arts. Reporting and use groups could then identify problems that arise, for subsequent annual or biennial meetings.

2. A study group composed of publishers and others in the private sector, the Commerce Department, USIA, etc., should identify ways in which statistics on exports under $500 in value might be acceptably estimated, ways in which ultimate destinations of transshipments might be established, and ways in which multinationals producing books in English abroad might provide at least quantitative information on those books of American origin. Funding might be provided by governmental and private institutions to allow the production of such studies on an annual basis. (The Commerce Department, as it is the principal data producer, could be an appropriate source of funds.)
3. A system should be developed within USIA or in the private/independent sectors—such as INCINC—to record U. S. titles on which English reprint and/or translation rights have been sold and titles that are subsequently published. Catalogs of such books published, by language, would be a prime resource for USIA in its programming and publishing abroad, a resource that would promote sales of such translations to the benefit of both U.S. rights holders and foreign publishers. The dollar value of rights sold could be requested on an aggregate annual basis to maintain competition.
4. Related to copyright licensing is the matter of piracy. Assuming that the new commitment to identifying pirated works is pursued by the various organizations concerned, some central reporting system is needed—perhaps within INCINC, the Copyright Office, or the President's Special Trade Representative's Office—so that remedial action will follow the identification of pirates (using the accumulating resources described in chapter 3).

The results of these statistical studies should be widely promoted by public and/or private sector institutions so as to ensure their availability to U.S. newcomers on the international publishing scene. The Reid Foundation Study Group found that industry discussants not presently in the international mainstream were unaware of the existence of many statistics already available and the fact that such compilations were in part the result of their own customs reports. Access to such material, which could be analyzed in many different ways by those accustomed to doing so with similar information on the domestic book scene, would seem to be a pre-condition to getting newcomers into the international markets in any substantial numbers.

12

Market Research for Export, Reprint, and Translation Rights Facilitation

Donald E. McNeil

For many foreign booksellers interviewed by the Reid Foundation Study Group researchers, information on how to buy American books abroad is relatively arcane, and certainly complex. Booksellers, institutions, and libraries find that frustration of their procurement efforts is almost a routine occurrence, if not an understandable one. One result of this state of affairs is that overseas USIA posts alternatively join, leave, and rejoin circulating book exhibits provided by USIA Washington in cooperation with U.S. publishers (chapter 5). USIA officers abroad wonder whether displaying books that cannot be bought locally, and that a post cannot even afford to buy for its own library, may not be counterproductive in terms of public relations: a surely angry scholar is one who, having been invited to an event and having determined that the books he has just examined in a display are those he or she wants to buy, is informed that they are not available.

It will not surprise those in publishing with international experience that, in the case of many professional works for which appetites are whetted through scholarly meetings and reviews and citations in journals, these observations about unavailability come from USIA officers in London, Paris, and Rome, as often as they do from officers in "remote" Third World cities. In London, for example, a mimeographed flier, listing booksellers that USIA has surveyed and received assurances from concerning willingness to take orders for books from the U.S., is distributed to callers asking for such information; however, those who use the list find that most of the booksellers will only take orders under certain circumstances, and are unable to indicate how long it might take for books to arrive. In Paris, the *International Herald Tribune* has adopted the practice of including the full addresses of publishers in all book reviews it publishes, so as to direct readers who are unable to obtain the books reviewed through European bookstores toward the U.S. producers rather than toward the newspaper.

Hence, access to American books is a problem of global dimensions. Some publisher discussants question whether limited governmental resources should be spent on Europe and other developed areas, in light of the critical shortage of U.S. books in the developing world. When the situation is viewed strictly in business terms and as a question of the need for economic development assistance, such questions are valid. However, the experience of USIA officers—whose primary mission in developed countries as in the Third World is cultural and political, and their constituencies academic and professional—leads them to consider Europe a critical area. These apparently differing viewpoints produce friction between government and industry that Reid Foundation Study Group researchers feel is unnecessary. Scientific literature for developing countries and works in the humanities for all countries need not be mutually exclusive emphases in joint USIA and publisher promotions. USIA's mandate is being expanded in the course of this study to include science as an important element of American culture; the publishing industry will need to respond with increased emphasis on USIA's concerns—the serious works in American studies, admittedly most often needed in smaller quantities but needed nevertheless (and needed everywhere). Journals in the humanities and arts in addition are also inadequately promoted.

How to Buy American Books

For foreign booksellers, the books of the large multinationals, which have overseas offices and warehouses, are the most accessible. Even so, a buyer in Nigeria who orders books from the U.S. office of a particular publisher will have his order passed on to London, since Nigeria is within the marketing territory of that office: the order must be filled from London, taking more time and creating additional cost for the London service. In the case of U.S.-based export representatives like Feffer & Simons, which also has overseas offices and warehouses, the service cost will usually be reasonable in the case of books from publishers that have contracted with Feffer & Simons to represent them, but not in the case of the works of a publisher from a country that has been excluded under the representation agreement. In the latter instances, the sales representative may be a foreign distributor for a country or region with whom the publisher has done business in the past and the publisher may prefer to continue the relationship, rather than consolidate all export sales. The fact that a U.S. publisher may, rather than tackling international markets in general, have sold English-language reprint rights for a large segment of the globe to a British publisher only complicates the idiosyncrasies of international book-world sales mechanisms.

Some informed booksellers abroad are aware that orders consisting of small quantities of books from a large number of publishers are most successfully filled if they are channeled through independent U.S. wholesaler firms, originally established to service U.S. booksellers, libraries, and institutions. The largest of these have been expanding into international markets for more than a decade. Such wholesalers are not required to report to publishers whether their customers are domestic or foreign (nor are such firms knowledgeable about assignments of rights which may reserve particular sales areas to overseas publishers). They may benefit, therefore, from sales promotion by a U.S. publisher, by the overseas subsidiaries of those publishers who have them, by an export representative, or by a British publisher. An example of the public relations damage that can result from such distribution was provided by an anthropologist in India who wanted to buy a copy of B. F. Skinner's *Beyond Freedom and Dignity* soon after its publication, while it was first widely discussed among his professional peers. He was informed from the U.S. that the rights for India had been sold to a London publisher, and that he would be required to wait until the British edition appeared to obtain the book! Meanwhile, what was he to do at conferences? He resolved the matter by having an American friend buy it in a U.S. bookstore and mail it to him. There are, regrettably, far more of such one-on-one personal book services in scholarly circles than one might reasonably expect necessary.

Such problems are so deeply rooted that only time will bring their resolution. U.S. Books Abroad Task Force recommendations should be concerned with fostering industry conferences or market problem studies (that do not conflict with antitrust laws), perhaps convened by the Commerce Department and/or the Eximbank. That the complicated process must be untangled if U.S. book exports are to flourish is certain: how to do this is another matter. Perhaps the new Foreign Sales Corporation and Export Trading Company concepts, in which collaborative efforts by publishers for joint promotion, marketing research, and sales are permitted, will help cut the Gordian knot. With their monolithic government-owned industry, the Soviets do have an advantage over American private entrepreneurship in this area. All Soviet books can be purchased from a single exporter, Mezhdunarodhaia Kniga. In France, Libraexport, established with initial funding from the French government to promote and handle small multiple company orders and the exports of smaller publishers, is reported to have become so successful that government funding is no longer necessary. Publiexport in Madrid also seeks to simplify selling by combining forces.

Meanwhile, there is an immediate need overseas for materials that explain the complexities of U.S. book exports and America's current distribution system and allow foreign buyers who respond positively to improved promotion and distribution efforts outlined in this study obtain the books for which appetites are stimulated. This is an essential element of an enhanced

U.S. government book promotion program if developing world booksellers are not to be forced, often against their will, to turn to book pirates to fill their needs. Such publications as "How to Buy British Books," published by the British Council, and "How to Obtain French Books," published by the Cercle de la Librairie, are standard references in the bibliographic resources of foreign booksellers, librarians, and academicians as a result of their distribution by British and French government and industry. Each of those publications explains ordering procedures and requirements, and terms of payment, as well as where one buys the works of various British or French publishers.

USIA, the Department of Commerce, the AAP, and the AAUP have held discussions on the need for such publications, to clarify the U.S. "maze" described above, and to direct book buyers toward the most effective sources. Such an American publication seems specifically commercial enough for the Task Force to propose it as an ongoing project of the Commerce Department International Trade Administration. Content should be assembled by professionals who understand the special problems involved, however. Either an annual or a biennial edition could be considered, with updated material between editions available at overseas commercial offices and USIA libraries, and/or distributed in the private sector abroad by American embassies—probably at book fairs. Some professionals suggest that there are enough differences between areas of the world on purchasing to recommend regional editions, which would be more physically manageable in size, and lighter in terms of shipping costs.

How to Buy English Reprint or Translation Rights

Acquisition of rights to U.S. books is a less difficult process in Japan and Western Europe, where the rights industries are well developed. For Europe, an estimated 80 percent of all translations to be published in the following twelve-month period on the continent are initiated and/or contracted in the five days of the Frankfurt book fair each October. Such rights sales are the primary business in the International Hall at Frankfurt, and the situation there reflects the general complexities of rights acquisition elsewhere. Publishers sell rights to many books through their own subsidiary rights specialists at their own exhibits; potential buyers of rights not held by the publisher are directed to the U.S. literary agents in the agents' section of the hall, who represent particular authors, and in some instances the entire lists of particular publishers. (It has gradually become standard in the U.S. that translation rights to literary works are retained by the author, while rights to reference works are most often retained and developed by the publisher.) Whether the rights are controlled by a publisher or an agent the buyer may also be referred to the stand of a foreign literary agent. In today's sophisticated rights markets, there are regional specialists and country or language specialists. For example, Spanish and Portuguese translation rights to an American title might be controlled by

Carmen Balcells in Barcelona, by Lawrence Smith in Buenos Aires, or by International Editors' Co., with offices in both Buenos Aires and Barcelona. In turn, each of these agents might place rights for a single book with a publisher in the country of the other, as well as with publishers in Mexico, Colombia, and their own country. Probably, four editions in Spanish is the maximum for any one title. In English, the possibilities are global. As long as currency convertibility remains a problem, demands for multiple editions will grow, since it is less expensive in terms of available dollars to import rights than to import the actual book. Most recently, *Publishers Weekly* international editor Herbert R. Lottman reports from the Bologna (1985) Children's Book Fair that selling rights plus the film with which to print is growing even with respect to Europe, as U.S. publishers seek to overcome the high value of the dollar. (Among the new breeds of rights specialists, it should be noted that there are now rights agents to deal with rights agents. Many publishers in Japan, for example, prefer to have a Japanese rights agent in Tokyo handle the acquisition of Japanese language rights to foreign books.)

Once again, the marketing advantage goes to the Soviets. A single, monolithic rights agency that bears the acronym VAAP is the sole source for all foreign rights to books by Soviet authors. Reid Foundation Study Group researchers have not identified any similar organizations elsewhere, nor have they unearthed "How to Buy . . . Rights" publications issued by any foreign governments. For the Frankfurt fair itself, the British Council publishes compilations of brief reviews of British books on the rights block, together with the location of the rights holder at the fair, and U.K. addresses for follow-up work after the fair. In this area, at least, the U.S. has been a leader. American University Press Services, Inc., a profit-making offspring of the AAUP, has twice produced a "Foreign Rights & Marketing Guide," which USIA distributed through its posts. Such a guide for U.S. publishing in general would be a valuable aid to USIA book programs. In some of the programs described in chapter 15, the agency fosters direct publisher-to-publisher dealings on translation rights for books it promotes, in order to build long-range private sector publishing relationships. A rights agent publication would reduce the number of rights agent inquiries by USIA on behalf of foreign publishers. It might also produce independent translations without reference to USIA, and most certainly would improve the process.

It is suggested, in the context of enlarging INCINC's role in the reprint and translation rights business of the developing world (chapter 3), that INCINC might become the central source for all copyright facilitation needs of foreign publishers, and assume publication of a "How to Buy U.S. Rights" guide for or with USIA. In addition, a related activity that might be lodged in INCINC is the recording of U.S. rights sold, and the eventual publication for promotional use of catalogs of American books published abroad in translation by language and as English reprints.

Eventually, INCINC might also take on the role of publisher or co-publisher with USIA of the catalogs of American books available in translation, intended to promote the sales of those books by distribution of the catalog abroad. In the context of the present chapter, strengthening INCINC's image as a U.S. rights center in international circles would further make clear that, while the U.S. is serious about using its economic strength to eliminate piracy and ensure that authors' rights are protected, the U.S. also takes seriously its responsibility for assisting developing countries in the acquisition of rights to American books on legitimate terms. As noted in chapter 3, the AAP has in the past expressed the view that INCINC should be located in the government, specifically the Copyright Office. It may be, however, that INCINC is too much of an operationally oriented institution for the Copyright Office: it could be an adjunct of some other already existing institutions or of one that may be developed to enhance U.S. overseas book publishing and promotion programs discussed in chapter 13 on the role of other institutions.

How to Sell American Books Abroad

It is not the intention of this study to teach salesmen how to sell books internationally, but rather to encourage more of them to learn to do so. For those operating beyond the water's edge as well as a great number of small and middle-sized American publishers who do not, the risks of selling books abroad merge with the required international financial legerdemain and a maze of single-country rules, regulations, and procedures to create a seemingly insurmountable barrier to trade efforts. Despite the Florence Agreement and other multilateral agreements that pledge to eliminate barriers to the free flow of trade and information, international bookselling remains complex. Not every country has its seaports and airports as open to the printed word as does the U.S. Country "X" requires two pro forma invoices for currency exchange purposes, while country "Y" requires seven. Country "X" places no duty on children's books in English, but has a high one on books in Spanish that originate in a country where Spanish is not the first language. Catalogs and other promotional material are admitted free of duty in country "X," but the duty is quite high in the case of country "Y." Like the complexities of ordering books from the U.S., the complexities of selling and shipping abroad are numerous. Those in publishing who have made such information an integral part of their professional lives and those in government who deal primarily with such publishers need to be aware that much of the hesitancy among publishers thinking of entering exporter ranks is due to a lack of knowledge, and, indeed, to not even being sure of whom to ask questions.

Two kinds of information are needed for the neophyte exporter, the complicated kind of information described above, and the marketing research that publishers themselves conduct in domestic markets. Facilitating trade and investment is a prime responsibility of the Commerce Department's U.S. Foreign Commercial Service. Each FCS post, for example, develops a country marketing strategy and action plan in collaboration with the Commerce Department's Export Development Office. These plans allot time and resources for active assistance in response to U.S. business requests and for identification of local trade and investment opportunities. FCS officers initiate promotion activities at their posts and manage promotional programs developed by the Commerce Department. It is at this decision stage that book sales promotion needs to be incorporated into Commerce Department country plans, as a trade item of importance beyond immediate dollar return. Just as the Commerce Department will need to work closely with USIA and the publishing industry in identifying book promotional needs, FCS offices in the field will need to call on USIA specialized book knowledge in embassies in order to develop and execute programs. Conversely, USIA will want to ensure that its overseas offices coordinate book activities with those of the FCS, preferably having the book promotional elements of its country plan attuned to those of FCS in the field.

The FCS gathers data on host-country trends affecting trade and investment, analyzes industry sector prospects, and identifies and evaluates importers, buyers, agents, distributors, and joint venture partners for U.S. firms. In addition, FCS officers also monitor and analyze local laws, regulations, and practices that affect market access and business conditions. These data include the status of (and changes in) standards, licensing import and investment restrictions, subsidies, taxes, patents, trademarks, and, as a result of recently issued instructions to FCS offices mentioned in chapter 3, local adherence to copyright and the monitoring of piracy. These data gathering responsibilities, pursued by FCS in response to a mandate to expand the book trade, will produce the materials that are essential to increasing the export activities of publishers. It is encouraging to note in this regard that subsequent to the initiation of this study, USIA and the Commerce Department have begun working jointly to research book distribution in Central America.

The prospective FCS research materials mentioned above should be given to USIA regional book officers abroad. USIA should also conduct and collect important research in its special areas of competence, e g., academic, professional, and governmental use of books. This material can be combined with that of the Commerce Department and communicated to the book industry by both agencies, or whichever one has the better apparatus for distribution. In this area, USIA's activities vis-a-vis the domestic distribution of its materials will need to be clarified as part of the new mandate—it should be made clear, by legislation if necessary, that the congressional restrictions on domestic dissemination of USIA products does not extend to information designed to enable private sector groups to help achieve USIA objectives through use of such information.

Market research and the distribution of information enabling books to cross boundaries are givens among America's allies and competitors. The Cercle de la Librairie produces a variety of reports in this area, e.g., "Le Marche du Livre Aux U.S.A." (Book Markets in the U.S.). A British Council sampling includes "German Agents for British Books," "British Publishers Representatives in India," and "British Book Markets in France"—the latter an extensive analysis of French education, as well as French library and bookseller networks. (In that regard, a USIA publication series from the 1960-1970 period that it has been suggested should be restored is "Low-Priced Book Markets in Africa," together with counterparts for Latin America, the Near East and South Asia, and East Asia.)

Travel by Publishers

Sales efforts by mail and assistance by the U.S. government can never be as effective as publisher visits to marketplaces themselves. The AAP has on several occasions announced in its international division newsletter that USIA wants to hear from prospective publishing industry travellers so that their itineraries and their objectives can be communicated to American embassies along the route. The same applies to the Commerce Department, and publisher representatives should be encouraged to recognize that American embassies are a base for them. Not only can the embassies facilitate contacts in education and informational fields (USIA) but also in trade and financial circles (FCS). Fully coordinated embassy efforts will include AID, and the objective should be not only to assist the publisher but to obtain his professional assistance on book and library programs of concern to the embassy (e.g., see chapter 7). Visiting professionals can advise USIA posts on indigenous libraries, importers, and booksellers where placement of American book review and bibliographic publications will be most appropriate and effective.

As the foregoing suggests, the topic of export facilitation blends easily into the topics of education for the international marketplace (chapter 10) and statistics and data (chapter 11). It should be emphasized that the need for education expressed in those chapters exists equally among most publishing personnel, at home and abroad, and officers of USIA and the Department of Commerce assigned to book and library programs. Orientation seminars arranged jointly by industry and government would be an excellent start down a difficult road, a field so specialized and unique that some corporate conglomerates that have absorbed publishing houses have abdicated management, quickly returning responsibilities for it to the book people, or have soon cast off their new acquisitions.

PART V

INSTITUTIONAL RESPONSIBILITIES

13

The Role of Private, Public, and Independent Organizations

Donald E. McNeil

Curtis Benjamin concluded his review of U.S. book publishing efforts since World War II by asking a question: "Whose responsibility is it, anyway?"[1] He was referring to the "yawning book gaps that exist in all Third World nations of the world," for whom he clearly had a humanitarian concern. Mr. Benjamin referred also to the decline in American government assistance to those countries that had taken place, a decline that is a major concern of the Reid Foundation study and the U.S. Books Abroad Task Force Report. We have sought to depict the intricacies of international book publishing and promotion and identify specific problems and their solutions. For the most part, this investigation has taken literally the statement in the NSC memorandum that declared it is time for a new *government* commitment to American books abroad.

Undoubtedly, Curtis Benjamin would agree with that statement, and would have been pleased to know of the NSC response to his study, published only two months after his death. He had anticipated that the government would not respond, and urged that the private and independent sectors take action. His own suggested approach was the creation of a "not-for-profit organization, under some such title as 'National Coalition on Books for Developing Countries' or 'U.S. International Book Council.'"[2] He proposed a

[1] *U.S. Books Abroad*, Part 9, pp. 71–74.

[2] Ibid., Part 10, p. 75.

broad coalition of individuals, institutions, professional societies, trade associations, and corporations. Benjamin held out hope for eventual government restoration of abandoned international publishing programs by including government representatives on the organization committee of his proposed not-for-profit organization.

In a very real sense, therefore, the U.S. Books Abroad Task Force is the organizing committee Benjamin proposed, and the NSC has given it four interrelated questions to address, based on Benjamin's ideas.[3]

1. How can we stimulate more direct involvement of the American publishing industry?
2. How can we best utilize the expertise and professionalism of existing organizations?
3. Are programs better managed through official U.S. involvement, or by nongovernmental organizations?
4. Should we establish an International Book Council or foundation as a Title VII entity under the State-USIA Authorization?

Finding answers to these questions has not been easy, although the Reid Foundation Study Group tapped as many of those persons experienced with past and present international book publishing programs as would respond to inquiries. Questionnaires were twice distributed to the entire membership of the AAP International Division Executive Board, with the cooperation of chairman Pierre Balliett and executive director Saundra Smith. Some Task Force members wrote out their views on those subjects for which they felt most qualified; some wrote extensively and eloquently on all topics. Others talked with Reid Foundation Study Group members at length.

Unexpectedly, the one point on which there was little enthusiasm at this time as a response to the ideas proposed by the NSC and USIA was the Benjamin book council concept. The objectives of the proposed council are quite in harmony with the task presented by the NSC and this study, albeit it is necessary to determine whether existing institutions might not preempt it if the many recommendations made by the Task Force are accepted as responsibilities of particular existing agencies of government or existing industry organizations. If this is not to happen, nothing precludes the nongovernmental sector from pursuing the Benjamin concept. Indeed it could well do so as a complement to public sector initiatives.

A Government Advisory Group

The Government Advisory Committee on International Book and Library Programs (1962–77) was the organization that most professionals in the private sector and some in the public sector felt had contributed most to

[3] See Appendix 1.

private-public cooperation on books during its lifetime. The USIA Book and Library Advisory Committee (that produced the U.S. Books Abroad Task Force) was considered valuable in relation to USIA book programs, but in the view of critics was insufficient for what should be a government-wide effort on behalf of the book publishing industry. The U.S. Advisory Commission on Public Diplomacy, created in 1979, was preferred over the USIA committee as a model.[4] Created by an act of Congress, the commission reports to both Congress and the president on its concerns. Its membership is appointed by the president, with the advice and consent of the Senate. Although its secretariat is in USIA, discussants noted that its broad substantive purview of "public diplomacy" encompassed much more.

At the same time, publisher discussants stressed that creating additional responsibilities for the existing advisory commission was not what they intended. They believe expanded book publishing programs would take up as much of the time of a private sector advisory group as that membership could spare; in addition, they stated professional experience was needed. At an early meeting of a Task Force drafting committee, it was suggested that Theodore M. Waller, a former Grolier vice-president and now President of Waller & Associates, should be asked to prepare a review of the book development council idea and the workings of the Government Advisory Committee on International Book and Library Programs, preliminary to any book program advisory commission recommendation. This was done, and his report appears at the end of this chapter. In sum, he suggests a commission structured as to membership and purpose like the earlier advisory committee, but with the legislative status and mandate of the Public Diplomacy Commission.

Interagency Coordination

It became clear that these Task Force discussions reflected publisher beliefs that past U.S. book programs had often floundered because of a lack of interagency government cooperation, as well as a lack of cooperation between government and industry. One of the advantages of the earlier advisory committee, in the publishers' views, was the fact that while it was housed in the Department of State, its membership included not only publishers, librarians, and representatives of academe but representatives of the departments of State and Commerce, USIA, AID, and observers from other governmental agencies. When it was explained that the definition of a government advisory *commission* precluded membership by representatives of a department or agency of government, several discussants drew on their familiarity

[4] The United States Advisory Commission on International Communication, Cultural, and Educational Affairs was established by Section 8, Reorganization Plan Number 2 of 1977. In a 1979 amendment to the U.S. Information and Educational Exchange Act of 1948 (Sec. 604, 22 U.S.C. 1469), that commission was redesignated by the Congress as the U.S. Advisory Commission on Public Diplomacy.

with Washington structures to suggest that what the Task Force wanted on the executive side was a Senior Interagency Group (SIG).

SIGs are established to focus on matters of concern to the National Security Council on an ad hoc or long-range basis, reporting directly to the NSC. They include representatives of all agencies concerned with the particular problem or programs, and ensure that both action and coordination will take place at the executive level, with the agency designated as having central responsibility chairing the SIG. Assured that nothing in the SIG structure prevented meetings between it and/or its chairman with an advisory commission, Task Force discussants proposed that their final recommendations include a SIG as well as an advisory commission.

Those who had prior experience with program deterioration due to lack of continuity believed that the effectiveness of the new approach could also be ensured if it were the result of a national policy statement or presidential executive order calling for government-wide cooperation to alleviate some of the more urgent needs of the book world. Apropos of the role of the private and independent sectors, several discussants suggested that a national policy statement might also urge that the private sector enhance its own responsibilities by new efforts to meet the book crisis. If a program were also presented to Congress in a legislative package that asked for approval of a commission, a truly non-partisan or bipartisan initiative might result.

With these basic Task Force concerns about public sector—private sector and interagency coordination at least put down in written form, it is necessary to address the NSC's specific institutional questions.

How can we stimulate more direct involvement of the American publishing industry?

Discussants in both domestic and international publishing candidly question, whether the great majority of publishers are ready, interested, or even informed enough to take part in a stepped-up book export initiative unless considerable promotion and education efforts are made. Without intending their comments to be specifically critical of publishers, several discussants in government agencies concerned with the funding and facilitation of export activity believe that publishers have the same "isolationist" tendencies found in other industries with whom the government has tried to enhance international trade efforts. It is, they say, a serious national problem when the U.S. must increase exports as a permanent new element of the country's business life.

This isolationism does not consist simply of caution in approaching something new or different; rather, it is a result of the fact that the publishing industry, like other American industries, has had the largest single educated, literate market in the world in which to produce and sell its products. There are ostensibly no boundary barriers, customs problems, or exchange concerns for domestic producers, yet according to Leonard Shatzkin,[5] the industry has not even created an efficient and effective book distribution system in the U.S. On the positive side, Reid Foundation research suggests that the publishing industry, while of course must be interested in profits, at the same time has cultural objectives—providing links between author and reader, abroad as well as at home. This will be the appeal of addressing the book gap for many in the industry, particularly if they know that there are government resources available to support their efforts—including help in filling the gaps in their knowledge.

At the same time, some of the problems with which the developing world is trying to cope also affect U.S. publishing operations abroad and are fostering hesitancy and even withdrawal from unstable foreign situations, even as U.S. publishers are being urged to go forward with overseas sales efforts. Some of the responsibility for this complicated international situation, and hence for strong counteraction, rests with government and its years of neglect concerning American publishing abroad.

In this regard, W. Gordon Graham, chief executive of the U.K. Butterworth Group in London, writing about recent American publishing industry moves such as Macmillan's sale of all but one of its foreign subsidiary groups, observed, "More federal support and collaborative promotion would have helped. But the United States government's economic aid and information agencies . . . had lost interest in the book."[6] He was referring to the 1970s, when the ebb tide began. The 1984–85 budgetary situation of the Association of American Publishers itself, forced to absorb a 20 percent funding reduction, reflects current retrenchment that is unfortunately timed in terms of this project.[7] The AAP International Division was to be abolished in the reduction, and was saved only at the last minute through cost-saving measures that brought two other AAP divisions under the aegis of its executive director. On the international front, only book piracy remains a priority AAP concern in 1985, and the AAP Education for Publishing Committee was eliminated entirely. The latter development occurs just as there is an important role for such a group in helping meet the educational needs identified and discussed in chapter 10.

The Association of American University Presses (AAUP) has traditionally been strapped for funds with which to emphasize the development of international markets and translations. Although they are nonprofit organizations, university presses have been as affected by the fortunes of their parent universities in recent years as any other departments of those institutions.

---

5 Leonard Shatzkin, *In Cold Type: Overcoming the Book Crisis* (Boston: Houghton Mifflin, 1982).

6 W. Gordon Graham, "The Shrinking World Market," *Publishers Weekly*, May 4, 1984.

7 Lisa See, "Literacy, Freedom to Publish, Survival of the Book," *Publishers Weekly*, March 29, 1985.

Nevertheless, many of those presses have rich community ties with foreign educational institutions through the area studies programs of their universities, and have existing scholarly book publishing relations whose development would most meaningfully support the serious, scholarly objectives defined in this study. USIA has recognized this special importance of university press products over the years by emphasizing them in its book exhibit activities, and by funding travel by press professionals from time to time to consult with foreign counterparts. This study can only recommend that such efforts be continued and expanded. It is encouraging to note, meanwhile, that the AAUP has given new emphasis to international activities in 1984–85. A substantial segment of the 1985 annual meeting of the AAUP was given over to discussion on development of international distribution and publishing. For the first time in many years, the AAUP was present at the 1985 Jerusalem book fair, and will have exhibits at *Liber* '85 in Madrid and at the Frankfurt fair in October. Demonstrating the seriousness of its new efforts, the association has engaged a consultant to study the special needs of university press marketing and promotion abroad. As past USIA experience reflects, the nonprofit nature of these presses enables more flexible cooperation with them in support of the objectives of this study than is often the case with commercial publishers. They are, for example, logical adjunct organizations for the publishing education discussed in chapter 10.

The focus of the AAUP on the dissemination of scholarly knowledge is shared by the Society for Scholarly Publishing (SSP), an organization which partially overlaps with the AAUP in its membership but includes other nonprofit and profit-making organizations in the field of scholarly book and journal publishing. In addition to an institutional membership of 84, the SSP is open to individuals involved with scholarly writings and has a membership of 1,100 in that category. SSP involvement in the educational activities proposed in chapter 10 would be valuable in achieving the goals of the Task Force in that its membership and their seminars are concerned with problems of knowledge transfer that permeate this study. *Scholarly Publishing*, a quarterly journal produced by the University of Toronto Press, is not an official SSP publication. However, it is an essential resource in this area of concern and is included as part of an SSP membership. Like the AAUP until recently, the SSP has not had much international involvement, but should clearly be included in government-sponsored exhibits, meetings, and other activities involving foreign professionals, as reflecting the special social science and liberal arts concerns of this report.

Study of this problem of industry involvement by the Reid Foundation Study Group leads it to conclude that only persuasiveness and considerable evidence showing that the government has changed its position on the book gap will lead to significant increases in publisher involvement abroad through existing organizations. Those publishers and exporters who have long been involved in promoting American books abroad will continue to do so. However, even they hesitate about entering new fields until the international economy changes, and they are not likely to make many new moves without at least some government funding and assurance of protection against the risks. Discussants hope that Mr. Graham is wrong about government assistance coming too late to stem U.S. industry withdrawal. However, they are waiting to see how much and in what form the assistance will come.

How can we best utilize the expertise and professionalism of existing organizations?

Considerable expertise and professionalism in the private sector can be tapped for the American books abroad program, but that expertise will need to be identified and possibly put into a database before effective advantage can be made of it. Lois Spice Haig, a member of the U.S. Books Abroad Task Force, is currently engaged in research on this topic and the closely related topic of education for publishing (addressed in chapter 10), both at home and abroad. She is in the process of preparing a directory of nonprofit organizations representing expertise and professionalism in publishing, for which she has thus far identified some 200 institutions and associations. Her scope is somewhat broader than that of this study, and we have therefore included in Appendix 5 only the 103 associations most immediately representative of book publishing and international concerns in this area. (The omitted groups are related to writing, editing, and the graphic arts, the broader range of book world activities, although certainly such groups can be called upon for input as needed.)

It is important to reiterate that, for those book programs requiring professional expertise—and discussants believe that all participants in such programs must have professional publishing knowledge to be effective—USIA will need to train its own book program officers (see discussion on this point in chapters 10 and 14). Backed by the expertise and professionalism available in private and independent organizations, it should be possible to obtain professional results. In fact, it would be negligent not to take advantage of existing talent outside of government, either in the capacity of consultant contractors, or as employees of private sector agencies that might be appropriate project grantees for execution of projects, particularly in the nonprofit institutional world.

That does not, however, preclude the use of profit-making publishing firms and their professionals to achieve government objectives. Indeed, when considering how to provide low-priced English language texts for Third World students, the Reid Foundation Study Group and Task Force members are in agreement that international publishing operations already in existence should be utilized to produce such student editions as rapidly as possible (see discussion of this recommendation in chapter 6); here, profit is the glue motive that brings together expertise and effective performance. (This is true not only of U.S. publishers and exporters of books but of foreign professionals as well.) Reid Foundation investigators believe that the use of existing publishing concerns is the most economical and effective way of producing, promoting, and selling books, whether the companies are American, American subsidiaries, or completely foreign-owned operations abroad. Discussants have noted that when USIA staffers have not heeded the advice of foreign experts, or sought to press impractical formulas or approaches on them, the natural results have been ineffective book programs.

Are programs better managed by official U.S. involvement, or by a nongovernmental organization?

The answer to the question immediately above is also at least a partial response to this question. There must be official U.S. involvement in book programs, if the purposes for which the government establishes such programs are to be achieved. Good management can be found both within and outside of government, and the decision as to where to administer a program should be determined by the circumstances surrounding that program, rather than by rigid guidelines that exclude either the government or the private sector from a project. The Reid Foundation Study Group and Task Force members have not found any nongovernmental organization that can perform all of the broad range of activities described in this study, not even among professional publishers themselves or the internationally oriented publishing support industry of exporters, promoters, and distributors. However, a partial exception to this general observation was the Asia Foundation. It has offices in ten Asian countries, and distributes books from its Books for Asia program in fourteen others. Beyond donations, however, the Asia Foundation has many programs that need only be modified to include certain Task Force-generated projects.

Asia Foundation President Heyden Williams (a Task Force member) and his staff reviewed with the author functions related to the U.S. Books Abroad project which the foundation might undertake. Subsequently, a study was prepared by the foundation that pointed to those of its present activities already extant in areas related to the U.S. Books Abroad program, or at least close enough to the program that modification or adaptation would make it economically feasible to undertake some of them in Asia.[8] Disseminating information about the content of books, for example, is something that the foundation already does, and it could readily expand this aspect of its functioning with additional resources. In addition, training courses are already a basic part of many of the foundation's projects, i.e., present programs training librarians

[8] The Asia Foundation Paper . . . on "Books For Asia" (San Francisco: Asia Foundation, 1984).

in a number of countries could be expanded to familiarize those librarians with American bibliographic information and procedures for ordering books.

While the foundation does not have publishing professionals on its staff, it has experience in conducting training classes and seminars abroad and needs only the professional component. Unless these projects increased to a level that would require its own resource staffs of specialists, the foundation could develop such seminars and classes in consultation with existing industry organizations (e.g., AAP, AAUP, ABA), or other nongovernment institutions might bring together seminar groups to be programmed by the foundation. It has already arranged one successful publishing advisory delegation, for the National Book Foundation in Pakistan, and in several country programs, specific books were translated and published with foundation funding. It is unfortunate that the Reid Foundation Study Group was unable to find other nonprofit regional organizations with personnel in place and some emphasis on educational seminars and training programs.

Not surprisingly, the Asia Foundation already conducts technical and developmental projects with grants from AID. Reid Foundation Study Group members found also that the Asia Foundation is actually in the process of restructuring its book-related activities and expanding them beyond book presentation programs to include more library and librarian development. Part of this change is the result of the fact that book procurement on behalf of Asian institutions aside from donations has increased to the $500,000 level, requiring considerably more bibliographic resources than were needed in the past. In addition, foundation presentation of special gift subscriptions to journals has grown considerably and will be integrated with book activities. There are, however, no plans to engage in book publishing support except in a case-by-case situation where projects originate within an Asian country.

Should we establish an International Book Council or Foundation as a Title VII entity under the State-USIA Authorization?

The Reid Foundation Study Group and the U.S. Books Abroad Task Force did not so much answer this question in the negative, but rather shifted their focus to the more specific concerns of industry-government relations and intra-governmental relations. The two groups' conclusion was that these latter needs, given the form of a government advisory commission and a senior interagency group, should take priority over a nonprofit book council in this study. As noted earlier, this approach does not preclude a council or determine that it is not useful to create one, but defers the matter to the independent, nonprofit sector for development as Mr. Benjamin proposed originally. For the immediate future, a commision and a SIG can seek assistance from existing groups.

The Center for Book Research of the University of Scranton is, for example, finding its way into many areas of book research that need study, both domestic and international, after having been founded in 1983 as a department of the university. The center is headed by John P. Dessauer, a publishing analyst who has been the book industry's statistician for many years and is the author of the opening chapter of this study. The center has issued the first volume of *Book Research Quarterly*, based on a 1984 seminar, "The Book in the Electronic Age." Mr. Dessauer expects the center's efforts will focus on the quarterly, on conferences, and on sponsored research, providing a unique research resource for the publishing industry.[9] Too, the Asia Foundation, for example, has indicated its willingness to extend its expertise to organizations operating in other world areas and its assistance to projects in Asia that do not conflict with its modus operandi. The Reid Foundation is prepared to do likewise.

Not to be overlooked in this examination of ongoing public and private sector activities is the role of the Center for the Book in the Library of Congress, which can claim paternity of the U.S. Books Abroad Task Force and this study. The Benjamin Report and its aftermath, which developed from the Center's International Book Program, is a good example of the catalytic role that Librarian of Congress Daniel J. Boorstin envisions for the center: "a seminal and kinetic influence, encouraging other people to do things for books they might not otherwise have done."[10] Center Director John Y. Cole, its only federally salaried official, has access to private sector leadership and support through a National Board of Advisors, currently chaired by Simon M. Bessie of Harper & Row, that includes publishers, educators, librarians, authors, etc. Hence, to address the international book gap, the Center brought together private and public professionals with first-hand knowledge of the problem. From this group came a request for a study for which the AAP International Division provided funding. Publication of the report was funded by a private grant from Leo N. Albert of Prentice-Hall. The process can serve as a model and guideline for future studies that the Task Force or successor groups may want to develop.

Throughout this study, the role of governmental agencies, such as the Department of Commerce, the Overseas Private Investment Corporation, the Eximbank, and the Agency for International Development, has been discussed and recommendations made. Except for the Commerce Department, however, the participation of those agencies in the U.S. Books Abroad project has been limited. The Reid Foundation Study Group has, therefore, focused in this chapter on the immediate objectives of the NSC memorandum and

---

[9] John P. Dessauer, "Founding the Center for Book Research," *Scholarly Publishing*, October, 1984.

[10] Robert A. Carter, "The Center for the Book: Seeking Outreach," *Publishers Weekly*, January 4, 1985.

believes that the participation of those agencies, encouraged through whatever inter-agency coordination the NSC deems most effective in creating sustained government book programs is long overdue.

USIA has been identified in the process of this study as the federal agency with primary responsibility for governmental concerns about American books abroad. Thus, the following chapter is devoted to USIA's programs related to book publishing and promotion—past, present, and future—and how they ought to be improved, either independently or in cooperation with other agencies and the private and independent sectors.

Before addressing the USIA role specifically, it seems important to reiterate what has been expressed and implied throughout these chapters concerning the private sector. In the final analysis, as experience has shown, all effective government book programs will build on what the private sector has previously done, and is currently doing. If the book-related activities of government agencies (other than presentations) do not build industry-to-industry relationships whenever they can, they will at least be uneconomical in the long run and certainly suspect in the immediate future. Moreover, such programs do not last beyond the government support that spurred them. Even when USIA is dealing with a foreign publisher publishing a translation, it is better that the additional time be taken to connect the foreign publisher and the U.S. rights holder directly.

As Dan Lacy points out in chapter 2, what the U.S. book has achieved so far—and this achievement is considerable despite the problems addressed in this study—is the work of the U.S. private sector. More impressive in dollar trade terms is the fact that all of the millions of American books exported, reprinted, or translated abroad have been paid for by the foreign buyers—publishers, institutions, and readers themselves. Against the background of that fact, it will be seen that every dollar expended by government agencies in support of commercial book programs can be expected to eventually be returned to the U.S., its mission of disseminating understanding of the U.S. and its culture having been completed. This money will, in addition, bring other dollars, from the trade that follows the book.

Operation Through Existing Organizations and/or Establishment of a Nonprofit Book Development Council

Theodore M. Waller

There are a number of precedents/models for a possible international books council: the Government Advisory Committee on International Book and Library Programs, the Franklin Book Programs, in some degree and in some of its aspects, the British Council (having in mind the overlap between that council and USIA), among others. Fragments of the concept are dealt with by various donated book programs, the most successful and valid of which is the Asia Foundation.

Organizationally, there is also something to be learned from the Public Advisory Committee on Public Diplomacy and the National Endowment for Democracy.

Critics of the books council idea might well argue that the functions contemplated for the council either are already being performed by private sector organizations or might better be performed by such organizations. I believe both arguments are fallacious. The government is uniquely qualified to perform the coordination of catalytic, interagency, and intragovernmental functions for which the council would be designed. Many private sector organizations have interests and programs that are germane to the books council concept. These organizations and activities should be evaluated; and where they are valid and found to be functioning in harmony with the public interest, every encouragement should be given them and they should benefit in various ways from the activities of the books council.

It will further be argued that all or much of the funding for a books council should come from the private sector, e.g., the book publishing industry or foundations. Some funding, particularly for specific projects, might flow from such sources, but it seems exceedingly unlikely that foundations would bear the major burden of financing a books council and unthinkable that the book publishing industry would make such a committment. If there is to be a books council, it must be financed primarily with federal government funds, presumably USIA funds with perhaps some support from the Department of State and AID.

Having consulted rather extensively and weighed the alternatives, I strongly recommend that the USIA proceed forthwith to organize a books council which would have the following characteristics:

1. The council probably should be congressionally chartered.
2. It must be nonpartisan.
3. It should be in the form of a presidential advisory commission reporting simultaneously to the President and to Congress.
4. The council—hereafter called the commission—should be charged with the responsibility for oversight of all U.S. government international book-related activities and for coordinating such activities with the appropriate private sector efforts.
5. A major responsibility of the commission would be to maximize communication and coordination among the federal agencies involved, and between such agencies and private organizations.
6. The commission need not have the authority to implement international book programs or to make grants or private funding other than what may be required for research uniquely appropriate to its purposes and capability.
7. The commission should be concerned with the reciprocal flow of books between the United States and other nations. This is an area that has received extensive lip service over a period of many years but where little or nothing of significance has been accomplished by either public or private efforts.
8. The commission should have funding sufficient to provide for an adequate professional staff, member travel, and appropriate research.

Commission members should without exception have demonstrated interest in, and expertise with respect to, its mission. Marginally qualified political appointees would be devastating to the hoped for success.

In concert with the above recommendations, the President should establish a senior interagency group to meet at least biannually with the commission to assure appropriate coordination among the government's international book-related activities and between such activities and the private sector.

Careful thought must be given the involvement of private sector organizations in planning the commission and its membership. It is strongly, nay fervently, recommended that the members of the commission be representative of their constituencies but not formally designated by the various private sector organizations. Members should be recommended to the President by the lead agency after appropriate consultation with the private sector.

It will be agonizingly difficult to designate the organizations and professional groups of which members should be representative. There must, of course, be knowledgeable book publishers with extensive international experience and similarly qualified librarians. But what about magazine publishers? Not for this commission; this is an international books council. What about people from the information industries? Same answer. Should people representative of such educational organizations as the International Reading Association be included? Difficult, but probably not.

Selecting members of this commission is a little like recruiting international civil servants who must, while being loyal citizens of their countries, have an overriding commitment to their international organization. Our commission members must understand the special problems and objectives of their professions while being fundamentally committed to the public interest purposes of the organization.

These recommendations are made in the belief that, on the one hand, the national effort of the United States, public and private, must greatly expand the distribution of U.S. books abroad if this country is to be competitive in the world idea and technology markets and, on the other hand, that this goal is achievable only if there is heavy coordination within the government and between government agencies and the private sector.

It seems clear that there is no existing organization within the government or in the private sector which could be developed into a body adequate to performing the indicated functions.

The active interest and wholehearted cooperation of the various major organizations in the book world are much to be desired, but formal concurrence by those organizations should not be a condition of proceeding with the project. If the commission has sufficient governmental support and is appropriately structured, compelling self-interest will guarantee private sector cooperation.

It is imperative that the industry groups and professional organizations most concerned be kept fully informed from the beginning in order that the organizers not be plagued by industry and organization representatives rendered paranoid by rumor.

It may be that the cognizant government agencies will conclude that, while the answer to the NSC query on this subject is affirmative, no significant funds can be made available and that for the near future the objectives of the commission should be pursued by improvising within existing organizations. Before abandoning the commission idea, however, all concerned should be encouraged to reflect on the importance of an expanding international trade in American books to American foreign trade generally. The British, the Germans, the French, and the Spaniards know that "trade follows the book." It should be possible to demonstrate the truth of that proposition here.

Finally, a word of caution. It is usual now to focus on the inadequacies and failures of Franklin and the Government Advisory Committee on International Book and Library Programs. One should not have to defend these efforts in order to profit from the not inconsiderable experience gained by those concerned.

14

A Book Publishing Program for USIA

William M. Childs

USIA Book Publishing—A Review

Book publishing and promotion programs operated by USIA from the early 1950s until today are descendants of several agencies created during and after World War II, including the Office of War Information (OWI), the Office of the High Commissioner for Occupied Germany (HICOG), the Economic Cooperation Agency (Marshall Plan), the Office of the Coordinator of Inter-American Affairs (Rockefeller Program), and other international efforts of that era. When President Harry S Truman dissolved the OWI, the International Information Administration (IIA), created in 1950 as part of the Department of State, absorbed the book and library programs of the OWI as well as those of HICOG, the Marshall Plan, and the other aforementioned agencies. In August, 1953, President Dwight D. Eisenhower established the U.S. Information Agency by executive order, giving it responsibility for the staff and operations of the IIA and the status of an independent agency.[1] In the nearly 35 years between 1950 and the present, USIA and its predecessors have facilitated the publication of well over 150 million American books in 57 languages, a very successful record. A comprehensive account of USIA book publishing and promotion activities of this period, "Book Program Review—1950 to 1980,"

[1] Reorganization Plan No. 8, President's Advisory Committee on Government Organization, 1953. The advisory committee was appointed by President Eisenhower in January, 1953, to restructure the wartime growth of the executive branch.

was prepared in 1981 in response to Director Charles Z. Wick's request that USIA book publishing be reexamined and that a policy for future programming be developed. Much of the following chronicle of USIA book publishing is taken from that review.[2]

Traditional Publishing

The rubric, "traditional," includes identified worldwide efforts to assist foreign publishers in bringing out translations of American books, on a title by title basis, as an integrated part of the annual production of those publishers. Subsidies took a variety of forms, all with the objective of making books available for commercial sale; most of these books were gradually introduced as objectives and USIA policies changed; they were published without special identification or pricing so that they did not appear to differ from the publishers' regular production. Such efforts produced an annual average of 5.5 million books during the 1950s and 1960s, excluding those produced in the low-priced book programs discussed below. The decline of USIA's book publishing that began in 1965 occurred primarily because distribution through commercial channels did not satisfy changing USIA concepts of specific, targeted audiences to be reached directly by agency officers.

Not surprisingly, European-oriented publishing programs were the first to be eliminated as budget cuts became necessary. By 1960, the Scandinavian language programs had disappeared; German was a modest program of 10 titles per year that began as a major effort in the HICOG days, and ended with USIA in 1964; a French-for-worldwide-use program had also been reduced to about 10 titles per year by 1962; the Spanish program had three sources for books in 1960—Spain, Argentina, and Mexico. USIA support for publishing in Spain was discontinued in 1963, while the low-priced publishing operations in Argentina and Mexico were vastly expanded. The language programs that remained stable for more than 25 years were those in Chinese (averaging about 350,000 books per year, almost all in traditional Chinese characters until 1970), Korean (160,000), Japanese (300,000), Burmese (80,000), and Arabic (100,000 books divided between Cairo, Beirut, and Damascus, until the 1967 Arab-Israeli war). Other minor language programs were created and dissolved as overall USIA media techniques changed, primarily in the direction of electronic media.

Low-Priced Books in Translation

In 1955, with congressional funding, USIA launched a low-priced book program in world as well as single-country languages. The theory behind the

[2] Memorandum, August, 1981, from Donald E. McNeil, Chief, Book Programs Division, to Richard Moore, Director, Cultural Centers and Resources: "Book Program Review—1950 to 1980."

program was that there was a mass audience for books that could be reached with low-priced paperback editions in large print runs produced by publishers in the country where the language was used. Japanese, Chinese, Farsi, seven or eight regional Indian languages, Thai, Urdu (Pakistan), Arabic, Greek, and Turkish were the principal languages chosen for this program. Aside from 100 percent subsidizing to reduce retail prices, and print runs of 10,000 or more copies, this program also was distinguished by a complete emphasis on commercial channels. In its brief four years of existence (1956–1960), the translations section of the Low-Priced Book Program produced 4,346,800 books. It was terminated when it became apparent that the book distribution infrastructure of those countries was simply insufficiently developed to move large quantities via sales (a deficiency still plaguing distribution efforts in much of the Third World and Eastern Europe today) and that, lacking the ready avenues from volume sales, the price structure would not support booksellers. Remainders in 1960 were donated, and the program was largely redesigned along traditional lines.

Low-Priced Books in English

Unlike the two program categories described above, this major series of low-priced reprints in English was produced exclusively in the U.S. by American paperback publishers. These publishers turned over specially produced "student editions" to their export representative firms, and the latter, in turn, marketed them through regular overseas commercial channels. The first titles in 1955 were produced in 25,000- to 50,000-copy editions: however, unlike the more widely dispersed low-priced translation program, Student Editions were quickly reduced to maximum printings of 25,000, copies. In the case of serious scholarly titles maximum printings were reduced to 15,000 or 20,000 copies, due to the lack of international commercial distribution outlets capable of dealing with large quantities of anything but the most popular best sellers. Retail prices of student editions began at 10 cents, but soon rose to 20 cents and then 25 cents to make the profit margin more attractive to foreign importers and booksellers. However, the Student Edition program fell victim to budgetary problems in the 1960s. In a very real sense, the series was ahead of its time. Low prices per unit and a large volume of unit sales were fueling the "paperback revolution" in the U.S. in the 1950s, but the developing world was not structurally ready for that revolution, lacking sufficient retail outlets. As chapter 6 reflects, the concept is very much in demand in 1985.

Ladder Editions were developed for the low-priced books in English program in 1957, and out-lasted student editions that had paved the way for them by almost 10 years. Ladder books were paperback editions of American books abridged and rewritten using controlled vocabularies of 1,000 to 5,000 words for the use of young adult readers of English as a second or foreign language. Although they were to become very popular as instruments of

English teaching, they were first produced in 1957 to provide students or graduates of English training with an introduction to American culture. (The idea for Ladder Books developed from a report by the USIA post in Tokyo to the effect that Japanese students without access to American books in English appropriate to their level of competency were reading boyhood biographies of Lenin, Marx, and Stalin.)

The Ladder Books became the most widely used and successful series that USIA produced on a worldwide basis. Approximately 70 percent of the more than 9 million books published were sold as exports, and the balance was used by USIA overseas posts with their English teaching classes, in USIA libraries, and for sales promotion. Like the student editions, they were produced in large editions and with a low retail price. They were, however, able to finesse the lack of sufficient retail outlets via volume sales to English-teaching institutions. Terminated in 1976, the series remains popular, being published independently in a few countries by local publishers.

Low-Priced Books in Spanish and Portuguese

USIA responded immediately to President Kennedy's 1962 "Alliance for Progress" initiative by introducing low-priced translations of American books into Latin America. This program was, at its peak, probably the most expensive publishing enterprise that the agency has undertaken, and was a major component of the extensive book publishing activities of the 1960s reflected in Table 1, "USIA Book Publishing Production 1950–1983," at the end of this chapter. As previously noted there had been a small USIA book program in Spanish since 1952, first in Spain and then in Argentina and Mexico, all prior to the Alliance for Progress. The program in Spain was stopped in 1963 in order to focus all resources on "industry building" in Latin America, an Alliance for Progress objective,[3] and Argentina became the major producer of books with USIA support. Unprecedented funding and support were now given to the large scale and highly visible Latin American (rather than "Spanish") Book Program. With full support from President Kennedy, USIA Director Edward R. Murrow gave the program his personal stamp of approval and continuing attention.

By 1964 these Latin American publishing centers were completely operational and had achieved their targeted production goals of 1.3 million books in Portuguese and 1.5 million in Spanish. In the next year, the high water mark for USIA book programs, USIA's Latin American Book Translation Program produced 2 million books (188 titles) in Spanish.

One clear lesson for those who propose reviving USIA's book publishing

[3] The Agency for International Development responded also, setting up a Regional Technical Aid Center (RTAC) with offices in Mexico City, Buenos Aires, and Rio de Janeiro. RTAC supported translation into Spanish and Portuguese of American technical and scientific books which supported AID development projects in Latin America.

programs can be drawn from the Latin American experience of the early 1960s: with strong unstinting support from USIA's top management, sufficient funding, and experienced book publishing professionals as managers, a USIA book publishing program can be quickly mounted and can soon turn out large quantities of quality books. What is less clear, however, is whether ways and means can be devised to efficiently get these books into the hands of their intended readers, short of giving them away. During the peak years of the Spanish programs, USIA evaluations showed that its books were effectively distributed (commercially) within the producing countries and, to a certain extent, within neighboring countries as well. However, getting books produced in Argentina into Mexico and Central America, or those published in Mexico into Argentina and other Southern Cone countries in adequate numbers, was another matter. Continent-wide distribution was never satisfactorily achieved by the USIA program, and, in fact, is an unattained goal for the book industries of those countries today.

P.L. 480 Textbook Program

In 1959 Congress enacted the P.L. 480 "Food for Peace Program," designed to give developing countries with food shortages and insufficient dollars to satisfy their needs access to American agricultural commodities. The P.L. 480 Act authorized acceptance of local currencies in payment for American goods, and then authorized the expenditure of those currencies in the countries of origin on educational and cultural exchange activities mutually acceptable to the U.S. government and the foreign government. One such agreed-upon activity was production of American textbooks in English reprint editions or translation. Consequently, textbook programs in Egypt, India, Korea, Pakistan, Spain, and Yugoslavia were launched. USIA administered these programs, with AID participation and funding in the case of some scientific and technical textbooks. Subsidy agreements were made with local publishers wherein a portion of production costs (80 percent in the case of India, the largest P.L. 480 textbook reprint program) was paid with local currencies received for American agricultural goods.. Under government-to-government agreements, P.L. 480 reprints were titles approved by the host government's ministry of education and were sold at low prices, usually as low as one-fifth the price of the American hardcover original.

Nearly 12 million American textbook reprints were produced for universities and libraries in the six participating countries during the 16-year history of the P.L. 480 Program from 1959 to 1975. India alone accounted for over half this total: 8.2 million textbooks were published there between 1962 and 1972, in 1,885 editions (see Table 2, "Joint Indo-American Textbook Program 1962–1981," at the end of this chapter). These programs were considered invaluable for local university education by foreign government officials, educators, and publishers, as well as by many in USIA and American publishers (who made rights available through publisher-to-publisher contracts, with the foreign government authorizing payment of royalties in dollars.)

U.S. publishers consulted in the preparation of this chapter are in general agreement that the presence of these low-priced reprints has promoted sustained use of American textbooks through introducing educators, scholars, students, and librarians to advanced thought and literature, especially in basic sciences, medicine, engineering, and technology. Publisher-to-publisher contacts made through P.L. 480 have opened doors to commercial relationships for American publishers enduring to this day. In the case of India, P.L. 480 can take credit for the present day joint Indo-American publishing companies that grew out of this program, e.g., in chronological order of establishment, Prentice-Hall of India, Affiliated East-West Press (American Book and Van Nostrand), Wiley Eastern Limited (John Wiley & Sons), and Tata McGraw-Hill.

French Language Translations for Africa

The return of Charles DeGaulle to power in France in the early 1960s led to the rapid transformation of Francophone Africa from colonies to countries. Belgium reacted to the tenor of the times by giving independence to the Congo. Faced with a void in communicating to these newly established countries, USIA responded in part with the creation of a French-for-Africa Book Program in 1962. As there was little indigenous French African publishing industry upon which to build, the African Regional Service Center (which turned out 800,000 books in its first year of operations) was established in Paris to work with publishers there. As was largely true at the beginning of the Latin American program, USIA also found French Africa's commercial book distribution system to be practically non-existent. (It would be misleading, however, to fail to note that much more of a book selling and distribution infrastructure existed in Latin America in the 1960s than in Africa then, or today for that matter). The lack of a commercial network led USIA to create one (at considerable expense), funding a Paris office and a staff of five for the American firm selected to develop distribution in Francophone Africa.

Faced with numerous barriers, including low literacy rates, USIA was unable to infuse the African program with the funding, staffing, and enthusiasm it had given to the Latin American program of the same era. The first-year African production total of 800,000 copies was not to be surpassed, or even equalled, again. Five years later, in 1967, production had dropped to one-fourth that level, and by 1979 it had fallen to 67,000. In 1983, it was 59,850 copies.[4]

---

[4] Book Program Division, USIA. *"Books Published in Translation and in English; 1983"* (Washington, D.C.: USIA, 1984).

Book Programs in India

Because of the sheer volume of U.S. publishing activity in India, it is worthwhile to examine more closely the details of USIA's Indian book production programs. W. Gordon Graham, chairman of Butterworths, a venerable British publishing firm, is an old India hand who speaks from long experience in the publishing trade there. He wrote of the "sheer magnitude of the Indian market, India's widespread use of the English language, and the well-developed Indian institutions of higher education and learning" in an article published on the eve of India's Third Biennial World Book Fair in 1978.[5] He noted that India "in its (then) 30 years of independence, has become a major publishing country as well as a major market . . . each of its 14 primary languages supports a publishing industry equivalent to that of a small unilingual country."

With its strong determination to increase literacy and with increasing enrollments in primary, secondary, and university education, India's literacy rate has exceeded 30 percent: that means "that there are almost as many people able to read in India as in the U.S." As a consequence, India has become "the third largest publisher of books in English."[6]

USIA produced some 20 English titles in India annually between 1952 and 1958. By 1964 this English reprint activity, separate from P.L. 480 textbooks but always considered a supplement providing relevant reading for university students, had reached an annual total of 511,000 copies. The India program was expanded even further, and significantly, beginning in 1961, with the introduction of books in the major Indian languages. In 1965 this USIA production included 663,400 in Hindi, 53,000 in Malayalam (the Indian state boasting the country's highest literacy rate), and 156,000 in Marathi. With the addition of production in Telegu (94,000), Tamil (113,000), and Gujerati (225,000) in 1966, USIA's India program of English reprints, translations, and P.L. 480 textbooks combined became the largest USIA book program in the world. However, in 1968 USIA managers in India decided that the agency's target audiences were all reachable in English and that Indian regional language books were no longer required. Hence, a major segment of the Indian book program was dropped. Books in English then became USIA's bridge to Indian readers.

The USIA Book Publishing Scene Today

The data presented in Table 1 at the end of this chapter showing that only 539,717 books were produced under the aegis of USIA worldwide in fiscal year 1983 illustrate the current diminished status of books as a USIA commu-

---

[5] W. Gordon Graham, "Publishing in a Major World Market on the Eve of the New Delhi Book Fair," *Publishers Weekly,* February 6, 1978.

[6] Ibid.

nications medium. The reasons, most related to budget restrictions and the agency's search for more current, more exciting electronic communications techniques, have been explained earlier. Some observers have suggested also that a lack of understanding among some senior USIA officials concerning the importance of books to foreign intellectual leaders, educators, and professionals contributed to the demise of the book as a medium of public diplomacy.

Whatever the reasons, a steep downward slide in USIA-supported book production began in the late '60s, continuing through the '70s until today. Book programs no longer rank with radio, TV, motion pictures, or even other print media as mainstays of USIA communications techniques. In 1972, an active and successful Japanese translation program was eliminated on grounds that media-rich Japan did not need a book program, and resources were needed for newer, faster, better "targeted" media approaches. (The Japan program is the best example of "innovation" gone awry, in that successful traditional media programs were replaced at great expense simply because of enthusiasm for new technology. Not only did book publishing activity end, all USIA libraries became "Infomats" housing microfilm, tapes, VTRs, and something called "electronic dialogues": U.S. book collections were limited to 2,000 titles and to titles no more than two years old. Opened with fanfare, "Infomats" were eventually closed and quietly reopened as "libraries" about 1981. All of this cost money, of course, but more importantly it reflected the suspicion concerning books encountered in USIA policy circles. Only in 1982 did a new library program policy statement require substantial justification in the future for any proposed major changes in a USIA library, and the concurrence of several Washington officers, including the director.[7]

Under USIA auspices books have been published in 58 languages (including English) since 1950; in 1983, there were books in only 14 foreign languages plus English recorded in the USIA book translation program.[8] Futhermore, production in only six languages now exceeds 15,000 books in any one year: Arabic, Chinese, French, Spanish, English reprints, and Korean—all world languages except Korean. USIA policy in the 1970s determined that textbooks in scientific and technical fields were not relevant to agency program themes, and so P.L. textbook programs were eliminated in all but the social sciences. Scientific, technical and medical books were and still are precisely the kinds of books that are priority items on any list of American

---

[7] Charles Z. Wick, "USIA Library Program" USIA policy statement, Washington, D.C.: USIA, 1982.

[8] Books Published in Translation

books desired by Third World countries. Textbooks on American achievement in the social sciences, economics, and international relations are also important and in demand, but the humanities are not the most immediate concern of such developing nations. In a "total" program, it is advantageous to the U.S. to have all categories of books available; however, with limited budgets, USIA selection must inevitably take place.

A USIA Book Publishing Program—Urgency and Opportunity

The preceding review of the development and decline of USIA book programs provides some indication of the approaches USIA should consider in restoring the book to its repertoire of public diplomacy resources. The authors of this study would remind those concerned with restoring book publishing and promotion to USIA's communications options, however, that the book gap is the consequence of not just the curtailing of USIA (and AID) publishing activities over the past decade. As USIA and AID were eliminating books from their overseas programs, American publishers themselves were steadily losing foreign book markets to alternative sources. (It is ironic perhaps that American publishers were losing ground in developing countries at a time of increasing international literacy rates, due in many cases to U.S. aid.) Inflation and a strengthening dollar pushed the already high prices of their books beyond the reach of increasing numbers of readers, especially in Third World countries. These problems and possible remedial actions are the subject of other chapters, while we focus here on USIA's purpose and role in rebuilding its long-dormant overseas book publishing and promotion programs of the 1950s and 1960s.

Those involved in the preparation and publication of the Benjamin Report should know that as a direct result of the interest among the Reagan administration, the Congress, and the publishing industry in the report, USIA Director Wick ordered the preparation of an "American Books Abroad" budget for fiscal year 1986. USIA has proposed to spend a minimum of $12 million annually over several years to support publication and promotion of books related to agency interests and book-related activities, including development and publication of Ladder Books and other instructional materials in support of USIA English teaching programs.

USIA refers to this funding level as "optimal": whether it will be truly optimal is too early to say. However, it is important to keep inflation in mind in setting an initial funding level. For example, in fiscal year 1966, the zenith of USIA book publishing programs, $3.5 million was allocated for translations, English language reprints, textbooks, Ladder Books, and for promotion of American books in general. In 1986, the same book program would cost well over $15 million per year. Yet, many informed observers did not believe that the number of books USIA published during those peak years was adequate for the challenges of the times.[9]

The 1986 "American Books Abroad" plan also calls for creation of a Foreign Service Officer corps of publishing specialists, to be supported by additional foreign national employees at key overseas posts. Decisions need to be made on how newly expanded book programs will be administered. Most of the experienced book program specialist corps including foreign national professionals are gone, dispersed into retirement. Mechanisms have fallen into disuse and have been forgotten. There is no longer a "corporate memory" concerning the process of getting books translated, published, and distributed in a *professional* manner in USIA, and mistakes wait to be repeated. (This study, by including the views of many in the U.S. industry involved in the earlier programs as well as those of former USIA staff now retired, is that corporate memory recaptured, in the belief of a number of those associated with the U.S. Books Abroad study.)

A major managerial question for USIA is whether it should attempt to rebuild a corps of publishing specialists or look to outside professionals to operate or oversee the expanded overseas book publishing operations being proposed. Even with the greatly increased funding that the U.S. Books Abroad Task Force hopes will be made available, it is doubtful that funding will be sufficient to maintain a career book publishing specialist in each overseas post where new or accelerated publishing activities might be launched. While prudence would seem to require that full-time regional publishing specialists be placed in charge of USIA's world language programs, now operated or being developed out of USIA Regional Book Offices in Buenos Aires, Mexico, Spain, France, Egypt and Hong Kong, USIA is not likely to install a career publishing specialist as full-time manager in smaller, single-country language publishing programs. Reid Foundation Study Group members anticipate that agency planners are likely to find that these latter programs could be effectively supervised by a Foreign Service Officer generalist as his/her part-time responsibility. The Reid Foundation Study Group agrees that if such career officer generalists were aided by a small staff of experienced foreign national employees, this tactic could work, *provided* there were periodic assistance and guidance by specialists, the nonprofit community, and consultant advisors as a regular element of the programs.

There was unanimity among Reid Foundation Study Group and Task Force members in the view that only experienced, professional management of reinvigorated USIA overseas book publishing and promotion programs should be considered by the agency. At the same time, doubts were expressed that the

---

[9] For more on the subject, see *International Book and Library Activities: The History of a U.S. Foreign Policy,* Paxton P. Price, ed. (Metuchen, N.J.: The Scarecrow Press: 1982).

agency would seriously consider rebuilding a career publishing specialist corps to manage programs it might be able to fund. Reid Foundation Study Group researchers have sensed a skepticism among many senior USIA planners that book programs really require a specialist group to manage them. Moreover, even if Congress were to provide the funding level proposed by the Task Force, these same agency officials tend to doubt that that level would be sustained long enough to justify rebuilding a publishing specialist group. Reid Foundation Study Group members believe, therefore, that the agency should consider use of outside specialists to work with regular career generalists assigned to overseas book programs on short-term consulting assignments helping the agency quickly launch publishing projects. These outside specialists could be brought back periodically to check on progress and direction. At the same time, we would urge agency consideration for developing a small corps of publishing specialists. Such a cadre would provide USIA with adequate in-house expertise to manage the large world-language publishing programs such as Arabic, Chinese, French, Portuguese, and Spanish.

To urge use of outside professionals routinely is an acknowledgement that most of the costly mistakes of past book programs were due not to incorrect concepts but to their incorrect execution. Reid Foundation Study Group members have noted that, as in all human endeavors, risks of management lapses will be present in a large-scale USIA book program. Anything short of professional management will jeopardize the achievement of objectives and the effective and productive use of taxpayers' money, as well as undermine the credibility of books as effective and worthwhile USIA communications media. Some senior USIA managers became disillusioned because of a few instances of past book program management lapses, and argued for cutting such programs down to size or eliminating them entirely. The authors believe that USIA should begin a revitalized book program not overly concerned with these past difficulties, but with full awareness that sound management will avoid them. Selection and/or training of publishing specialists is an obvious first step toward assuring that expanded book programs will be professionally managed. Frequent audits, not only by accountants but by experienced professional publishing specialists, should be part of USIA's oversight of its overseas book publishing operations.

Surveys and Operating Plans

The outside specialists and experts discussed above could be quickly marshalled to guide USIA toward publishing activities that it might restore and/or expand as quickly as funds are made available. Such specialists would also be useful in monitoring progress and generally evaluating programs as they are set in place. Reid Foundation Study Group and Task Force members and discussants consulted agreed that the agency should move ahead even before funding is finally settled. A desirable early step would be to enlist their assistance in conducting on-sight surveys at USIA overseas posts where new publishing programs are to be initiated as well as those with ongoing programs considered for sharply increased production (such as the Arabic, French, Portuguese, and Spanish programs). Such survey reports would serve as guidelines, especially for those posts with little or no experience, for working with local publishers, preparing publishing/procurement contracts, monitoring performance, assuring that production specifications are satisfactorily met, and observing the promotion/distribution process. In addition, they would provide USIA with the information on feasibility, cost, etc. needed in planning and budgeting for an expanded global book publishing program, thereby serving as a "pre-audit" for the oversight process discussed above.

These survey reports need not be long, in-depth research concerning the sociopolitical complexions of societies, nor even examinations of all the strengths and weaknesses of their publishing industries and book distribution systems. Brief reviews conducted at overseas posts by an experienced publishing specialist and meetings with selected publishers and booksellers could quickly produce an operating plan and cost schedule, along with details on how to proceed in a manner consistent and compatible with each post's personnel and budgetary resources and local publishing and bookselling capabilities. Such surveys would provide USIA overseas posts with an operating plan including the following elements:

1. outline of an annual publishing program;
2. inventory of staff, experience, and know-how, including recommendations for training in publishing;
3. catalog of translators, interested and qualified publishers, and structure of the local book trade;
4. some indication of local area literacy and readership;
5. estimated costs;
6. step-by-step procedures on working with translators, publishers, and booksellers from initial presentation of a proposal for book translation or reprint project, negotiating a publishing contract, reviewing publishers' cost proposals, monitoring promotion and distribution performance, etc.—subsequent review of a program on perhaps a bi-annual basis would ensure the continued success and further development of programs by bringing the global experience of veteran publishing specialists to bear on problems new to the post.

Translations and English Language Reprints

It must be assumed that readers targeted for a reinvigorated USIA book publishing program are primarily professionals, educators, students, government cadres, scholars, writers and journalists, and leaders, supplemented by a body of literate, informed lay readers interested in learning about the U.S. and

American people. (While readership should be checked from time to time, it is assumed that these are the intended audiences because they are consistently so identified in the USIA readership studies in domestic or foreign surveys Reid Foundation Study Group members have seen.) Also, the majority of readers in these groups can be reached through books in the six world languages (Arabic, Chinese, English, French, Portuguese, and Spanish). In fact, books in English alone, printed in countries with reasonably well-developed book publishing communities such as India and Pakistan, could reach a sizeable readership in much of the developing world in Asia and East Africa.

At the same time, there are important audiences that do not read in any of the world languages and/or may prefer to read books in their native tongues. Single-country languages likely to be most important to USIA are those used in Asian and Western and Eastern European countries such as Japan, Korea, Indonesia, Thailand, Czechoslovakia, Hungary, Poland, Pakistan, Turkey, Greece, Portugal, etc.

The following section outlines approaches for quickly launching more typical USIA overseas publishing activities in translation and in English.

Facilitating Co-publishing Ventures

Co-publishing—the simultaneous publication of a book by publishers from two or more countries, with each holding rights for their traditional market areas—a development on the international publishing scene over the past decade, offers new approaches for a reinvigorated USIA book program. Co-publishing has been viewed increasingly as a collaboration with great potential for cost savings in preparing translations and in producing books, especially those with costly engravings involved—art books, atlases, and similar coffee table publications such as travel books. However, a major reason for the trend toward splitting Spanish language rights noted by the Reid Foundation Study Group has been the search for ways to get around formidable export barriers erected in many countries in Latin America. With the Latin American economy in such disarray, serious dislocations in normal book distribution patterns have taken place. Traditionally, it has been difficult enough for publishers to distribute Mexican books in Southern Cone countries (Argentina, Bolivia, Chile, Paraguay, and Uruguay) and Argentine books in Mexico and Central America. Now, few Argentine or Mexican publishers have much success in getting their books much farther than their own borders. Even the successful publishers in Spain whose books have tended to dominate Latin American markets are losing ground. This is not due to indigenous competition, however, but to serious shortages of the basic currency of international trade—the American dollar.

One solution to the above-mentioned problems is co-publishing. Production is usually handled by one publisher, which prints the whole edition and puts its publishing partners' imprints on copies pre-ordered for designated market areas. Sometimes Spanish publishers, for example, will bring out a for-Spain-only edition and sell microfilms or printing plates to an Argentine and/or Mexican publisher for their own production. Publishers cooperating in the venture share the costs of preparing translations, editing the manuscript, and typesetting, and pay only for the paper, printing, and binding of copies they ordered for their particular markets, thereby effecting a considerable cost saving.

USIA opened a book program office in Barcelona in February, 1985, and will facilitate co-production of books by Spanish and Latin American publishing partners. It would be desirable for USIA to arrange for continuing, close liaison between its book offices in Barcelona, Buenos Aires, and Mexico City and facilitate as many co-publishing translation ventures as the three offices can work out among publishers in their respective countries. It has been noted that American publishers are discovering the practicality of "splitting" Spanish rights between Spanish and Latin American publishers in the dollar-short market: hence, USIA should find these publishers attuned to co-publishing ventures the agency may develop with collaborating Spanish publishers. This development in Spanish language rights brokering can serve as a model for co-publishing ventures in other world languages, and USIA should look for such opportunities in its other world language programs. A type of co-publishing is already being employed in the agency's French book program for Africa. Rather than produce a book alone, the USIA Book Office locates a Paris publisher interested in a book for sale in the developed country French market. Two jointly-produced editions result, at a saving to both publishers, and the book's audience is extended to countries outside of Africa.

Another opportunity for a stepped-up USIA publishing program may be available through the relationships American publishers have developed with foreign publishers—including their own subsidiaries in certain cases. As described in chapter 6, several of the larger American textbook firms have created overseas editions, especially of college textbooks, which are sold abroad at prices well below those charged for the book in the U.S. hardback editions. At least one publisher also produces translations in a wide range of languages, including Arabic, Chinese, French, German, Japanese, Portuguese, and Spanish as well as a number of Indian languages and a few African tongues. USIA should immediately explore collaboration with these American publishing firms, companies which could offer management of co-publishing ventures through their own overseas branches and/or with indigenous publishers. These firms could offer the professional handling of translation, editorial, and production phases of book publishing of which USIA is not likely to be capable. Marketing systems are in place that offer better-than-average distribution through local distribution channels, direct mail sales, and library and university promotion.

Textbooks in USIA Programs

In the past, many USIA officials responsible for determining the kinds of books to be published and promoted abroad under USIA aegis have viewed textbooks, especially those in science and technology, as being of peripheral interest. Textbooks are still viewed by many as support for educational development and not, therefore, as being relevant to themes related to American culture and society. It is suggested here that American textbooks, even in the basic hard sciences, medicine, engineering, and technology, also support American cultural themes. Furthermore, they demonstrate American preeminence in these fields, and are widely sought not only in the developed world but in Third World countries and the Eastern bloc.

While funding for textbooks produced under USIA programs has heretofore been provided primarily by P.L. 480 monies, there is no reason why textbooks cannot and should not be made available within the regular USIA overseas translation/reprint publishing programs under discussion here. There is an advantage, of course, in using surplus P.L. 480 currencies in countries where they are available, such as India and Pakistan (see Table 3, "P.L. 480 Excess Currency Countries, June 30, 1984," at the end of this chapter). However, in other priority countries (e.g., those in Latin America), P.L. 480 funds are not available. There, American textbooks at the secondary and university levels are eagerly sought but are priced beyond the reach of impoverished students and even school and university libraries. Over the years, USIA has tended to limit its involvement with textbooks strictly to P.L. 480-type programs and then favoring only those in the social sciences that supported its cultural objectives. AID in the past had been expected to take care of any needs for texts in science and technology, in the context of its technical assistance programs. But AID has dismantled its publishing activities other than providing some modest support for primary school educational development programs that may include providing school books directly to children far more completely than USIA has dismantled its activities. Clearly, a review by a USIA/AID inter-agency group is needed here, lest textbooks get lost completely in plans to make American scholarship, thought, and knowledge more widely available to overseas readers. Many express the view that science is culture, and certainly American culture, and should therefore be in the USIA province of a balanced program. Interviewed on this very subject Charles E. Scribner, Jr., said that "one of the worse events in the history of science was when the phrase 'natural philosophy' to refer to science was dropped."[10]

[10] Alexander Hellemans "Science for General Readers," *Publishers Weekly,* August 17, 1984, cites similar views by others in publishing and science.

Conclusions

Implicit for the U.S. Books Abroad Task Force in the foregoing review and discussion of USIA's book publishing activities, past, present, and future, are conclusions reached by the Reid Foundation Study Group.

1. USIA should take immediate steps to bring its overseas book publishing and promotion program to at least the levels of the 1960s, requesting funding adjusted for inflation in its next appropriation request.
2. As discussed earlier, USIA no longer has a corps of experienced publishing specialists to administer enhanced publishing and promotion activities that the agency may institute. Options for meeting this shortage of experienced book program managers include:
   (a) recruiting specialists from the publishing industry with international experience (there are trained younger professionals currently expendable to their organizations, as many publishers' international divisions are forced to cut back in the face of declining overseas markets, who may be interested in a career change);
   (b) "borrowing" experienced managers from international divisions of publishing firms for short-term assignments;
   (c) contracting with independent publishing specialists on a consultant basis to work with career officer generalists on short-term assignments; and
   (d) in collaboration with the industry setting up a short-term training program to introduce newly appointed USIA book program personnel to international publishing.
3. USIA may need to quickly launch publishing and promotion activities in some countries before it can produce trained career officer book specialists to manage them (if it decides to restore a publishing specialist corps). The Reid Foundation Study Group believes that USIA could start with less experienced officers in certain situations, calling on the nongovernmental specialists to prepare operating plans and budgets based on on-site surveys.
4. USIA should explore co-publishing opportunities between Spanish, Portuguese, and Latin American publishers, as well as those with potential in other world languages, e.g., in Chinese between Taiwanese and Hong Kong publishers.
5. USIA needs to establish closer continuing contacts with those American publishers who have charted the waters in publishing abroad. These firms have established publishing bases of one sort or another that could be enlisted to produce, promote, and market both book translations and English reprints of interest to USIA.
6. The Reid Foundation Study Group has already explored possible collaboration with American publishers that would produce "at home" overruns of selected books supportive of USIA objectives, books that could be promoted in selected Third World countries at low prices. This idea is

patterned after the British Council's English Language Book Society (ELBS) scheme whereby participating British publishers produce an overrun of a special low-priced ELBS edition for selected Third World countries. USIA is urged to pursue such a publishing avenue with American publishers.

7. As an immediate and high priority, USIA should give serious consideration to reactivating its P.L. 480 Textbook Program in India (Joint Indo-American Textbook Program) and/or establishing one in other countries where surplus P.L. 480 currencies have accrued. We recommend also introducing university-level textbooks in all disciplines in regular USIA overseas publishing and promotion programs, both in translations and in English. Collaboration with AID would be desirable where that agency's interests could be stimulated.
8. As we have seen, USIA overseas libraries predate USIA itself by many years, having their origins in OWI and the Rockefeller Program for Latin America at the outset of World War II. Although they are not technically a topic of this study, their existence in flourishing form has been presupposed throughout our considerated of the needs of book promotion. In 1948 when the Smith-Mundt Act gave the Department of State responsibility for U.S. information and cultural programming abroad, including supervision of American libraries overseas, there were four in Latin America which had been set up under the Rockefeller Program, a handful in British Commonwealth countries originated by the OWI, and a number of American House libraries set up by the U.S. military government in Germany (HICOG). As U.S. overseas cultural activities expanded during the 1950s and 1960s, the number of USIA libraries expanded in concert with them reaching a peak of 254 by 1965. With the decline of book program activities noted earlier in this chapter, so, too, these American overseas libraries reduced in size and number, falling to only 131 today, a drop of half. Implicit in the recommendations set out above for expanded overseas book publishing and promotion programming is one urging a greater role for USIA libraries in that promotion through re-opening the 130 or so libraries closed during the book drought from the mid-1960s down to the mid-1980s, rebuilding their collections, and strengthening USIA library operations generally.

This chapter has concentrated on a USIA book publishing program. Designated as the agency with primary responsibility for U.S. government overseas book activities, however, USIA must, of course, be concerned with much more than supporting publication abroad of books on public diplomacy themes. The agency program envisioned here would include a wide range of promotional activities as well: book exhibits, book reviews, provision of information on American books and how to order them, educational exchange, currency convertibility, and copyright—all concerns of American books abroad and covered in separate chapters of this study.

Table 1—USIA Book Publishing Production—1950–1984[a]

Fiscal Year	Translation Program	P.L. 480 Textbooks[b]	Published in the U.S.	Total
1950	10,000	—	—	10,000
1951	1,730,000	—	—	1,730,000
1952	3,310,000	—	—	3,310,000
1953	5,820,000	—	—	5,820,000
1954	4,360,000	—	—	4,360,000
1955	5,131,496	—	—	5,131,496
1956	5,987,666	—	633,624	6,621,290
1956–60[c]	4,346,800	—	—	4,346,800
1957	7,359,238	—	1,904,962	9,264,200
1958	6,814,000	—	873,046	7,687,046
1959	3,873,550	—	830,875	4,704,425
1960	4,746,350	—	659,867	5,406,217
1961	3,129,950	142,350	672,149	3,944,449
1962	3,545,422	476,150	1,082,624	5,104,196
1963	5,287,900	775,805	1,456,971	7,520,676
1964	8,317,151	1,078,396	1,776,196	11,171,743
1965	10,244,342	1,215,116	1,325,197	12,784,655
1966	8,855,243	789,100	1,599,016	11,243,359
1967	6,913,109	792,000	1,597,223	9,302,332
1968	4,999,557	696,052	835,310	6,530,919
1969	3,202,001	952,623	653,077	4,807,701
1970	2,593,922	1,761,806	517,723	4,873,451
1971	2,089,650	364,030	517,706	2,971,386
1972	2,029,840	1,436,519	655,170	4,121,529
1973	1,528,544	272,244	415,903	2,216,691
1974	1,256,390	229,202	620,374	2,105,966
1975	1,130,181	402,311	296,181	1,828,673
1976–5 qtrs.	1,344,546	441,195	—	1,785,741
1977	881,229	106,500	—	987,729
1978	768,204	23,275	—	791,479
1979	565,087	16,750	—	581,837
1980	502,040	23,000	—	525,040
1981	594,654	—	—	594,654
1982	567,035	4,000	—	571,035
1983	539,717	—	—	539,717
1984	463,964	—	—	463,964
Totals	124,838,778	11,998,424	18,923,194	155,760,396

[a] Number of copies.

[b] P.L. 480 textbooks, produced primarily as English language reprints of American editions mostly in India, were financed by foreign currency holdings of the U.S. government generated from the sale of surplus American agricultural commodities.

[c] Low-Priced Book Program under which translations of American books were produced in Third World countries under contract with an American publishers export representative firm.

Table 2.—Joint Indo-American Textbook Program (P.L. 480), Number of Editions and Copies Produced (1962–81)

Fiscal Year	No. Editions	No. Copies
1962	19	49,000
1963	34	88,900
1964	75	383,871
1965	146	493,300
1966	153	658,100
1967	154	595,600
1968	124	596,452
1969	212	879,173
1970	297	1,679,906
1971	78	329,330[a]
1972	289	1,390,019
1973	48	220,744
1974	51	172,002
1975	125	382,811[b]
1976	39	183,129
1977	18	67,500
1978	7	23,275
1979	5	16,750
1980	7	23,000
1981	4	10,500
Totals	1,885	8,243,862

[a] The sudden drop in production in FY 1971 was due to the temporary curtailment of the Joint Indo-American Textbook Program by the government of India at the time of the Pak-Indo War.

[b] Some residual AID funds from the $3 million made available to the P.L. 480 Program in the late 1960s were utilized in FY 1975, accounting for the sharp increase in textbook editions published during that year.

Table 3.—Excess P.L. 480 Currencies

Excess Currency Countries (Currencies held in Treasury in excess of two year anticipated uses for operating expenses and programs):

Country	Amount
Burma	$ 10 million
Guinea	13 million
India	360 million
Pakistan	135 million

Near Excess Currency Countries (Currencies held in Treasury in excess of one year but less than two year anticipated uses for operating expenses and programs):

Country	Amount
Czechoslovakia	$ 2 million
Ghana	1 million
Poland	127 million
Sudan	19 million
Taiwan	4 million
Yugoslavia	4 milllon

Source: AID Central Accounting Office, June 30, 1984.

15

A Matter of Content: Title Selection and the National Interest

William M. Childs and *Howard R. Penniman*

Two issues have an impact on the selection of titles to be promoted through a revitalized USIA book and library program and represent two extremes of opinion regarding USIA itself. First, is it essential to USIA's mission to ensure that American books are available to overseas readers that are broadly representative of the full range of opinion and writing on American culture, society, and experience? This view might be characterized as the "full range" position. Or, should USIA limit its efforts to making sure that foreign readers have access to serious, responsible American writing that explains, supports, and advances current American policies?

Some Task Force members and other discussants contend that titles to be published and promoted with USIA financial support, or to be purchased for overseas USIA programs, ought to be primarily related to American domestic and foreign policy interests. For example, one Task Force member stated "It is fair and proper to ask: will this book or program benefit the United States abroad? If books are to be our ambassadors abroad, as has been proposed in the NSC memorandum (see Appendix 1), then it is our obligation to select our ambassadors with knowledge of what they will say about us."

Others take the contrary, or "full range," position. Another Task Force member supporting this view maintained that "Books selected for the library ought to reflect the best available works reflecting broadly American life and culture." There is, in addition, a third position, however. Some professionals experienced in international publishing urge that selection criteria should include recognition of the needs and interests of overseas library users. One

Task Force spokesman for this position advised that "People abroad will not read books unless they want to; that is, unless they feel that books will in some way be helpful to them. Efforts to send abroad large quantities of books because they have a message we want to spread will be wasted unless they have a message the users want to read. For this reason, within very broad definitions of suitability, selection of titles for the program should be in the hands of foreign recipients, or, alternatively, of publishers who have had long experience in determining the market for American books and know what will be sought."

NSC Director Robert McFarlane noted in his April, 1984, memorandum to USIA that "the 'book gap' is serious," and began his request for a study with the premise that "the time is right for a major new commitment to the provision of U.S. books abroad": the justification for this commitment should be the *competition of ideas*. "The power of ideas," McFarlane wrote, "has been projected through the written word. Whether we are dealing with the 'war of ideas' or looking at the problem in terms of fostering the 'infrastructure of democracy'—twin goals eloquently stated by the President in London in June 1982—we must compete."

USIA, in its rationale for a new book program developed in November, 1982,[1] observed that "serious American books in English or in translation on themes of concern to USIA are essential to the agency's mission in public diplomacy" and stated that the purpose of an expanded USIA book program should be "to promote significantly increased publication and distribution abroad of books in translation and in English which *support or help explain our foreign policy, our institutions, and fundamental American values*" (emphasis added). Earlier, in June, 1982, USIA Director Charles Wick had issued a revised USIA library policy statement calling for all agency library programs to provide "the latest and most accurate information about the U.S. government and its policies . . . and in-depth information about American values, history, culture, and character."[2] More recently, in June, 1984, Wick issued a statement setting forth eight purposes for USIA, the first two of which are to "strengthen foreign understanding and support for United States policies and actions"; and "promote foreign awareness and knowledge of American society, culture, and values so that other nations can better understand our policies and objectives" (see Appendix 3 for the full statement of the purposes).

The issue to be decided, then (a major one for the U.S. Books Abroad Task Force and the government to address), is the content of a reinvigorated USIA book and library program. One Task Force member stated that issue

---

[1] Rationale, USIA Book Promotion

[2] USIA Library Program

best when he said, "There is a fundamental matter on which members of the Task Force have disagreed, reflecting in their deliberations a difference of opinion which exists in the USIA itself and among other Americans who are concerned with the issue. It is primarily a choice of emphasis: should the new initiative suggested by the National Security Council be aimed primarily at strengthening a program that disseminates abroad books which are 'broadly representative of the full range of American culture, society, and opinion?' Or, should it emphasize books which are chosen because they, on the whole, present American society and policies in a way that is supportive of American foreign policy objectives?"

A Look Backward

As can be seen from the previous chapter, USIA book programs grew from fledgling informational and cultural outposts created within pre-war and wartime U.S. government agencies, such as the Rockefeller Program in Latin America and OWI, and postwar operations including HICOG and the Marshall Plan.

By 1943, American libraries had been established by OWI in London, Sydney, Melbourne, Wellington, Johannesburg, and Bombay. Their purpose was basically to serve journalists and writers, radio, local governments, and educational, scientific, and cultural institutions and organizations by making information on the United States available and helping those groups to more accurately present the U.S. to their countrymen. Shortly thereafter, two more American libraries were set up, in Capetown and Cairo. An OWI Library Unit and a Book Division were established to provide policy direction for those libraries. Criteria were quickly determined for selecting books and publications to be sent to them. Thus, the issue of book selection and the national interest was automatically raised by the fact of creating a Library Unit.

Parallelling the growth of the OWI library program was the development of the Rockefeller Program, with 27 cultural centers established throughout Latin America largely for cultural exchange and the teaching of English, Portuguese, and Spanish; English to indigenous populations, and Portuguese and Spanish to resident Americans. All of these centers established libraries that developed collections of American books, initially for English teaching purposes, but eventually for cultural resources. By 1950, with the creation of USIA's predecessor agency, the International Information Administration (IIA) within the Department of State, to take over administration of these institutions, more than 100 U.S. Information Centers with active library programs were in operation around the world.

A Bibliographic Division, made up largely of professional librarians, was established within IIA in 1951 to review and select books for these overseas American libraries and other prospective book promotion activities. This division's functions included monitoring American publishers' annual output for the purpose of identifying books potentially useful to the IIA book and library programs. The librarians reviewed books and prepared descriptive and analytical appraisals of them in terms of their suitability and applicability for overseas book and library program managers. This large and visibly growing American overseas library service program soon caught the attention of the American press, citizens, and the Congress. In the early 1950s, as the Cold War became the dominant American foreign policy concern, pressure was brought to bear on the IIA director to establish criteria for selecting books for overseas libraries that would cast the best light on America.

By the mid-1950s, as American publishers began turning out rapidly increasing numbers of books in response to domestic post-war demand, the Bibliographic Division (in USIA after 1953) became overtaxed and fell short of workload demands. Some of the expanded book review workload was contracted to an outside research organization that was able to provide the expertise of university professors and other specialists and prepare in-depth book reviews and special bibliographies. The director of this outside research group participated regularly in Bibliographic Division meetings and acquired extensive knowledge concerning the various USIA overseas book and library programs as well as of the criteria for selecting titles to be promoted by them. Thus, he brought the title selection process into the academic community, thereby adding a sorely needed subject matter specialist resource pool to that process.

As new publishing and promotion programs were developed in the 1960s (see chapter 14 for a program chronicle), title selection criteria and procedures were adjusted to meet the special objectives of individual programs. The book selection process itself was substantially altered to meet USIA's accelerating overseas publishing programs. It was recognized that these programs represented a substantially larger investment in American books by the government than selection solely for U.S. overseas libraries. The simple purchasing of a book for USIA libraries often amounted to an order of only 30 to 40 copies. Book publication programs required the translation and production of perhaps 3,000 to 10,000 copies of a book for distribution to readers in several languages. Choosing books to support lecture and seminar programs might involve the purchase of 200 or more copies—again, considerably larger than the usual library order. Orders of books by USIA posts around the world for presentation to institutions or individuals might also involve purchasing several hundred copies.

Since these programs cost more money, policy officers from USIA's geographic divisions insisted on having a stronger role in choosing the titles to be translated and/or reprinted in countries under their jurisdiction. Their object was to ensure the selection of books which directly serve USIA goals for individual countries or geographic regions. When USIA established the Latin American Book Program, for example, a coordinator was assigned to provide guidance and direction. A Latin American Title Selection Committee was also established within the USIA book publishing division, under the direction of the Latin American book program coordinator, with representatives of the agency's Latin American policy and operations office participating. Later, similar committees were created for the French-for-Africa and Arabic translations programs.

This centralized, globally coordinated approach to title selection within USIA's Bibliographic and Book Program Divisions of the 1950s and 1960s has been gradually transformed over 20 years of operations. USIA field officers were limited to the use of books approved by those two Washington-based divisions in the 1960s. If a book were desired for a library, or for presentation to a prime minister, other high-level governmental officials, a journalist or scholar, or for translation into any foreign language, it was required that it be chosen from lists prepared by the Bibliographic Division, or be submitted for appraisal and approval by that division when not found on such lists. In the event that the Bibliographic Division did not approve a book, the Public Affairs Officer (PAO) in charge at the requesting post could still obtain it, but only by providing justification to the agency.

In December, 1969, USIA Director Frank Shakespeare, reacting to this policy, stated that he regarded the PAO as the "most knowledgeable authority and the best judge of library requirements within his country. He should be able to order his books without the need for justifying his choice in each case." Shakespeare called for a decentralized title selection mechanism and declared that the PAO "has the ultimate responsibility for the selection of publications for program use" at foreign posts. The Bibliographic Division was assigned responsibility for "applying professional judgement to the selection of publications through the review and appraisal process and for communicating professional judgments to the PAO to assist him in making the final selections" for use in programs under his jurisdiction. Meanwhile, the Book Program Division continued to select books for world language publication programs and to recommend titles for single-country translation programs.[3]

Title Selection Today

In 1979, USIA in effect placed responsibility for title selection for all book and library programs, with the exception of world language book publishing, with the Public Affairs Officer in the field. Individual title selection committees for the various world language publishing programs had been absorbed

[3] Circular "Dear PAO" letter from USIA director Frank Shakespeare to all USIA posts, December 10, 1969. The responsibilities of the Bibliographic Division and the Publications Division (now Book Programs Division) were spelled out in a follow-up Information Center Service Staff Instruction No. 53, January 2, 1970 on "Book Selection Procedures."

into a single Title Selection Committee in the Book Program Division responsible for determining titles to be translated. Thus, while field posts now selected books for all library and publication programs under their control, the Book Program Division continued to have final authority over the titles published in world languages in programs that it operated, and to recommend titles for single-country languages. But the most important change in the 1979 revision of book selection policy was the elimination of "hands on" review of books by the Bibliographic Division and outside reviewers.[4]

Budgetary considerations and shifting program priorities were responsible for the termination of the 20-year outside contract book review and bibliographic arrangements. Functions and responsibilities of the Bibliographic Division were sharply redefined and its staff and budget reduced. No longer would that division directly review books for purposes of preparing appraisals, making recommendations to field posts, and assembling substantive bibliographies. Rather, its function became "the compilation of authoritative special bibliographies in subject fields identified for attention by posts . . . (and providing) descriptions and judgments of titles by peers, commercial review sources, and other authorities outside" the agency. In general, books would no longer be regularly scrutinized by USIA bibliographers or by outside specialists under contract on behalf of USIA specifically. Outside reviews and "peer judgments", wherever published, have replaced a 30-year program that included not only substantive reviews but also addressed books with the USIA mission and policy considerations in mind.

According to informed discussants, the only substantive review USIA field posts now receive is the periodic book announcement prepared by the Bibliographic Division. Under the 1979 policy change, these notices provide judgments but do not constitute agency recommendations based on a Bibliographic Division review of the books in the announcement. In most cases, the announcement quotes from published reviews which, of course, were not prepared with USIA's mission in mind. If no published review is available (often the case with scholarly works of interest to USIA), the "Book Announcement" simply quotes the cover blurb or publisher catalog. With shrinking budgets and staffs, few PAOs have time to examine books requested from the agency after they arrive, as suggested by the 1979 directive, and must often leave title selection to foreign national employees in charge of the USIA library and/or other book promotion activities.

---

[4] Circular "Dear PAO" letter from Associate Director for Educational and Cultural Affairs Alice L. Ilchman to all USIA posts, May 11, 1979, enclosing a revised Section 730, USIA Manual of Operations (MOA) on "Selection of Publications."

Choices

Assuming that an expanded program is created, the central concern for the U.S. Books Abroad Task Force is whether internal procedures for title selection are adequate—or should be revised. Should the responsibility for choosing titles that USIA field posts will publish, promote, present to governmental and opinion leaders, place in their libraries, etc., continue to reside in individual posts as is now the case? Or, should that function and responsibility be returned to a strengthened title selection committee within USIA-Washington? In either case, can the present system of limited assessment of outside publications adequately support an expanded program? Can USIA itself provide subject matter experts from within its ranks to review books authoritatively and provide the other needed bibliographic services that a revitalized USIA book and library program will require? Should an agency-centered, strengthened title selection process be authorized to arrange for outside book review and bibliographic services providing academic and other subject matter experts? In the latter case, the Task Force will want to consider whether it would be desirable to include a provision for continuing consultation between USIA and such an organization.

Conclusions

Since the OWI days of World War II, it has been recognized that American overseas libraries are not intended to be replicas of U.S. public libraries. They are intended to make available to the foreign reader representative and balanced works that reflect American life, society, culture, and government policies. Only writings of qualified, authoritative, and responsible observers and chroniclers are deemed appropriate. In other words, titles selected for placement in USIA libraries, and for publication and promotion abroad, are expected to be the best available commentaries on American life, culture, arts and humanities, education, and science and technology—and on national policies.

A "local choice" doctrine, or a corollary of it, "local acceptability," was the predominant rationale of the now defunct Franklin Book Programs of the 1950s and 1960s, operated in its early years largely with financial support from USIA.[5] This program was developed by a group of internationally minded American publishers who were concerned that few developing countries could provide their readers with indigenously produced books. From its founding in 1952, the Franklin Programs' twin purposes were developing indigenous publishing industries with autonomous local management, and the selection of titles for translation on the basis of local needs and interests by that local management. Thus, "nation building" and "local choice" policies

[5] Curtis Benjamin's study, *U.S. Books Abroad*, contains the most current analysis of the Franklin Book Programs.

guided the Franklin programs for the two decades of its existence. USIA acquiesced to these goals in the early days of its relationship with Franklin, with the proviso that it have veto power on titles not acceptable to the agency. In fact, although USIA was one of the prime financiers of Franklin, this policy meant that virtually any title recommended by Franklin was approved, unless it was specifically prejudicial to the interests of the United States. USIA's role, in short, was a negative one, and, in the early years of USIA's problems with "censorship" charges concerning its own libraries, rejection was not a casual recourse in any agency book programs. However, as the accountability requirement for USIA book programs called for more and more attention to books supporting the agency's mission, cracks developed in the relationship and USIA eventually dropped support of the Franklin Book Programs in the late 1960s. Several of the program's founders currently serving on the U.S. Books Abroad Task Force believe that, with the growth of indigenous publishing and distribution infrastructures in the developing world and the outreach of many American publishers through inexpensive student-edition textbooks, there is no longer a need for a Franklin-type overseas publishing enterprise.

Title selection and book content policies for USIA book activities which involve no book purchases, but rather are (1) books donated for distribution overseas under agency aegis and (2) those commercially distributed under any agency currency convertibility programs should not be overlooked either. Reid Foundation Study Group members argue that, if USIA is to present a book donated by a publisher or to support presentations by organizations such as the Asia Foundation, Brothers Brothers Foundation, or Freedom House, as much consideration should be given to its literary and scholarly merits and its relevance to USIA's mission and purpose as is given to those books USIA purchases directly.

The U.S. Books Abroad Task Force should also take note that when USIA sought to limit the kinds of books exported under currency convertibility agreements with American publishers in the 1960s, cries of "censorship" arose (see chapter 5). In 1961, USIA Director Edward R. Murrow succinctly expressed the essence of USIA policy: "I find it a little tiresome to be called upon to deal with the charge of censorship repeatedly. We have no intention of trying to interfere with the sale of American books in the foreign market. As far as we are concerned any American publisher is free to sell, and any foreign purchaser is free to buy, any publication he wishes as long as he doesn't look to the United States Treasury for subvention of the transaction. When government financial assistance is involved, the taxpayers, the Congress, and this Agency have a right to insist that some benefit accrue to the achievement of our national purpose."[6] This USIA policy statement was

[6] Letter, from USIA Director Edward R. Murrow to President, American Book Publishers Council, November, 1961.

issued specifically in the context of the IMG convertibility program; the Task Force may wish to consider whether criteria on selection applicable to books in that program are not more clearly applicable to volumes purchased, or translated and published at taxpayers' expense.

PART VI

A NATIONAL POLICY

16

International Book Programs of Major World Powers

Donald E. McNeil

Before moveable type, the uniqueness of individual books, the skills, money, and time needed to duplicate them even approximately, endowed each one with a special value beyond its substantive value as the prime medium by which generation could speak to generation. The commissioning by royalty of books with carefully elaborated lettering and illuminating illustrations, as well as the similar reproduction of religious works and classics in the European monasteries and Arabic cultural centers of the Middle Ages, gave books status as art objects—a status that today means such books command prices equal to those paid for paintings and sculptures, no two copies being the same. In their time, these books graced royal as well as ecclesiastical collections and endowed those rulers who possessed them with implied wisdom as well as taste in the eyes of peers and subjects. Moving from there to the use of books, through gift and dowries, to influence other governments was a modest step.

The print revolution launched by Gutenberg meant, of course, books and knowledge for the many. Viewed as a dangerous thing by those in power, this development led to the earliest copyright laws, intended to restrict rather than extend the availability of books. Efforts to prevent tracts from reaching one's own subjects proved as ineffective then as now, although the approach is still very much in vogue. Ever since the age of the seventeenth-century French kings, who recognized the power of language and effectively promoted French as the international language of diplomacy, books have been an accepted means by which governments seek to influence foreign audiences and, hence, international relations. Even the smallest, poorest nations today still see the international availability of a body of published national literature as a cultural necessity in the age of public diplomacy. Access to the knowledge of the major developed countries has an equal if not greater priority.

National book trusts, councils, and foundations, as well as book and literacy programs and subsidized publishing, have mushroomed in the developing world since the end of World War II. Major power book export programs created to extend influence, win over readers to a course of action or belief, assist in national development, or promote understanding of culture have also blossomed. For the purpose of this study, the Reid Foundation Study Group has selected the programs of the United Kingdom, the Soviet Union, France, and Spain, for specific elaboration. Nevertheless, almost all governments today fund national book activities of some sort whether they are the larger programs of West Germany, India, Argentina, Australia, and Canada, or the modest presence of Outer Mongolia, Burma, Mauritius, and the Cameroons at the Frankfurt book fair. What they all suggest is a recognition of the global influence of the book, a recognition that has drastically declined in the U.S. government as expressed by action, even as it has grown elsewhere.

THE UNITED KINGDOM

"Trade follows the book" is an axiom that goes a long way toward explaining why the private and public sectors in the United Kingdom work closely on the export of British books. Trade is the lifeblood of the British Isles, and, for the British, books are the cutting edge, the promoters behind which follows other trade. "Britain is fortunate in having a language which people all over the world want to learn," one British Council *Annual Report* (1979–80) noted. "English is a national asset ultimately more valuable than oil." U.S. government leaders recognize the truth of those facts too, but this is not shown in their responses. Perhaps the difference can be explained by noting one basic fact: British book exports in peak years constitute 60 percent or more of production; U.S. book exports have reached a maximum of 8 percent of production and have, for most post-war years, hovered about 6 percent.

Cultural relations are a generational game, the same 1979–80 British Council report observed. British culture—used here as a collective term that includes much besides language and the arts—can influence people, but its impact is gradual. Meanwhile, American observers who have studied both the British book industry and British government support of book exports say that the relationship between them appears more seamless, less linked to immediate results, and more patient than in the U.S.[1] There is little doubt that the

[1] A key event of the year for British Council and the industry in 1984 was the extension of their annual meeting to a full five days, with some twenty council staff members concerned with books exchanging views with industry professionals to update their knowledge. (Publishers Association *Annual Report*, 1984–85.)

British Council is concerned with the commercial book trade abroad. Little time is spent distinguishing between social science and literary works, and scientific and technical ones, in terms of what the council will promote. (In fact, most subsidized books are texts in science and technology.) In addition, there is even less concern as to whether a British book is of domestic origin or, for example, American. Indeed, the British industry and the British Council would likely be all too happy if all copies of American books destined for Commonwealth countries bore a London imprint. When asked how the council and the industry avoid or minimize friction on book content in joint programs by a Reid Foundation Study Group member, a council officer replied, "Wisdom on both sides." The 1984–85 Publishers Association *Annual Report* notes that content differences do arise, but are kept manageable and resolved pragmatically.

The British Council

The British Council celebrated its fiftieth anniversary as the primary British cultural presence overseas in 1984—in some cases, such as in former colonies that are now Commonwealth members, the council is almost an indigenous institution. A quasi-public institution operating under a royal charter, the council performs many of the same functions as the U.S. Information Agency. It is, however, quite distinct from the BBC, and press functions are provided at embassies by regular embassy staff. In fact, in providing and promoting English teaching, conducting educational exchange programs, sponsoring cultural programs, arranging training programs in the United Kingdom, and promoting British books and journals, the council maintains a discreet distance from the embassy in most countries, with its own offices connected to its libraries and cultural centers.

Aside from removing the council from politics this semi-independent status has operational advantages. The council is able to contract with foreign institutions and governments, for example, which pay for training programs in the United Kingdom arranged and supervised by the council. The council is also able to sign contracts with international institutions such as the World Bank to provide consultants for their developing world projects. A recent example is World Bank assistance to Kenya for improving its entire primary-secondary curriculum and related textbooks. The council has contracted with the government of Kenya to provide British educators and professionals for consultation on the preparation of textbooks, as well as for production and distribution.

On the home front, the council's charter status enables it to receive support from diverse sources, e.g., (1) a grant-in-aid for overseas information services from the Ministry of Foreign and Commonwealth Affairs; (2) Overseas Development Administration contributions for management of technical and higher education programs; (3) payments for its consultation services to international agencies and other governments; and (4) its other earnings. Publishers, too, fund special projects and services by the council. The first two sources provide the council's operating funds. The earnings are from charges for its English language training programs and related courses abroad, and from the sale of its own publications.

Among the latter is the *British Book News*, a monthly journal editorially prepared by the council staff and printed by B.H. Blackwell's, the largest private sector book wholesaler and institutional sales company in the United Kingdom. Reviews in the *News* are not so much literary criticism and critique as they are statements of content and estimates of where the book stands in its field, provided by discipline experts. Each issue of the journal carries dozens of such reviews, arranged by topic, with one or two longer reviews on particularly significant books from each topic (if there are any that month). Supplements devoted to one field are issued throughout the year, to ensure that good books absent from the monthly issue for lack of space are at least listed. The *British Book News* is regarded in the international book trade as the leading publication of its kind, indispensible for publishers, librarians, booksellers, and educators. The council distributes a certain number of copies of the *News* through its offices abroad, but the magazine is also available by subscription from Blackwell's, and is now substantially self-supporting. "How to Buy British Books," and "German Agents for British Books" are only two examples of a category of publications produced and distributed by the council intended specifically to overcome barriers to the commercial book trade. Other publications are noted in chapter 12 as guides to what the Department of Commerce and/or USIA might produce for our own industry.

The Book Division of the council consists of the Book Promotion Department, the Libraries Department, and the Low-Priced Book Department. Book Promotion produces the review journal, works closely with publishers on promotion (primarily with the Book Development Council described below), and develops thematic book exhibits to which publishers donate promotional copies. In 1984, there were 750 showings by council offices abroad, either at their own libraries or at local institutions or events in each country. In addition, the council mounts its own stand at major international book fairs. Like promotional programs of many other countries, that of the council is launched each year at the Frankfurt fair. The stands of foreign counterparts may occupy more space than the council exhibit, but none compete in terms of volumes available at Frankfurt. The council exhibit contains more than 5,000 titles, a majority shown spine out and arranged topically as in a library, with space for browsers to stop. Flyers, leaflets on book buying, and issues of the *British Book News* are distributed at the booth, along with information on publishers not at the fair and on those that are present. In 1983, a computer terminal was added to link the fair with bibliographic data available in the United Kingdom. In addition to fairs, the council and the publishers' Book Development Council hold joint book trade seminars each year with counterparts abroad. In 1984, there were ten seminars in major publishing capitals of Europe and Asia.

The Book Presentation Scheme, conducted by the Library Department, has the straightforward purpose of maintaining and developing collections of British books at specific institutional libraries throughout the developing world. Some $5 million worth of British books are purchased each year at concessionary prices from publishers, and this program assures that there are one or more in-country collections of British books, aside from those in the smaller libraries of the council itself, available in all developing countries. In fact, since there is turnover in the council library collections, the presentation recipients are in effect depository libraries, much like the Federal Depository Libraries concept supported by the Library of Congress and the Government Printing Office in the U.S. Council presentations are accompanied by bibliographic assistance from council librarians, including bibliographic materials, assistance on determining needs, and training of library staffs. Some of the funding that the council receives from the Overseas Development Administration is expended for library training programs that bring individuals to the United Kingdom for that purpose or to send British librarians abroad. It should be noted that there are no donated book programs beyond these purchased presentations, except those that operate independent of government and industry. (The Ranfurls Library Service distributes about 300,000 books per year largely to Commonwealth institutions.) In fact, even those books donated by publishers for exhibit purposes are intended for inclusion in council library collections when their display usefulness is ended and not intended for other in-country libraries that are or will soon become customers.

The Low-Priced Book Department is concerned with commercial access to British books in developing countries, and is identified with the English Language Book Society (ELBS), a subsidy to British publishers using the overrun approach. The price of a book in its first printing includes a publisher's fixed costs: editorial work, graphic design, and the cost of producing type. Second and subsequent printings costs are limited essentially to paper, ink, press time, author's royalties, and ongoing promotion, and are the more profitable sales. When reprints are contemplated, publishers inform the council of their plans and provide a sample copy of the book for approval. Copies beyond those intended as the reprint are overrun copies and, with council subsidy, will be sold in designated developing countries at prices substantially lower than the regular edition. These low-priced editions are all printed with similar covers that identify them as a distinct series, regardless of publisher, so that they can be promoted in catalogs and promotional materials of their own. Unlike past USIA and AID programs, except for the Student and Ladder Editions in their earliest years, orders for ELBS books are directed to the British publishers that produced the books, and are fulfilled and billed by those publishers directly to the customers. The books brought out under the ELBS program are almost entirely in scientific, technical, and medical fields, and are primarily textbooks. Some 1.5 million were sold in 1983.

The International Book Information Service (IBIS) is an example of how effectively the British Council works with industry. The interests of the industry are in promotion, those of the council in contact identification. Using the resources of the council's library staff, usually selected for their instincts for and interest in book promotion in addition to their basic librarian skills, lists of institutions and individuals in categories such as professors in a discipine, librarians, etc. were gradually compiled and delivered to IBIS for sorting, computerizing, and selling to the industry for use in mailing promotional material and, as the mail systems in certain developing countries have become more reliable, for direct mail order sales on an international level. IBIS soon became a self-supporting institution, although council librarians abroad are still called on from time to time to assist in revising lists. IBIS has become profitable enough to establish IBIS Information Services, Inc., in New York, which sells its lists to American publishers as well as to others who may need mailing lists of scholars and professionals in most recognized fields. Today, IBIS New York claims lists containing over 650,000 faculty member addresses worldwide outside of the U.S., among others.

The Book Development Council

Although direct relations between British Council officers and individual publishers are common, the institutional link is the Book Development Council (BDC), a company registered in the early 1950s as "A British Enterprise for International Cooperation." The BDC was funded at the outset by subscription from some 60 British publisher members to "ensure that adequate supplies of British books are available on reasonable terms wherever they are needed; and to study how best it can support or complement local educational or publishing and bookselling enterprises."[2] Eventually, although remaining a company to enable it to enter into agreements with governments and private institutions both at home and abroad, the BDC has become in effect the International Division of the Publishers Association, with some similarity to the International Division of the AAP in the U.S., but with a staff (thirteen in 1984) large enough to undertake the projects that the Publishers' Association, the British Council, the Overseas Trade Development Board, and the Overseas Development Administation envision for it.

[2] At the time the Book Development Council was formed, Britain was in the process of losing its colonies, while the American book industry was beginning to flex its muscles internationally; there was great concern in the British industry about holding traditional markets, and forming the BDC was only one of the responses.

As in the U.S., piracy is a major British concern at this time, and the Campaign Against Book Piracy (CABP) of the BDC has been successful in raising a substantial fund from the industry—including ongoing commitments of 1 percent of export turnover from some companies. In the first three years of the committee's existence ending in 1984, 400,000 British pounds had been raised. An anti-piracy officer in the Book Development Council office in London works with two BDC anti-piracy officers in Hong Kong and Singapore, with the latter providing on-site reporting and action. The CABP promotes legal action and/or embassy protests where piracy shows up, and is also working on the problem of "compulsory licensing" where it has appeared in Asia; the major current activity of the AAP is in part a response to the U.K. Publishers Association urgings at Frankfurt meetings, and the two associations are seeking to work closely with each other (although the American effort to raise its own "war chest" has not yet been markedly successful). The CABP reports funding made available for court action by Nigerian, Indian, and Singapore publishers, against identified pirates. The CABP has identified cases of "compulsory licensing" in Korea, Indonesia, the Philippines, and Pakistan that alarm them. Like the American copyright industry (chapter 3), the CABP is awaiting the effect of changes in Indian copyright law that provide for "compulsory licensing," but reports that in 1984 an amendment to the Indian Copyright Act has greatly increased penalties for piracy. A major victory for the CABP in 1984 was the decision in a Singapore suit that British books *were* protected by the Singapore copyright law against piracy there.

In other endeavors, the BDC coordinates the presence of British publishers at international book fairs and exhibits in cooperation with the British Overseas Board of Trade. Depending on the event, the BDC will in certain circumstances develop combined stands for publishers and facilitate publisher participation at others. In 1983, the BDC sponsored and administered joint ventures at eight major book fairs, including the American Booksellers Association (ABA) convention, and over eight hundred exhibitors benefitted from the Trade Board's total subsidy for the year of 250,000 British pounds, or approximately $500,000 in 1983 dollars. (As noted earlier, British Council exhibits are separate from these displays, albeit the council is present at the same events.) In 1982, the Overseas Board of Trade paid, for example, some 90 percent of the cost of the British presence at Frankfurt, where British publishers were the largest contingent. A startling exhibit statistic: trade board support to publishers for the single event at Frankfurt is greater than the board's support of exhibits at all overseas events for any other industry. Even when the BDC recommends that there not be a major collective presence at a fair, publishers are paid one-half the travel costs of one company officer, and receive a rebate for the cost of their individual stands.

The BDC Development Aid Project Service is funded by the subscription of a limited number of Publishers' Association members, and by BDC earnings from the sale of consultant and training services to overseas publishing projects. Although the BDC runs training courses abroad as requested by foreign publishers or governments, consulting by professionals sent from England is another DAPS activity, as well as an information service for subscribing publishers on foreign projects. In 1984, BDC provided such data for ninety projects in fifty countries, and also made visits to the World Bank in Washington, D.C., the European Development Fund and UNESCO in Paris, and the Asian Development Bank in Manila. The British Council textbook assistance programs contracted by that body with foreign government and international institutions, as described earlier, are developed with the BDC, which assists in assembling professional personnel for such contracts. Linked to those activities is the BDC Overseas Bookseller Training Officer, who conducts seminars and workshops abroad for retail booksellers and the British Council Bookshop Management Course for foreign booksellers held in London each summer. The tenth such workshop occurred in 1984, the last to be funded by the Overseas Development Administration. Henceforth, the British Council will finance them.

The Export Information Service is also a BDC responsibility, with the monthly *Export News* being supplemented by a steady flow of circulars on all germane matters, e.g., increases in import duties, foreign exchange restrictions, quotas, and license requirements. In addition, the BDC publishes the spiral *Export Handbook*, providing updated pages each year. Funded through subscriptions by publishers, these materials are one of the BDC's many sources of income that supplement Publishers Association funding and funding by the Overseas Trade Board, the British Council, and the Overseas Development Administration. All in all, the cooperation of the three governmental bodies and the BDC, together with supplementary activities by other organizations, have created what competitors consider the most efficient, effective book trade development program existent in the West.

UNION OF SOVIET SOCIALIST REPUBLICS

Soviet propaganda reflects a very high regard for books—not only for their persuasiveness in advancing the cause of socialism abroad, but also for the statement about cultural development that the book publishing activities of a country make. Considerable book-related publicity from Soviet sources stresses the size and diversity of the book industry of the U.S.S.R. The interest in literature of their socialist society receives great emphasis, e.g., the interest of the Soviet Union in the culture of other countries demonstrated by translations of foreign language books in the U.S.S.R., and by Soviet purchases of books in foreign languages.

The Soviet publishing industry translates more titles than any other country in the world; one out of every four books produced in the world is published in the U.S.S.R.; and the Soviet Union has no peers on the publication of Soviet books in non-native languages for the benefit of readers in foreign countries. One cannot attend an international book fair or publisher meeting at which Soviet participants are present without being informed about those basic book facts, which Soviet leadership clearly believes to be significant in developing countries that traditionally hold books in high esteem. What is sought by the Soviets is prestige, and their extensive publishing activities show their conviction that books can provide it. At book fairs where books can be sold at stands, such as the Cairo International Book Fair, the sales at the U.S.S.R. exhibit of books in English and Arabic certainly support the Soviet thesis.

For Soviet strategic purposes, books fall into only two essential categories: those that advance the cause of socialism and those that are detrimental to that cause. There are no "neutral" books in Soviet theory. Thus, while American strategists may, as described elsewhere in this study, debate whether scientific and technical books warrant governmental expenditures for promotion in the context of public diplomacy, the Soviets have no doubt. By their very existence abroad in the hands of scholars, students, and professionals, such American books are, *inter alia*, propaganda for capitalism, and detrimental to the cause of socialism, while Soviet texts on the same subjects advance socialism. Hence, the Soviets publish books for export that seem devoid of political purpose to many Western eyes.

Discussants who are professional observers of Soviet political and economic policy stress that the need to earn hard currency with which to finance their own imports is a factor in the expanded Soviet book promotion in recent years; there seems little doubt, however, that in developing countries where a lack of hard currency forces a reduction in book imports, ideological objectives have first priority. Neither currency exchange problems nor lack of local buying power keep Soviet books away from Third World bookstores and book fairs—often well-bound hardcover books, at subsidized low prices that students and the working class can afford. The Soviets consider themselves to be in a struggle with the West for the minds of young future doctors and scientists through medical, scientific, and technical textbooks, even when the U.S. does not.

The Soviets have published books on socialism and communism for the foreign market since the 1920s, but a more sophisticated, professional, large-scale approach to the international book world has arisen since the early 1970s, following the establishment of detente with the United States. Probably the most significant change in Soviet policy toward books in recent times was expressed in a decree of February 28, 1973, by which the copyright law of the U.S.S.R. was revised to provide protection for the copyrights of citizens of other countries. It was a change in a deeply rooted Russian policy, since not only the Soviet government but the previous czarist governments had resisted any and all pressures to join the international literary community of nations in that fashion. Moreover, not only did this historic step amend Soviet copyright law, the purpose of the change was to bring Soviet copyright law and regulations into conformity with the Universal Copyright Convention (UCC) and enable the U.S.S.R. to become a signatory to that convention. Indeed, the Soviet Union did sign the UCC almost immediately, and its accession went into effect on May 27, 1973.

This clear reversal in Soviet thought on property rights was one that the Western publishing world had been seeking for a very long time. Martin P. Levin, former vice president for Book Publishing, Times-Mirror Company, has prepared a highly readable, enlightening study of the events in Soviet-American publishing relations leading up to the Soviet accession to the UCC, the results, and new concerns that immediately developed in the West subsequent to that historic investiture.[3] There is far more than a suggestion in Mr. Levin's paper, as he describes the many efforts of U.S. publisher delegations to negotiate arrangements that would protect copyright holders against Soviet piracy, that the Soviet actions in 1973 were not a pre-meditated strategy but the result of quid pro quo negotiations between Soviet and American government representatives pursuant to the Nixon-Brezhnev detente agreements at the 1972 summit. In reporting on the copyright position of Soviet publishers in meetings with American counterparts during the 1960s, Mr. Levin lists Soviet objections to protection of foreign copyrights that are substantially the same as those of developing world countries at the present time (see chapter 3). Because of their substantial translation activities—for example, their need for Western books—Soviet publishers feared high royalty charges that would stretch their dollar accounts and/or reduce the number of translations possible.

The Western response to the new Soviet copyright law was by no means all favorable.[4] The Soviet copyright agency, soon to be known abroad by the acronym of VAAP, consolidated access to copyright on all Soviet literature in one government institution. Dissident writers such as Solzhenitsyn and Sakharov warned that the new Soviet law would be used to restrict Western access to their works, thus bringing about the direct opposite of the broad purposes of the UCC—repression rather than enhanced dissemination of works by those who disagreed with the government. Conversely, VAAP stirred controversy among Western copyright holders that first year, by offering to pay a modest royalty for rights to certain journals, with what some thought to be threats in certain cases to print without royalty payments if the Soviet terms were not accepted.

Protests followed, as detailed in Mr. Levin's account, from those who saw

[3] Martin P. Levin, *Soviet International Copyright: Dream or Nightmare?* (unpublished), New York, 1982.

[4] Ibid.

(as had the dissidents) Soviet use of the new copyright law to circumvent the UCC rather than to conform to it. But U.S. publishers visiting Moscow in the spring of 1973 concluded after meeting with Soviet counterparts that Soviet publishers were simply unprepared for the revision of their copyright law, and that patience was required. This confirmed the view, described by Mr. Levin, that the change in Soviet copyright policy was a trade-off for a tax concession the U.S.S.R. wanted, in negotiations with the Americans pursuant to detente. It was not the most auspicious way for a major publishing country to enter the field of international copyright protection, but history reports many important political changes achieved by accident.

Once the Soviets comprehended the dimensions of their act, however, they exploited politically their accession to the UCC in international publishing circles. In fact, some twelve years later, VAAP has become a cutting edge of the Soviet effort to disseminate information on Soviet society and culture in book form and, of course, pursuing the global objectives of the socialist system. In UNESCO and other organizations where developing world access to Western copyright is debated, the Soviets can and do stir copyright problems for the West by sympathizing with, indeed actively encouraging and promoting, the current approach of the Third World to meeting their need for Western copyrights via compulsory licensing and/or arbitrarily deciding what are "reasonable royalties" that they will pay. In UNESCO, if one takes as the measure of what is "reasonable" the Soviet offer, i.e., free rights or minimal royalties as necessary, the advantage of a VAAP-type copyright structure can be recognized. All rights to the output of Soviet writers are available through the one, monolithic government organization, and the hard currency royalty—if there is one—can be arranged without undue concern for the interests of the authors.

Despite publisher exchanges at the Frankfurt fair in which VAAP giveaway prices are sometimes used half jokingly as a "negotiating point" by Third World publishers seeking rights to an American title, it would be a mistake to underestimate the effectiveness of VAAP. It is a primary avenue for subsidization of the many Soviet books published outside of the U.S.S.R.—books seen in bookstores throughout the world but especially in the developing world. They bear the imprint of legitimate, usually private sector publishers, whose editions may contain little to identify their original source beyond the fact that the authors are Soviet and the subject matter is much in accord with Soviet thinking.

The nature and size of Soviet subsidies to foreign publishers is closely held information, not advertised or reported, and consequently can not be cited in assessment of Soviet foreign book programs for the world except in general terms. Fortunately, for the comparative purpose of this study, VAAP promotional literature on its commercial programs does describe some of the variety of forms of cooperation available. Books may be translated in the intended country of publication, with VAAP funding the translation, the printing, or both. In some arrangements, VAAP offers the foreign publisher both a translated manuscript in the appropriate language, and rights to publish in that language, delivered as a package. Depending on the country and its printing import regulations, VAAP will arrange to have the printing done in the U.S.S.R., thus saving hard currency.

For those who would compare Soviet and U.S. government book subsidy for readers of other countries, the writer offers a word of counsel: if statistics were available on Soviet publishing projects through foreign channels discussed above, it is those unknown production figures that should be compared to the half million books per year presently published abroad with assistance from USIA, rather than the quantity of books published in foreign languages in the U.S.S.R. However impressive the latter figures are, some professional observers of the Soviet scene believe that the "quiet" production in foreign lands is larger. In the open society in which USIA operates, "Books Published Abroad in Translation and in English," an annual agency report, lists languages in which American books are published with USIA support, the titles published, the number of copies produced, and the U.S. dollar equivalent of the retail prices. Although the Soviets provide no such information on their foreign publishing, information is of necessity available where the books are to be sold, and USIA's research staff or an independent sector research institution might consider collecting it.

There is little secrecy about book production in foreign languages *in* the U.S.S.R. for export sale. This is due to the logical reason that it would be as difficult to promote sale of these Soviet products without catalogs and other literature as it would be to sell U.S. books. In addition, there is the previously mentioned prestige factor in Soviet policy, that requires some promotion. The Soviets have tended to limit such information, however, contributing little to UNESCO data beyond the number of titles they produce. Only more recently have statistics seeped out through the Soviet industry's own literature, enabling the USIA research office to produce the study on Soviet export publishing that fortuitously became available in 1984 as the Reid Foundation Study Group and the Task Force began their assignments.[5]

The core of the USIA report is production. Soviet publishing houses produced some 74.5 million books in 56 non-Soviet languages in 1982. English is recognized and accepted as the preferred language of international communication in many fields—the 24.3 million books produced in English make up by far the largest single foreign language portion of 1982 Soviet production. Its Spanish language production (11.6 million books) makes the

[5] Soviet Book Exports 1973–82.

U.S.S.R. either the fifth or sixth largest producer of books in that language in the world. (Since Cuba, too, does not publish data we can only suspect that the U.S.S.R. is fifth and Cuba sixth.) German language production in 1982 was almost 11 million books, making the Soviets the third largest world publisher in that language. India is clearly a major focus of Soviet interest, confirmed by Soviet production of 2.3 million books in 13 Indian regional languages. In addition, India takes a major share of Soviet-produced English language editions, as well as being the location of the largest Soviet book publishing program outside of the U.S.S.R. Other significant statistics for foreign languages include 6.6 million books in French and 1.3 million books in Portuguese. The overall quantitative trend over the 1972–83 decade surveyed in the USIA study has been upward, although it appears to the USIA staff to have begun to level off in the last two years surveyed, 1981 and 1982. During these two years, there has at the same time been a notable shift toward languages of the developing world.

Soviet production of its foreign export editions is concentrated in six export publishing houses: Aurora Art Publishers, Mir Publishers (science and technology), Novosti Publishers (current events), Progress Publishers (social-political literature), Raduga Publishers (fiction and children's books), and Russkii Iazyk (Russian language). A telling comment on this Soviet export publishing activity is a discussant's report that Soviet citizens attending the Moscow International Book Fair crowded into the exhibits of these six Soviet publishers, attracted by the prospect of seeing Soviet art books reserved for export. This is, of course, not the impression that Egyptians and Reid Foundation Study Group members carry away when they visit the Soviet stand at the Cairo International Book Fair. The very low-priced books found there seem to represent the high quality, affordable works that an advanced socialist society makes available to its own citizenry. That is a misconception of which the Moscow fair-goer is well aware.

Being able to deal with only six American publishers instead of the complex export system discussed in chapters 2 and 13 would be a welcome development for U.S. foreign customers. However, for the foreign buyer of Soviet books the process is even less complex. All Soviet titles are available for export from a single foreign trade company, "Mezhdunarodnaia Kniga" (International Book); "Kniga," as foreign buyers and sellers prefer to call it, is also the sole Soviet importing agency. Statistics extrapolated from Kniga literature point to a steady increase in exports over the 1973–82 decade of 250 percent, or an average of 25 percent per year, according to the cited USIA research study. In support of "peace and progress," Kniga claims 1,000 "trading partners" worldwide. Kniga also reports staging book exhibits at some 1,500 events throughout the world each year that support bookstore sales with promotion and, where permitted, direct sales at the event.

Task Force members, publisher and librarian discussants, and Reid

Foundation Study Group members have among them visited all of those events identified as international book fairs in chapter 8. There is no doubt that the Soviet presence is impressive, if for no other reason than the great number of titles displayed and the fact that the Soviets almost invariably have multiple copies that are actually sold where fair rules permit, moreover at low prices and in large volume. The cost of participation in such events on that level is rarely feasible for commercial publishers in Western countries, who display their titles in single copies, can take only bulk institutional orders, and refer individuals to the sales stands of local booksellers who are their customers in that country. What the Soviets do with the proceeds from their sales at such events puzzles Western publishers, since exchange problems and shortages of dollars affect Soviet international traders as much as they do any private entrepreneur. The one year that USIA officers estimated funds needed for U.S. participation at the Soviet level in a sizable international fair, the cost was a minimum of $75,000 for one event, beyond what sales might return.

The flagship of Soviet international book activities is the Moscow International Book Fair, a biennial event held for the fifth time in September, 1985. Although the fair could have been justified as a logical next step after accession to the UCC, it was not undertaken until 1977, and then, at least initially, as a response to the Helsinki Agreement—the kind of prestige event described earlier as particularly attractive to Soviet image makers. The Final Act of the Conference on Security and Cooperation was signed in 1975: Basket III of the act dealt with cultural exchanges and specifically called for "more frequent book exhibitions"; the first Moscow International Book Fair was announced for September, 1977, with the theme of "Books for Peace and Progress."

From the outset, poor public relations and promotion of the fair dampened foreign enthusiasm. Although the Soviets hoped for broad participation from as many countries as could be persuaded to attend, no one was left in any doubt that "Books for Peace and Progress" included many titles and excluded many others. The exhibit literature attempted to define what was acceptable, but it was clear that the Soviets expected participants to make their own preselection or "self-censorship," as a few American publishers described the process. Moreover, participants were asked to submit lists of the titles they were bringing to the fair in advance. The Soviets had no intention of exposing their citizens to undesirable literature; hence the Moscow censors used the required title lists to note dubious titles that would be given closer examination when the crates of books were opened in their presence.[6]

---

[6] Joseph S. Drew, *Through American Eyes: The Moscow Book Fair* (Washington, D.C.: Political Science Department, University of the District of Columbia, 1983) provides a profile of varying U.S. publisher views on the selection process. *A Bowl of Burning Gold: American Publishers and the Moscow Book Fair* (December 1983) extended his evaluation following the September, 1983, fair.

Frequent participants have gradually learned the workings of the Soviet censorial minds and have accepted the concept of pre-selection. The prevailing rationale is that the Moscow fair is the only opportunity to do business with Soviet booksellers and publishers who do not travel frequently to events outside the country, and who do not therefore have the opportunity to handle books and to become acquainted with their foreign publishing counterparts on the familiar terms that are the *sine qua non* of successful publishing cooperation. For foreign publishers, who are also paying their own way to a costly fair, it makes little economic sense to take books to Moscow that importers will not buy, publishers will not translate, and censors may remove at the outset. Consequently, a significant imbalance in the content of non-Soviet bloc exhibits in the direction of scientific, technical, and medical works occurs. For national displays of Western countries to go beyond that, subsidy is needed for their publishers.

There is no common agreement among Western publishers on pre-selection and censorship, but it should be noted that it is American publishers who have been most active in challenging the Soviets on this matter, as well as on Soviet political decisions to ignore the applications of certain publishers and, indeed, entire industries from certain countries: disputes at various times over the exclusion of Israel and South Korea come immediately to mind. Ardis Publishers, a U.S. publisher of books in Russian, has also been denied exhibit space, while Robert L. Bernstein of Random House was temporarily denied a visa in 1979, even though his company was permitted to attend. Mr. Bernstein is known to the Soviets as a member of the "Helsinki Watch" and the "Freedom to Publish" activities of the AAP, and is the publisher of several Soviet dissidents, e.g., Alexander Solzhenitsyn.

Views on how to approach this most political of book fairs do vary, with other Western publishers (e.g., from the United Kingdom) criticizing the Americans for their "confrontational" methods. Their view is that the Soviets have been "maturing" on their approach to display content, as well as on exclusion of countries or individual publishers for political reasons. Some suggest that the Soviets have a "tiger by the tail" and realize that non-Soviet bloc publishers are in a position to do great damage, not only to the fair but to the Soviet foreign book business in general, if their views are not accommodated. The only real Soviet alternative would be to cancel the fair in this view, and the Soviets now have too much invested to do that.

When the U.S. challenged the pre-selection concept with an AAP national exhibit in 1979, funded in part by USIA, for which themes were chosen but title selection for those themes left to the individual U.S. publisher, there was considerable noise from Soviet officialdom, including the removal of some titles. But the Soviet citizenry at the fair that year was nevertheless exposed to a substantial selection of 3,500 books on American culture, in addition to the scientific and technical titles at individual U.S. publisher stands. Andrei Sakharov was among those who urged the Americans to return to subsequent fairs with their cultural collection, despite the problems. However, requests for USIA support for exhibits at subsequent fairs were denied in 1981 and 1983 for the specific purpose of protesting the Soviet invasion of Afghanistan, and for the additional reason in 1983 that the cultural agreement between the two countries had expired and has not yet been renewed as of mid-1985. Only official support through government funding was denied in 1981 and 1983; USIA and the State Department carefully took no position on whether or not publishers should go without their support, and some did go.[7] There appears to be a change in the current (mid-1985) private sector thinking on the Moscow fair, and Baker & Taylor, the largest American library supplier/wholesaler, was scheduled to participate in the fair in September, 1985, with a collective exhibit of over 1,700 books from a minimum of 191 publishers, funded commercially by the participants.

Unless new, serious differences arise in U.S.-Soviet relations, a majority of discussants and the publishers profiled by Professor Drew in his studies conclude that there should be an American national presence at future Moscow fairs. They argue this because the fair has, according to most reports, grown in size each biennial, and is likely to continue to grow as long as exhibitors return home with a sense of accomplishment, i.e., book orders and rights sales to Soviet publishers. Since few go to Moscow to deal with each other—which they can do equally well at Frankfurt—the sales to Soviet buyers are economic results that influence them and are within the control of the Soviet sponsors.[8] A national presence is argued by some as an important cultural statement, made through the showing of U.S. books to Soviet fair goers who have little opportunity to learn about American culture otherwise. How culturally useful are the present commercial collections by American publishers? The answer would seem to be "not much." As long as the Soviets won't buy them, individual publishers cannot be expected to take cultural works to Moscow without government funding. Perhaps the content of the Baker & Taylor stand in 1985 will give some answers and point to future directions on the day the fair opens.

It would appear that the present wave of Soviet book programs began expanding at the beginning of the 1970s, possibly, as we have seen, as the result of an accident—the addition of copyright to a tax treaty as a concession of less interest to the Soviet negotiators than some others they sought. We cannot be certain of this, however, since the beginning of enhanced activities also coincided with the rapid decline in U.S. government book programs in the developing world. For example, by 1973, the U.S. had completely

---

[7] William E. Freeman *The Moscow Book Fair*, (Washington, D.C.: USIA 1984.) See also Joseph S. Drew *Through American Eyes*.

[8] Freeman reports that Kniga claims $135 million was spent by VAAP and itself at the 1983 fair for imports and rights.

withdrawn from an Indian book publishing program that had been the flagship of U.S. programs: the Soviets decided promptly to replace the U.S. with an enlarged program of their own. Whatever the origins of the new Soviet book efforts, they have grown in size and effectiveness, whether the criteria are its book fair at home and its book fair participation abroad, book publishing at home for export, or subsidized publishing abroad.

It was not possible to find many professional discussants who felt comfortable hazarding estimates of what all of this book activity costs the Soviet government. There are too many statistical gaps, too many American contacts abroad with publishing professionals who seem to have all returned from subsidized business trips to Soviet publishing centers, too many Soviet delegations of professionals travelling to meet with developing world publishers to help improve their production and train their staffs, or to participate in seminars that accompany book fairs and make up industry meetings.

"They are there," says Task Force Chairman Paul E. Feffer, "and many of their expenditures on book programs abroad are in *dollars*, as difficult for them to come by as it is for any developing country. It makes no sense that a democracy like ours, one that has such trump cards as quality of production and quality of content that no totalitarian system can beat, should lose by default. They are affording far more than we are in this war of ideas. Fortunately for us, there is one ingredient that they can *not* afford, and that is freeing the minds of their intellectuals, their scholars, their scientists, so as to produce books of the quality that we do. We should show such books at Moscow, just as a beginning."

FRANCE

The thesis that a government's attention to the language and culture of the nation, including literature, is so important that it is a political issue is not an American one. It is, however, a French belief, or rather a reality that helped the Socialists to gain office in 1981. Expanding the use of French (and protecting the language) abroad as well as at home has been an obligation of royal as well as republican governments for more than two centuries. It is a policy that made French the required language of global diplomacy, and French culture that by which the "civilization" of others was to be measured. It was and is what might be called generic public diplomacy and, if others debate the need for it, the French do not. Rather, as in that 1981 election, French debate revolves around how effectively the party in power is performing its cultural responsibilities and what the opposition would do to improve that performance. Charles deGaulle personified French culture as a factor in international relations for the twentieth century. His successors, both at home and in Africa, have welded Francophone countries into a close cultural alliance that is the basis of continued French influence as a major power, and books are a critical element of both domestic and foreign cultural policies.

Francois Mitterrand strongly criticized President Valery Giscard d'Estaing during the 1981 election for not keeping a promise to increase the Ministry of Culture budget to 1 percent of the total government budget. Rather, under Giscard d'Estaing's administration, modest budget increases were not even adequate enough to offset the erosion of cultural programs by inflation. Books for provincial libraries were severely affected by this, as were those for overseas book programs. Institutionalism complicated the situation by continued library building at home, and the opening of cultural centers in new locations abroad, both without adequate new funds. Meanwhile, the publishing industry itself was undergoing a depression, in part a result of reduced government support for books. From 1977 through 1980, titles published went down in France.[9] A finance ministry decree prohibiting publishers from setting retail prices on their books added to the d'Estaing government's woes. It was intended to reduce the price of books to consumers: the Socialists effectively used it as evidence that the government viewed books as "a produce like any other product." The decree had the effect of favoring discount sellers, damaging the ability of the small bookstores on whom the industry depended for sales of serious works to survive.[10]

Perhaps a most damaging event in the cultural area for the government was a 1979 government study group recommendation that programs abroad should deemphasize the French language in favor of reaching local elites in their own language. According to Prillaman, such an approach had actually been in operation in Africa as early as the 1960s.[11] It was, however, a matter of outrage in 1981 for the opposition party. A meeting of the *Haut Comite de La Langue Francaise* (an organ of government located in the office of the prime minister) followed the study, at which d'Estaing announced that the use of French was in danger. Socialists pointed out that the *Haut Comite*, which is made up of high officials of all Francophone countries, had not met in five years under d'Estaing, and pledged that protecting and expanding the usage of the French language abroad would be central to a Socialist government's cultural policy.

To the extent that these Gaullist cultural negatives concerned books, they produced a Socialist call for a conference with French publishers and intellectuals at Valence in March, 1981, concerning the straits of books at home and abroad. A Socialist party policy was developed at that conference that became an effective campaign document in pamphlet form.[12] Cultural policy alone did

---

[9] Herbert R. Lottman "France: A Changing Rights Scene," *Publishers Weekly*, December 11, 1981.

[10] Jerry Prillaman *The French Book Trade and Book Policies in Sub-Saharan Francophone Africa*. Washington, D.C., March, 1982. Unpublished.

[11] Ibid.

[12] Ibid. p. 82. Cited by Prillaman on p. 137 as *"Le Livre et le Lecture: Une Autre Politique." Communes de France* No. 13, Valence, March, 1981.

not win for the Socialists, as the economy of France had many grave problems in 1981; but cultural policy, including books, did play a significant role in the election results, which made Mitterrand president and gave the Socialists a working majority in the French parliament.

Mitterand, himself an author and intellectual, made clear almost immediately that cultural affairs would indeed be an important element of his government's program. According to *Livres hebdo* for November 24, 1981, his first budget provided for an increase in the portion of the Ministry of Culture from 0.47 percent of the total budget to 0.75 percent, and he set 1 percent as an early budgetary goal. This translated into a tripling of the budget for the Ministry's Book Division beginning in January, 1982. The *fonds cultural du livre*, a fund specifically designated for book export promotion, was increased from 16 million francs to 40 million ($8 million in 1982 U.S. dollars). A *Commission du Livre et de la Lecture* was in place by July, 1981, and delivered a report to the Ministry of Culture on October 1 containing 55 specific proposals intended to enhance the status of the book at home and abroad. Proposals Nos. 35–39 dealt directly with the need for new efforts on all aspects of book exports. "To sell is also to export," the commission observed, and noted that French book exports, already ten times those of audiovisuals, television, and cinema, could be substantially better. The commission also proposed that all commercial export relations between the book industry and government be centralized in the Ministry of Culture.[13]

The Public Sector[14]

Under the d'Estaing government, the aid ministry handled the cultural centers and book programs in Francophone Africa and Haiti as an extension of its responsibilities for assistance programs in those 26 countries. That meant, however, that even within Africa there was little coordination with French cultural relations in English-speaking countries or North Africa, which, like cultural relations with the rest of the world, were the responsibility of the foreign ministry. As of January, 1982, all cultural programs including book programs were removed from the aid ministry and transferred to the foreign ministry. Reconstituted as the Ministry of State for Development and Cooperation, the aid ministry had its assistance program responsibilities extended beyond the original 26 countries to encompass assistance programs for all of the Third World.

In effect, this was a swap of functions. From the foreign ministry, the aid ministry received some 7,000 to 12,000 teacher and technician positions to be

[13] Commission du Livre et de la Lecture. *55 Propositions sur le Livre Francais* (Paris: Ministere de la Culture et de la Communication, Paris, 1981).

[14] Jerry Prillaman, elaborates the 1982 public sector reorganization on pp. 60–84, *The French Book Trade. . .*

filled each year for countries outside of Francophone Africa. Added to the 12,000 positions for which it continued to be responsible, in that sector of Africa, the total aid ministry cadre positions available abroad in 1982 numbered between 19,000 and 24,000. Similarly, some 6,000 scholarships for the Third World outside of Francophone Africa were transferred from the foreign ministry and, added to the 7,000 already under aid ministry administration, produced a total of 13,000 scholarships. The 1982 budget for the reconstituted ministry was 5 billion francs, or more than $1 billion in 1982 U.S. dollars.[15]

Bringing foreign students to France for training and sending French professionals abroad, especially teachers, can not realistically be considered a non-cultural activity and such a distinction was not the intention of a programmatic reorganization in pursuance of efficiency. The teachers and technicians contract to work for short periods of time, and others who qualify can opt for this work abroad in lieu of military service. Hence, there is a substantial turnover of personnel that provides a natural constituency in France for support of the government's overseas cultural activities. Other ties to the book world were also maintained in the aid ministry. The Ministry of State for Development and Cooperation also administers funds from the prior aid ministry organization responsibilities intended for the purchase of equipment, of which a significant amount had been expended on the purchase of printing presses and other publishing equipment for Africa. Along with these purchases, the grant funds include allocations to allow book and printing professionals from France to go to Africa and train indigenous workers, as well as funds for travel by foreign nationals to France for similar training.

Book program responsibilities of the aid ministry for Francophone Africa now reside in the Book Division, Cultural Affairs Bureau, Ministry of Exterior Relations, formerly the Ministry of Foreign Affairs. All other aid ministry cultural programs—television, film, etc.—along with the administration of the 37 cultural centers in Africa were also transferred to the exterior relations ministry Cultural Affairs Bureau, where they are now joined with similar programs for the rest of the world. These cultural activities, including book programs, are the responsibility of the Cultural Counselor at each embassy abroad, a prestige appointment for a limited period of time from the French cultural scene. The counselor develops the annual cultural program (including books) for the country in which he is located that, approved by the ambassador, is sent back to the Ministry of Exterior Relations in Paris for coordination with other country programs and budgets for that year. Since January, 1983, the book division of this ministry has worked with the Ministry of Exterior Commerce to develop detailed marketing studies for French publishers on some 140 countries. These detailed reports include import regula-

---

[15] Jerry Prillaman, *The French Book Trade. . .* p. 67.

tions, the country's publishing and printing industry, and the channels of local distribution (wholesalers, importers, book clubs, etc.). Specifics are also provided on the status of the French language in the country, the number of French teachers, the importance of French culture, and the disciplines in which books are most frequently translated from French). The Book Division also as of 1982 had a budget of 7.5 million francs for review of books to be distributed abroad, and a budget of 5.5 million francs for distribution of review materials. Some 6,000 copies of the monthly magazine, *Le bulletin critique du livre,* are printed and distributed abroad containing reviews of books in the humanities, arts, and sciences. *New French Books* is a quarterly version of this publication in English, produced in 3,000 to 4,000 copies for the U.S. market. It contains some 300 reviews taken from *Le bulletin.*[16]

The Book Division of the Ministry of Culture has responsibility for commercial book programs on a worldwide basis since the 1982 reorganization, as a specific recommendation of the Commission Du Livre in 1981.[17] This division is responsible for book exhibits, French publisher participation in book fairs, credits to compensate publishers for exchange losses in priority countries, grants to publishers abroad to translate books in special fields, e.g., scientific and technical, to make French thought in those areas available abroad, and funding of book air shipments to distant customers. Mailing lists of overseas bookstores, credit information, and market surveys are accomplished in cooperation with the private sector. The Ministry of Culture Book Division coordinates its activities with those of the Ministry of Exterior Relations Book Division described above, the latter having the advantage of access to a large foreign service staff located overseas.[18] The *fonds cultural du livre,* mentioned previously as having been increased in 1982 to 40 million francs by the new Socialist government, is administered by the Ministry of Culture Book Division solely for export promotion. A variety of private sector projects are assisted with these funds, and there is apparently flexibility in its use, the Ministry of Culture working closely with the French publishers association in expending it.[19]

The Private Sector

The Syndicate National d'Edition (SNE) is the French equivalent of the AAP in the U.S. SNE works closely with the Ministry of Culture on both domestic

[16] Alain Zecchini, *"La situation du livre Francais dans 140 pays etrangers," Livres Hebdo,* Paris, September 5, 1983.

[17] Commission du Lire et de la Lecture. Proposition 36.

[18] Alain Zecchini, "La situation. . ."

[19] Prillaman, p. 351, footnote 17. A study of this fund is recommended by Prillaman as a model for the American industry.

and foreign book matters, receiving support for its studies, marketing activities, and research from that ministry. The Bureau d'Information et de Liaison pour l'Exportation (BILE) is SNE's counterpart to the AAP International Division, except that its staff and projects are more like those of the U.K. Book Development Council in size and activities. BILE is the channel through which government assistance is provided to publishers; BILE also provides the link between government and exporter on information about markets coming from the Ministry for Exterior Relations as well as the Ministry of Culture. A major function of BILE is the provision of statistics on book export activities and annual reports for both the industry and the government. Raw data for its studies are received from French customs and from the publishers.

Le Cercle de la Librairie is an inter-professional organization made up of the principal publishers, more than 500 bookstores, and major graphic arts and printing firms. It is funded by its membership, the Ministry of Culture domestic and export sections as appropriate, including *fonds cultural*, the publishers association (SNE), and sales proceeds from its own publications. *Les livres disponibles* (Books in Print) is produced annually, with more than 200,000 titles listed. *Livres hebdo* is the French equivalent of *Publishers Weekly*. *Livres du mois* (for export) and *Livres de France* are two of its monthly publications focusing on new books and their content. Irregularly published (as funded by industry and government) are marketing publications such as *How to Obtain French Books* and *American Markets for French Books*. Every second year, Le Cercle produces *Editeurs et diffuseurs de la langue Francaise*, a reference work comparable to *Literary Market Place*. In addition to its research and publications, Le Cercle serves as a clearing house and umbrella organization for interests of its diversified membership.

Libraexport is an organization set up with funding by the Cultural Ministry Book Division and SNE to process orders from abroad for the books of many different publishers, and small order not handled by publishers or larger exporters. It has been a significant success, and now is essentially self-supporting. Groups of small publishers get together on joint catalogs and other promotional materials that *Libraexport* distributes, and for which *Libraexport* then fills orders. *Sodexport* (French Association for the Export Distribution of Scientific, Technical, and Medical books) has been in existence since 1970, a creation of publishers of this genre that now has 39 publishing house members. The *Fonds Cultural* provided some 3 million francs in 1982 in support of book exhibits by *Sodexport* abroad and for travel by publisher delegations to foreign countries.

In 1984, the combined expenditures of the ministries of Culture and External Affairs in support of the overseas dissemination of French books had reached 5 to 6 percent of the value of French overseas sales, or between $12 and $14 million.[20] Prillaman, head of USIA's Book Programs Division, estimates that this would compare to an expenditure of $30 million by the U.S. government ($39 million, based on 5 percent of U.S. 1984 exports). In fact, Prillaman says that a French audit report on the activities of ten French ministries found that in 1982 government book aid came to 753 million francs, or some $80 million! In 1984, the French Ministry of External Affairs placed books third in public diplomacy priorities, behind only audiovisuals and the French language itself.[21]

Perhaps one of the better perspectives on how seriously the French take their cultural and linguistic role is provided by the treatment accorded to the products of the USIA book program office in Paris. Since those books are in French, and the use of the French language is what receives priority attention in the French government, USIA is invited by the Office de Promotion de L'Edition Francaise to have its American books in French included in collective international exhibits at events in countries where they are to be sold, on the same terms as the books of any French publisher. In addition, translations in this USIA program have twice been singled out for awards as the best translations of the year.

SPAIN[22]

What we refer to as "Spanish" is actually Castilian, originally one of the major regional languages of Spain.[23] It was the Castilian kings and captains who came to dominate Spain and provided the conquistadors who colonized so much of the New World. Through them, Castilian became the unifying language of Spain and the legacy of Spanish speakers in the Americas. The language, as linguists would observe, transported to New World soil the culture that originated it. In some ways, therefore, Spanish overseas book policy mirrors that of the French. The difference: it has been many generations since governors sent from Spain to the New World could directly influence the textbooks that were used, the books and journals that were read, and the quality of language as both read and spoken. The book publishers of present-day Spain have had to produce a high quality product and convince distant, divergent intellectual markets that it is the product they need. In both of these endeavors, the publishing entrepreneurs of Barcelona and Madrid have re-

---

20 Jerry Prillaman, "Trip Report." USIA memorandum of November 1, 1984, on travel to book fairs in Algeria, Spain, and Frankfurt in September-October, 1984.

21 Ibid.

22 A substantial part of this section on Spain is taken from the author's work in progress on book publishing in the Spanish world.

23 Andalucian, Basque, Catalan, and Galician are the others.

ceived sustained support from the Spanish government. As in France, the crucial interlinking of cultural influence with political relations, economics, and trade is considered a given, not a matter for serious debate.

The role of Castilian as the *lingua franca* of the Spanish world must be emphasized. In a family of countries that have been independent for some time, cultures have diversified and both the spoken and written language have become fractionalized, idiomatic variations of one another. Pure Spanish, correct Castilian, is that which originates in Spain. If the teacher, the student, or the scholar in any country has a choice between an edition of a book translated in Spain and an edition translated in one of the other major Spanish book-producing countries (Argentina and Mexico), there is no contest. Indeed, except for the works of writers of one's own country or the authors of another country whose very fame results from their literary skills in their own idiom, Castilian writing is a benchmark against which Spanish world sophisticates evaluate the quality of books produced outside of Spain. The publishing world itself is influenced by this perspective. Whether in Argentina, Mexico, or Colombia—whether or not it is actually the result—publisher contracts call for books to be rendered into "Castellano"[24] by the translator. There is no reason why the cultural establishment in Spain would want to change this and there are in fact national and international institutions in Spain concerned with the perpetuation of the Castilian language and culture in which intellectuals of all Spanish-speaking countries participate.

It is also important for market control that quality Spanish is being used to produce quality books that meet the needs of the reader, and one reflection of this is the translation industry. The Soviet Union, as we have seen, promotes its cultural image by advertising that its book industry translates more books from foreign languages than any other country. The publishers in Spain can promote the fact that their country is the second largest producer of translations in the world. Viewed in a global perspective, translations serve the same purpose for Spain as they do for the U.S.S.R.; they demonstrate that Spain is a cultured country. But more important, this translation effort demonstrates that Spain's books are the most diversified of the Spanish-speaking world, and the logical source to which readers of that language should turn. In 1982, some 30 percent of the editions published in Spain were translations. In 1984, there were as many as 4,000 U.S. titles alone available for sale in Spanish from Spain.[25]

---

[24] Some Latin American countries, particularly Argentina, refer to their language as "Castellano," and rarely, "Espanol."

[25] Mary C. Turner, compiler, *Libros de los Estados Unidos Traducidos Al Idoma Espanol*, (USIA, Washington, D.C., 1985.)

Another important gauge of a booming publishing industry is the number of titles it produces. Some 29,484 titles were produced in Castilian in Spain in 1982, despite the condition of its Latin American markets, or quite on a par with the production level of prior years (27,629 in 1980). These numbers of titles are considered necessary by publishers to give serious readers a wider range from which to choose. It has been noted that editions of books are 3,000 to 5,000 copies now, quite small by the standard of other publishing industries. However, the total number of titles available remains sizable, *Libros Españoles en Venta: ISBN* (Books in Print, although transliterated as Books on Sale) containing in excess of 200,000 titles in its annual edition. Such figures do, of course, include the translations reported above as making Spain the second largest publisher in that category in the world. In addition, these statistics win for Spain the position of the seventh largest publishing country in the world, and the fourth largest book exporter. A growing element of the Spanish effort to emphasize to the Spanish reading world that its book industry is cosmopolitan, but one on which there are few data, is the publication of authors from other Spanish-speaking countries. Literary agents in Barcelona also have a substantial number of Latin American writers whom they represent in rights sales for languages other than Spanish.[26]

A relevant political factor for an effective international publishing industry is whether or not there is freedom to publish in the country. Many Spanish intellectuals, including publishers, fled to Argentina during and after the Spanish Civil War. In addition, censorship in Franco's Spain forced Latin American intellectuals to look elsewhere for certain kinds of cultural and political nourishment, and the liberal political Spanish origins of many Argentines directed intellectual attention southward. During the 1940s and 1950s, also due to World War II and the temporary cut off of Latin America from the books of Spain by the war at sea, Argentina was the primary source of books for Latin America. In the 1950s, Spain recaptured first place in production and distribution, backed by substantial government support of book exports—an official policy intended to reinstitute Spain's cultural hegemony in the Spanish world through the language affinity. The halcyon years for Argentine publishers ended, as that country began to go through its own political upheavals. With the death of Franco, freedom to publish returned to Spain, and Barcelona and Madrid were once again centers of intellectual challenge, while Argentine publishers were being restricted by their military regimes. With democracy restored to Buenos Aires in 1983, it will be interesting to see the extent of the challenge to Spain that publishing industry is able to mount in Latin America.

---

[26] Herbert R. Lottman, "Spain: A Booming Rights Market," *Publishers Weekly*, July 17, 1981.

The Public Sector

The *Instituto Nacional del Libro Espanol* (INLE) in the Ministry of Culture has been the primary government channel for support to book publishing in Spain, although its future is now in question. *El Libro Español*, the Spanish equivalent of *Publishers Weekly*, is produced by INLE, as is *Libros Españoles en Venta: ISBN*, the country's annual volume. Most export support to publishers has been channeled through INLE, which has engaged also in a variety of promotional activities. The flagship effort was the large and attractive national stand at Frankfurt, whose cultural design made it a landmark for regular visitors to that fair. INLE and/or publishers receiving government support for independent stands could also be seen at the Argentine and Mexican international book fairs and other book events in Latin America.

Because of the cultural role of the book, government financing in the export field has been quite generous. A "reintegro" of 20 percent of the cover price has been provided on book export earnings, to make the complexities worthwhile. (Receipts of 100 pesetas in dollars for exports, for example, becomes, when the dollars are deposited at the bank, 120 pesetas.) Low interest loans have also been available for up to 60 percent of the value of export accounts receivable, at a subsidized interest rate of half that available for ordinary loans. Other support has included comprehensive insurance on export sales based on a government credit rating of the Latin American buyers, travel funding for major importers of books from Spain in Latin America to visit the Madrid and Barcelona publishers, and funding of air shipments to assure that books reach distant customers, e.g., in Chile, in a timely fashion and at competitive shipping costs. (At one point, this support made shipments to Chile actually less costly than those from Mexico.)

The Private Sector

The *Federacion de Gremios de Editores de Españia* is the national publishers' association of Spain. As "federation" suggests, it is an association composed of associations, those of Madrid and Barcelona being the major ones. Since the death of Franco, the profile of this association as the activist group of Spanish publishing has grown, while that of INLE has diminished. In fact, INLE is viewed as gradually disappearing. One discussant says that a principal reason for this development is the fact that INLE membership was mandatory under Franco, and that some of its actions and directives were authoritarian, leaving resentment behind in publishing circles.

At Frankfurt, the Spanish national exhibit has been sponsored by the federation since 1982, although still receiving government support, and INLE no longer appears. The Spanish *Salon de Libro (Liber)* was initiated by the federation in 1983, and several steps have been taken to promote the sale of Spanish books in the United States, a market that Federation Secretary General Jaime Brull considers very much underdeveloped. Partial funding was provided by the government to bring U.S. book importers to *Liber* '83 in Madrid, and again to *Liber* '84 in Barcelona. (The site of the salon alternates each year between the two publishing capitals.)

Plans to have the private sector take over more of the activities of INLE have been slowed, due to the economic crisis in Latin American markets. It is, however, expected that *El Libro Español*, and the *Libros Españoles en Venta: ISBN* volume will be produced by the publishers association. The book fairs in Spain have become shared responsibilities already, with the participation of the *Instituto Nacional de Fomento do la Exportation* (National Institute for Export Promotion), being expanded.

Publiexport is the Spanish response to the complexities of ordering books from many different publishers. It is an association of some 300 publishers in Madrid and Barcelona for whom export sales are consolidated. *Publiexport* promotes sales through mailings, combined catalogs, and exhibits at most book fairs and events in countries where Spanish books have a potential or present market. It also has its own offices abroad, and announced at the American Booksellers Association meeting in San Francisco, May, 1985, that an office is planned for New York.

Problems and Prospects

At this time, with so many Latin American countries—particularly the major markets of Argentina, Mexico, and Venezuela—tied up in restructuring their foreign debt, there seems little possibility that Spain's export book trade will operate at the level that it did prior to 1982 in the foreseeable future. It is impossible to overstate the effect of devaluation of currencies in Latin America and the shortage of dollars in that region on the Spanish industry, which has depended on markets there for two-thirds of its total book sales. Interviewed at the 1985 ABA meeting, Jaime Brull reported that the Spanish publishers are filling current orders from Latin America from accounts that can pay in dollars, which means a higher peseta price because of the cost of the dollar. Back debts (accounts receivable) will be amortized over a period of time. The Spanish government had to fund a substantial portion of the accounts receivables of some publishers in order to avoid extensive bankruptcy.

Government support to the Spanish book industry will continue, although much of it will come through the international trade office of the Ministry of Commerce in the future, rather than INLE. The forms of support will have to change, however, as a result of Spain's entry into the European Economic Community, which insists that trading partners compete on equal terms vis-a-vis government support. The "reintegro," for example, must be eliminated; Spain will have to deal with the value added tax (VAT) in relationship to books. The publishers' association is itself studying the book programs of other governments to determine what is applicable to Spain, particularly the support European governments already in the EEC are giving to their industries.

Mr. Brull is optimistic about *Liber*, which in 1985 returns to Madrid. Some 134 foreign exhibitors took part in 1984, and the number signed up for 1985 has already grown beyond that. Professionals visiting the 1984 salon numbered 1,136 with some 680 from Latin America. The government will fund 100 percent of the cost of bringing 1 representative of each Latin American *camera* (publishers association) to Madrid, and 50 percent of the travel cost of 15 major Latin American book importers to *Liber* '85.

Meanwhile, changes in the way that many publishers do business with Latin America are underway.[27] Some have sought to have their Latin American sales offices begin local printing. Some are selling film[28] so that publishers in Latin American can publish their own editions. Others are entering into co-editions from the start—an important new reason for the *Liber* book fairs as a meeting place. Still others are sharply reducing the advances against royalties that they are willing to pay for translation rights, in view of reduced export expectations, and are signing for editions limited to Spain. The Spanish government's dedication to Spanish cultural hegemony in Latin America will be sorely tested in the book field over the next several years.

---

[27] Herbert R. Lottman, "Barcelona: What's New In Spain's Publishing Capital?," *Publishers Weekly*, September 14, 1984.

[28] Negatives of pages of the original book that can be used to photo offset the same book in another country.

17

American Books Abroad: New Directions and Approaches

William M. Childs and *Donald E. McNeil*

I have long been a convinced enthusiast of the importance of overseas markets to American publishing. And I remain convinced of two things: (1) We publishers can do better in the international marketplace than we are now doing; (2) It is essential that the U.S. Government put real effort into giving reality to the widely accepted slogan: "Books can be our best ambassadors." (Simon Michael Bessie, a Harper & Row director and member of the U.S. Books Abroad Task Force)[1]

For most discussants involved in the U.S. Books Abroad project, the term "national policy" denotes a set course of *government* action to be identified and recommended. It was after all, the National Security Council memorandum that initiated this study and that memorandum was explicit in requesting professional guidance for a major new *government* commitment—one that would involve legislation, regulatory changes, administrative action, and funding to close the book gap. The problem was identified as critical, and as a matter of national security concern (a first time linkage of books and national security by the government). The NSC emphasized the importance of the commercial, nonprofit, and quasi-public sectors, but there was little doubt expressed by Task Force members that "national policy" and "major new commitment" were intended to signify the federal government as the primary focus of Task Force attention.

This is understandable, in view of the long-standing neglect of American books as ambassadors by the government (as recounted in the Curtis Benjamin report). However, the editors believe that there is a crucial flaw in this perspective: i.e., the necessary book industry front of U.S. authors, agents, publishers, research institutions, and traders oriented toward action in the international arena on the levels being considered does not now exist. In addition, the editors would be less than candid if they did not note that among

[1] Adaptation from an address given by Simon Michael Bessie at the AAP seminar on selling books abroad printed as "My Say," *Publishers Weekly,* August 16, 1985.

that small group of publishers and exporters principally responsible for the success that American books have enjoyed abroad, there are skeptics who are not certain that the U.S. government is capable of mounting the sustained, long-range commitment that characterizes the successful book policies of other governments identified in chapter 16. Such skepticism was expressed most emphatically by those experienced older hands who had been most heavily involved in earlier book programs that died of neglect (or its opposite—bureaucratic impatience).

Federal funding for a new book policy is an undisputed necessity. So, too, is a national policy—a policy recognizing that the impact of the book is far-reaching, and that commitments must be long term; a policy that involves both the private sector book community and the government, in funding as well as in planning and commitment; and a policy that is non-partisan and has the support of both the executive and legislative branches. Such thinking shaped the views of professional discussants as well as those of Task force members. Well before the drafting of recommendations began, a consensus was forming among discussants and Task Force members that a national policy, originating with the president and accepted by the Congress, was *the* priority on which others would depend. Several discussants concerned with strengthened private sector support stated that such a goal can be considered analogous to developing popular recognition and support for foreign aid and defense by characterizing them as being in the common national interest. The funding may change, but the policy remains unquestioned.

Skeptics concerned about vacillating support for government book programs from past experience stressed the importance of the fact that the current study had been set in motion by the White House, and persuasively presented the case for Reid Foundation research and Task Force deliberation on a book policy in the broadest context of national security—not just as a cultural program for USIA. The result was a three-pronged approach in which USIA remains America's primary "agency of the book" overseas, but the U.S. Books Abroad project stresses the importance of the book to U.S. trade and foreign aid programs, as well as the necessary national security role of the book as a cultural ambassador. (As discussed in chapter 13, such a tripartite role would require far more interagency cooperation and coordination on book activities than has been previously the case.)

An immediate change in USIA cultural programming to be undertaken, in the minds of most discussants, is to include children's books among those books promoted abroad by that agency. It is not only the child who is the audience for such promotion; the adult social and educational communities primarily concerned with child welfare also are fundamentally affected. Excluded from USIA programs and libraries since 1962 as insufficiently "programmatic," the lack of such books has created an unfair and incorrect image of the U.S. in the developing world, in which Soviet books for children are widely known and used by parents and educators who may find no use for other kinds of Soviet books. Task Force members in favor of programming U.S. children's books emphasize that they are not advocating any major new publishing programs; rather children's books can become a natural element of activities such as book fairs. USIA could cooperate with the Children's Book Council and spin-off some of its projects at minimum expense.

An especially urgent priority, however, is scientific, technical, and medical books—the American books most in demand abroad in the developing world—that present a major new target for the government, as proposed by Task Force members and professional discussants. All Task Force members emphasized the importance of textbooks in science and technology and professional books in all fields to American aid and technical assistance programs in developing countries, to trade promotion, and to U.S. cultural activities. Yet, except for the relatively few years of the Alliance for Progress in Latin America and the P.L. 480 Textbook Program in India (see chapter 14), neither the promotion of such books nor their publication abroad in English or in translation has been a significant element of any U.S. program (except for donated books—which receive no specific supportive or directional policy).

Under a national book policy, AID, USIA, and the Department of Commerce should, Task Force members propose, address book programs in these areas in interagency meetings. Many discussants concerned with educational development argue strongly that if AID does not consider such books integral to developing country needs, then the way should be cleared for USIA to support them as a fundamental element of American culture—which America's rise to pre-eminence in science and technology surely is. Those publishers most familiar with past government efforts view the result of diffused and unfocused policy—useful and badly needed U.S. books falling into the cracks between agency chairs because of jurisdictional and semantic disputes—as distressing, and note that virtually all other major governments include an essential role for scientific and technical books in national security as presented in chapter 16: particularly when used in educational systems abroad, scientific and technical works are powerful transmitters of the cultural system that produced them.

Scientific and technical books also lead naturally into new directions for book promotion in trade policy, since those categories of books give credence to the maxim "trade follows the book," which is a fundamental of book promotion in a trading nation such as Britain. It is equally important for the U.S., as America's trade deficit reaches startling dimensions and the expansion of all exports becomes imperative. Educational and professional texts in the sciences, including scholarly journals, provide state of the art information from which professionals decide what technologies should be procured and from where.

Similarly, the student taught today with American texts is tomorrow's

U.S. market. Thus, trade follows the book, and more books in turn follow other trade, a cycle that the editors have not found disputed in their research. Sophisticated government leaders around the world (especially in the Third World) recognize the importance of understanding the cultural, social, and educational settings that best stimulate ingenuity and inventiveness. Even Japanese educators, Americans might be surprised to learn, are studying the U.S. educational system in that context, and American educators examine the methodology of the Japanese, West Europeans, and even the Third World and the Eastern bloc in search of ideas. Some book/technology interaction is synergistic. Awareness of American leadership in many areas provides product demand that stimulates demand for the texts that produced the individuals who created the products.

The major importance of exported books to U.S. trade does not result, however, from their potential as trade promoters, but from their intrinsic value as commodities. While great gaps in American book export knowledge have been identified in this study, statistics demonstrate that recorded book exports have increased 25 percent over a decade. The Commerce Department has reported total book exports of $643 million in 1984. The best estimates of reprint and translation rights sales, based on empirical data, increase book income from international sources to more than $1 billion. With the addition of returns on U.S. publishers and exporter investments from their overseas sales offices and publishing subsidiaries, also not currently reported in government book statistics, some discussants believe that the book industry is already beyond the $1.5 billion export earnings point. Illegitimate foreign sales, the sordid work of pirates whose proceeds do not return to the U.S., are not, of course, counted in U.S. book industry export earnings. They are estimated, however, at $750 million. If these existing illicit book sales returns are added to the legitimate receipts as "current potential," they produce a 1984 total estimate of the export trade in American books that exceeds $2 billion.

Can American book exports expand only incrementally, or does the potential for geometric progression exist? Some book export professionals lean in the direction of the latter possibility, for the balance of this century, if the proper mix of trade promotion and market development by government and industry can be achieved. They cite data that show the market, in terms of expanded education and increased literacy in the developing world, has far outpaced world book production—and certainly American book production aimed at those countries. An important trend for the American book industry in this connection is the increasing number of countries adopting English as a second language (and/or the popularity of English as an elective where language choice is left to the student). Educators also point to the growing use of English as the language of instruction at the university level in such areas as American studies, comparative social sciences, engineering, the natural sciences, and medicine.[2] (A student must be proficient in English to major in these fields in a growing number of countries.) Estimates of English-language book markets by the year 2000 are at least triple today's production—which itself only partially fulfills existing demand.

The country that corners the largest portion of these English language markets will also be a predominant political and cultural influence as the growth of English usage continues into the third millennium. Because of the world-wide popularity of American books, the editors believe that that predominant country could easily be the U.S. if government and non-government institutions collaborate under a national policy to overcome the barriers and fill the promotional gaps. Such a position of market leadership will not be *given* to us, however: it must be *earned*.

Other governments are also aware of this linguistic trend, and not just in the teaching of English. India, a country where publishers are quick to note that English is one of the national languages[3] and *not* a foreign language, has become the third largest producer of books in English, and is now looking seriously to foreign markets. West Germany has become the third largest international book trader, behind only the U.S. and the U.K., due in part to expanding production of books in English. The U.S.S.R., as we have seen in chapter 16, produces some 35 million books in English, recognizing the necessity of doing so in order to communicate with literati and the intellectual leadership of the world.

Assuming that the U.S. will take up the cultural challenge of the book world, and assuming that equal attention will be given to translations, it is not difficult to predict new areas of geographic emphasis. Commerce Department export reporting breaks down 1984's book export sales of $643 million by country and, as we have seen in chapter 11, convincingly shows the developing world as the market to which the U.S. has been inattentive, if not indifferent. To repeat the earlier analysis for purposes of emphasis: the incremental increase in U.S. book exports is approximately 2.5 percent per year over a decade. Aside from being generally low, almost all of that gradual increase has been in sales to the developed world. In fact, the stark reality of the statistics is that in 1984 a few developed countries were the destination of 83 percent (in dollars) of all books the U.S. exported.[4]

In the developing world, particularly Latin America and Africa, there is

---

[2] Not to be overlooked, of course, is resistance to the growth of English language usage in education; English is viewed by some Third World societies as a threat to their cultural heritage.

[3] English is the official language of government, including the parliament and the court system, and is widely used in university instruction.

[4] According to Commerce Department statistics reported in the August 2, 1985, issue of *Publishers Weekly*, three developed countries alone accounted for 62 percent of U.S. publishers' total 1984 export sales: Canada, 40.4%; the U.K., 13.4%; and Australia, 8.4%.

not so much a *book gap*, where American books in English are concerned, as there is a *book chasm*. It grows wider and deeper when one recognizes that, for price reasons, in 1984 more than 40 million fewer copies were shipped than in 1982, although the dollar value of shipments in the two years differed by little more than $1 million. The developing world, then, is America's "new frontier" book market. In view of the reality, the promise, and the problems, this may be the U.S.' greatest cultural challenge: however, it *can* be met. The evidence for that view lies in the fact that total U.S. trade with the developing world already exceeds our trade with Western Europe and Japan *combined*, as cited in chapter 10.

The strong value of the dollar and the shortage of dollars may hinder book exports, but these conditions need not be considered either terminal or permanent. For the first time since 1981, the International Monetary Fund reported in July, 1985,[5] that 1984 developing country exports exceeded imports by $10.9 billion dollars, suggesting that problems previously considered unmanageable can become manageable. The surplus was not uniform, but in Asia only Pakistan showed a decline in exports. Nigeria, Mexico, and Brazil all posted surpluses.

Throughout this study, the editors and authors have come close to a statement on the need for American publishers to maintain control over their English language rights, if Third World market needs and U.S. technical assistance and cultural goals are to be met. What this translates to is the right to sell U.S. books in the developing world. Historically, the best means of selling books in English to developing countries has been to relinquish rights to the British publisher with whom a contract for a U.K. edition was signed. Before World War II, very few American books were sold in the Commonwealth except through such publishing arrangements. After the war, the acknowledged expertise of the British industry made it logical for American publishers to continue those arrangements, while they were giving their attention to the burgeoning markets at home (as described in chapter 1). The British Publishers Association, in fact, institutionalized such arrangements. Concerned about losing Britain's principal overseas markets because of the break-up of the colonial system, the Publishers Association required that a member publisher even forego the publishing of an edition of an American book in the U.K. unless the publisher secured the exclusive right as well to sell the book in the British Commonwealth, as it was constituted in 1947 (including the right also to sell reprint rights). Most U.S. publishers presented with such a requirement acquiesced, reflecting the fact that, except for the

[5] *IMF Memorandum* quoted in the *Washington Post*, July 8, 1985, "Washington Business," p 33.

pioneers described in chapter 2, interest of any kind in foreign markets was slow in developing at home.

In 1976, an anti-trust action was filed against a group of U.S. publishers naming the U.K. Publishers Association as an unindicted co-conspirator. A consent decree resulted from this action, under the terms of which the Publishers Association agreed to abolish this provision as a requirement in rights contracts with American publishers, and the latter involved in the action agreed to no longer acquiesce to such terms.[6] In effect, however, this decree meant only that compulsion was removed, and those U.S. publishers who chose to do so could continue to grant marketing rights to U.K. publishers if each publishing project was negotiated as a separate business transaction. It is a reflection of the extent of U.S. publisher disinterest or hesitation about entering the international arena that many continue to contract substantial shares of such market rights away rather than handle sales to those markets themselves or assign them to a U.S. export representative. This situation is one reason for the caveat in the opening paragraph of this chapter to the effect that structures and foreign trade orientation necessary to achieving the results which a national book policy seeks do not yet effectively exist in the U.S.

The reasons for holding English-language rights at home are not only economic, but also political. The anti-trust action described above originated in part from complaints by Commonwealth booksellers[7] and their governments, when told that although their country was now independent they must still go to London for their American books. (Incidentally, the process requiring that orders received in New York from dealers of some countries be referred to London for fulfillment is also irritating, more costly and time consuming as well as extremely complicated. The complexities of the U.S. book export trade are described in chapters 2 and 12.) A third reason for keeping English language rights is the fact that the present marketing system can seriously hamper U.S.-U.K. efforts to stem piracy. The British Publishers Association has announced in its 1984 annual report that its Campaign Against Book Piracy (see chapter 16) will be extended in 1985 to include "market infringement." In effect, this announcement means an effort to stop the trading in American books by American publishers or distributors in countries for which the British have acquired market rights.

The "culprits" in this particular type of market infringement are wholesalers and remainder houses in the U.S. book trade that buy from U.S. publishers. The latter have no control over those distributors, in terms of whether or not their books will eventually be sold in Illinois or a foreign

[6] *U.S.* vs *Addison-Wesley Publishing Co.*, 61,225 (S.D.N.Y. 1976).

[7] Australian, in the case of the cited litigation.

country for which rights may have been sold to a foreign publisher; these distributors are neither aware of nor interested in finding out about any limitations applicable to books they have purchased for resale. The shadow of anti-trust action looms over any concerted efforts to restrain these booksellers, along with monumental and unenforceable record-keeping procedures for all concerned.

It should also be noted that to a lesser degree, American publishers lodge similar market infringement complaints against their British counterparts. It is a no-win situation for the industries of both countries that the editors suggest might best be resolved by agreeing that publishers from each country have non-exclusive rights to editions of books from the other country for most markets. It is ironic that market infringement charges now arise most often concerning underpriced books in the Third World. The complaint is that remaindered books from one country are usually lower in price to the reader—an objective of developing world book programs of both countries—than the commercial editions from the other still on sale at full price. Admittedly, economic damage occurs in these situations, but not nearly enough to justify confusion of such issues with the more serious piracy both government and industry should seek to halt.

The main reason for recommending that U.S. publishers keep English language rights for such countries as India and Pakistan, however, is that a response to the challenges of the future will require flexibility in market approaches. The editors argue that an American publisher should want his own international division or export representative to handle sales to those countries where the market knowledge of those two approaches to U.S. export sales is now equal to that of their British counterparts. In other instances, likely to increase as markets grow and new technology makes reprinting still cheaper, the best decision may be to have books printed in-country by a subsidiary or by contract with a local publisher. (The need for low-priced editions printed abroad has been discussed in chapter 6.) In addition, it may well be that production by an Indian publisher for sale in India, for example, should also include market rights for neighboring countries. These variations need not preclude U.K. editions for which substantial parts of the world are left open to non-exclusive editions from all sources, as is the general case now with respect to European markets.

The objectives of U.S. national book policy should be the widest distribution of American books in all languages, at the lowest possible retail prices, so as to maximize their use by foreign readers seeking knowledge while simultaneously maximizing profits for U.S. publishers. To maintain the critical element of government support proposed in this study, far more publishers must take a hand in market development than now do so, directly rather than through intermediaries, and for books in translation as well as in English.

The editors believe that extensive changes in the ways American publishers do business are needed if they are to respond fully to a national policy on U.S. books abroad. In chapter 14, it was estimated that $15 million would be necessary simply to restore USIA book programs to their 1965 level, a level deemed inadequate even at the time. It is estimated that an effective currency convertibility program will eventually cost $50 million, and a U.S. book promotion effort that effectively deals with the problems identified in this study will likely cost several hundred million dollars in order to triple sales by the year 2000.

The federal government is not likely to be and, in the editors' view, ought not to be the sole source for this funding. Nonprofit foundations, private research groups, and philanthropic groups should be collaborators, along with the industry itself. Paul E. Feffer, chairman of the Task Force, has repeatedly proposed that the largest U.S. publishers devote 6 to 8 percent of their net income to research and development, without success. (His percentage is derived from the fact that export sales account for 6 to 8 percent of total publisher receipts.) Six percent of total U.S. 1984 export receipts of $643 million would add to $38 million. Obviously, Mr. Feffer is only seeking to stimulate debate. However, the industry will have to put far more money into market research, development, and promotion abroad than it does now, at the very least as a quid pro quo for what it expects from the government. Of course, when speaking of "the industry" and what it can and will do, it is necessary to distinguish between the thirty or so major multinationals and the majority of publishers. These thirty along with a few major exporters and wholesalers and perhaps 50 moderate to large other publishers, have been most responsible for the development of U.S. book export trade and subsidiary publishing abroad. The balance of the industry, some 90 percent of the total, are those companies described at the beginning of this chapter as neither a group in any usual sense nor, at present, particularly oriented toward either export activity or rights sales. (Some 500 publishers out of a total of 20,000 attend the Frankfurt Book Fair; some 250 belong to the Association of American Publishers.)

For the silent majority, this study itself is a how-to-do-it handbook and a promotional piece intended to arouse enthusiasm for activity in international markets where they have not gone before, pursuing export sales directly or working with an exporter, acquiring a rights agent, educating the subsidiary rights department on foreign markets, and participating at minimum cost in USIA and Department of Commerce international book promotion activities. Those with a more than fleeting interest in foreign markets should consider collective exhibits, and collective operations such as the Foreign Sales Corporations and/or Export Trading Companies discussed in chapter 4. More so than the larger publishers already involved in foreign trade, these publishers need educated staff and access to the various kinds of research identified as critical needs throughout this study. It should be noted pragmatically that, except for their willingness to take chances on the publication of a particular book—the critical cultural characteristic of their nature—money is less available than in many other industries, a peculiarity of what is also a high risk business. Thus, the Commerce Department approach of requiring that industry pay the cost of trade missions and exhibits in its trade centers simply will not produce the responses sought among publishers who in some senses still can be described as members of a cottage industry. While the Commerce Department must set rules applicable across the board on its activities supporting foreign trade, it should be possible to scale some of its fees. The same situation applies with respect to seminars and training programs. Such gatherings, which cost substantial money, are poorly attended by those who need them most.

Both English-language reprint programs and translation rights activities that the editors believe should be a major new direction for American publishers not now so engaged presupposes the knowledge, experience, and resources essential to action. The editors reiterate the need for an effective International Copyright Information Center (INCINC), as a nonprofit institution servicing rights needs of developing world publishers, and those American publishers who need information on the market for rights to their books and on how to proceed as well as guidance on copyright laws of Third World countries especially. If INCINC assumed the functions of assembling information and producing catalogs of translated books for distribution abroad (see discussion of a need for such catalogs identified for USIA in chapter 14), and data banks of information on rights holders and translations in process, it would have a base from which to effectively support the efforts of U.S. publishers, their associations, literary agents, and authors—support that will be essential to the proposed assumption of their copyright marketing responsibilities now often relinquished to British publishers. INCINC, with a broad base of connections with the world's book industries (reaching beyond those of trade associations) could also add an authoritative voice, based on solid research and experience in copyright transactions, to international copyright deliberations on other than governmental levels.

Another need identified by the editors, albeit not specifically focused on in the research for this study, is a clearing house or "umbrella" organization where the market research of government agencies and the book industry on the overseas book trade infrastructure (especially in developing countries) trade terms, and requirements could be assembled, analyzed, and made accessible to U.S. publishers. Similarly missing in the many proposals that cite need for education, training, seminars, and provision of information for general book promotion (chapter 10) is any consideration of a central institution or umbrella organization to coordinate and, as necessary, conduct research activities. It has been suggested by some discussants that, at the very least, the efforts of AID, OPIC, USIA, and the Department of Commerce in these areas be coordinated and complement one another. That approach, as seen in chapter 16, follows the pattern of the French government efforts (External Affairs, International Trade, Technical Assistance Programs, and Cultural Program ministries working in tandem, with the Ministry of Culture having primary direct industry support and coordination functions). The French also have the Cercle de la Librairie and several other semi-autonomous organizations through which government and industry support, coordinate, and cooperate with each other. As we have also seen the British feel the need for a Book Development Council independent of government and working with a somewhat autonomous, quasi-private sector British Council and the book industry's Overseas Trade board to meet their book development goals.

Curtis Benjamin settled in his study on a *private sector* organization, which he related by analogy to the British Council, as a most necessary element of U.S. book development. Because the Task Force was formed, as noted at the outset of this chapter, with the immediate purpose of addressing the needs for a new government commitment, a new government initiative, its report addresses, correctly, the priority of establishing new direct links between the industry and government and better links between government agencies (chapter 13). The editors have concluded that with the extent of information to be assembled, acted upon, and disseminated, the new links in the private sector that Curtis Benjamin saw to be necessary have become no less important—but are best left to the private sector (profit and nonprofit) to develop, e.g., a book development council.

Education and communication are the two areas that most need "umbrella" coordination, especially if one includes disseminating the results of foreign market research under education. With a relatively few exceptions in the form of actual degree programs or one or two term seminars, the field of education has not, one might argue, given the book industry as much as it has received in the form of meeting academic text needs. Lois Spice Haig, coauthor of chapter 10 on education for publishing argues that "The time has come to involve our educational institutions in the business of education for publishing, at home and abroad. Education is now an international affair, as never before. Technology has linked the world. Those countries that recognize the changing needs of the publishing world and act quickly will be the most influential, both culturally and politically. A redefinition of publishing to include electronic communication, specifically for educational materials, is a necessity.

"Educational institutions are banding together across the disciplines in order to coordinate and control the proliferation of information. The educational institutions now need to join hands with the publishing profession and industry to assist them to meet publishings' educational needs. After all, the publishing world traditionally has furnished the critical tools needed to accumulate, assimilate, and disseminate knowledge. It now needs educational assistance to maintain that role and to stay abreast of the new demands of the educational world."

Communication within the publishing industry and between government agencies and publishers (nonprofit as well as commercial) on foreign markets is lacking. It does appear that *Publishers Weekly* has been increasingly shifting its attention toward international affairs, including addition of a once-per-month "International Front" report and more frequent and extensive reports on book publishing abroad. Kenneth Giniger's *International Publishing Newsletter* was begun in 1982 in recognition of the sizeable knowledge gap; *B.P. Report*, from Knowledge Industry Publications, is also focusing more on the international book business, as well as government export and book promotion-related information. With due regard for the good features of each of these efforts, there are few chapters in this study that do not identify substantial elements of international industry development that need elaboration on a thorough, continuing basis and are not likely to get it.

What is true of the publishing media is unfortunately equally true of the industry itself. For example, in the best years of USIA's book programs, with 80 to 100 joint industry/USIA book exhibits annually, there were rarely more than 50 publishers participating. Without exception, the information channels of the AAP and AAUP brought forth only limited responses from only half of those publishers who subsequently did participate. The other half were "faithfuls," known to USIA officers as those to be contacted on a one-on-one personal basis because they would invariably participate *when notified*. However, most frustrating for USIA officers was disseminating the reports on showings that required publisher follow-up for successful results. Neither the AAP nor the AAUP has the publishing resources or personnel at this time with which to disseminate such materials to those member houses who could make best use of it. Perhaps the solution is some joint clearing house operation between the USIA and the Commerce Department. Perhaps the AAP, the AAUP, and the SSP need funding to expand their informational capacity: perhaps a new institution needs to be organized.

In any event, without improvement in communications concerning international publishing, a substantial share of the response to the problems and needs discussed in this study will constitute "wheel spinning." Similar needs for communication between government agencies were identified by the Reid Foundation Study Group, but these appear manageable, through improved interagency relations resulting from a national policy statement. However, they will not improve intra-industry communication, nor that between government and industry. The book, *Washington's Best Kept Secrets*, described in chapter 4, was more a demonstration of the extent of the problem than an answer.

Members of the U.S. Books Abroad Task Force and other discussants urged transforming the NSC memorandum (Appendix 1) into a Presidential Directive to government agencies. The editors would welcome a presidential statement of national purpose on American books abroad, and believe, in fact, that if such a presidential pronouncement does not result from the attention focused on the U.S. Books Abroad project, it is unlikely that a national policy on American Books Abroad will be stated at all, at least not in the very near future. As we note at the outset of this chapter, however, while federal funding is indispensable and participation of government agencies invaluable, the national policy which the sub-title of this book treats encompasses participation of private and nonprofit sector organizations and institutions as well. Indeed, the NSC memorandum notes that "The problem is not simply the weakness of current federal programs. Donation programs by private American publishers have been reduced. Funds handled by quasi-public/private organizations have been cut back. We need to renovate our total approach." That directive might have discussed as well book export problems of the industry itself identified in this study.

The thrust of a national policy and this discussion of new directions and new approaches, then, is that everyone concerned about the situation of American books abroad needs to revise their view of the dimensions and nature of the book gap, rid themselves of any habitual views that the responsibility rests with the government and that the task of dealing with the book gap can be turned over to the government. The industry—and government—need to recognize that just as the policies underlying a national security commitment to American books abroad are tripartite, so the responsibilities for taking actions are broader than government. The editors agree that by all means government must take an active role, instituting programs even larger and more varied than its book programs of the 1950s and 1960s. But for the 1980s and for the rest of this century as a matter of fact, public diplomacy calls for a much larger participation from the publishing industry *and* from all sectors of the American public policy community in seeing that American books are no longer "America's neglected ambassadors."

U.S. Books Abroad Task Force Report
... a new commitment

Paul E. Feffer, Chairman

U.S. Books Abroad Task Force Report ... a new Commitment[1]

Introduction

On April 4, 1984, Director Robert C. McFarlane of the National Security Council wrote to Director Charles Z. Wick of the U.S. Information Agency to say "The time is right for a major new commitment to the provision of U.S. books abroad." Mr. McFarlane referred to comments made by the late Curtis G. Benjamin in his book *U.S. Books Abroad: Neglected Ambassadors*, and pointed out that the United States has, in effect, unilaterally disarmed in the use of American books overseas in waging the "war of ideas" and in fostering the "infrastructure of democracy," two goals enunciated by President Reagan in London in June of 1982. He then called for a sharply focused report designed to develop a coherent strategy for the long term and, simultaneously, for the establishment of a task force drawing upon U.S. government expertise, the publishing sector, the academic world and quasi-public groups. USIA was asked to take the lead in commissioning a comprehensive study of the "book gap" and presenting a comprehensive package for legislative and administrative action.

In response to this initiative, USIA commissioned the Helen Dwight Reid Educational Foundation of Washington, D.C., to prepare the comprehensive study and established this task force as a subcommittee of the U.S. Book and Library Advisory Committee for USIA. Mr. Paul E. Feffer was appointed chairman of the task force. Mr. Leonard Marks was named as Special Advisor to Director Wick. Dr. Guy S. Brown was named as the USIA member on the task force.

[1] See Editor's Note on page 261 for topic organization.

During a period of intensive research, the Reid Foundation identified 11 topics to be considered in our new commitment to U.S. books abroad. The task force, in turn, addressed each of these topics and decided January 17, 1985, to make the following comments and recommendations in the order indicated. (See Editor's Note on page 261.)

Table of Contents

General Recommendations

The Task Force makes two general recommendations not directly tied to any of the individual topics:

1. The Task Force recommends that the main thrust of the NSC memorandum be transformed into a Presidential Directive to relevant departments and agencies instructing them to adapt their programs, funds, and other

resources, to the extent consistent with their other responsibilities, to accomodate the U.S. Books Abroad objectives.

This step is necessary in view of the cross-cutting nature of the challenge in promoting the increased flow of substantive American books abroad. It is particularly important in order to stimulate the development of financial assistance programs through USAID, the departments of Commerce, Agriculture, Treasury, and other agencies.

2. The Task Force also recommends that the U.S. government, through its overseas missions, encourage and assist those nations with a predilection toward open societies to acquire educational facilities and resources to meet their goals.

Dissemination of Information on the Content of American Books (Topic III)

The Reid Foundation has identified a number of factors combining to form a barrier to the export of American books: a strong dollar, shortage of foreign exchange, inflation, and other economic dislocations. Even so, in good and bad economic times the paucity of information on American books alone discourages importers and booksellers around the world from ordering them. Some American publishers maintain branches in countries where markets for American books are reasonably strong. They and others send representatives to visit booksellers, wholesalers, universities, libraries, etc., mail catalogs, and exhibit. But the really effective and productive information devices are the standard bibliographic tools such as *Books in Print, Publishers' Weekly*, and book review publications, such as *Booklist, Choice, Library Journal*, and book review sections of major American newspapers, including the *N.Y. Times Book Review Section, New York Review of Books*, and the *Washington Post Book World*.

Not to be overlooked are the journals of major American learned and professional societies that review serious American books. These publications collectively are the mainstays of information on American bibliographic output for the American librarian and bookseller and for intellectual leaders, academicians, students, and readers as well. Because of their high cost, unfortunately, they are off limits to overseas counterparts. Also, general malaise and disinterest on the part of the marketers of these publications in promoting bibliographic and review publications to potential overseas users make them somewhat of an unknown resource for much of the world, especially Third World countries.

Notwithstanding the unquestioned importance and value of promoting interest in making such tools available among user groups around the world, specific USIA interest in providing information on the content of program books argues for a specialized book review publication to give overseas guidance information on these books. One option is to model this after the short-lived agency review publication of the mid-Sixties, *American Book Review*. It carried content reviews of new and current American and foreign-authored books on agency-related themes. Another model is the current British Council publication, *British Book News*, which, in turn, was modeled after the agency's publication, nearly 20 years dormant. It is produced for the British Council by the prominent U.K. publisher and book export firm Blackwell's, and is largely self-sufficient through paid subscriptions, which Blackwell's promotes, and through U.K. publisher advertising.

Recommendations

1. Complimentary subscriptions to American book review journals, such as *Booklist, Choice*, and *Library Journal*, should be provided to booksellers, libraries, universities, and publishers in Third World countries.
2. Complimentary copies of book review sections of major American newspapers, including the *New York Times Book Review Section, New York Review of Books*, and the *Washington Post*, should be provided to leading journalists, writers, academicians, scholars, and other distinguished intellectual leaders in both the developed and developing worlds.
3. Complimentary subscriptions of academic and scholarly journals should be provided to leading members of the counterpart disciplines and professions abroad, with the purpose of giving these overseas scholars and professionals a sense of collegiality with their American colleagues and to inform them through articles of the status of research and writings in their respective fields and to provide them with information about current books through review essays and regular book reviews.
4. Back copies (not too old) of *Books in Print* should be provided to selected booksellers, libraries, and universities; these copies, while not inclusive of the newest books, still contain information on availability of current American books at lower cost.
5. The following options on how to identify and record recipient institutions, organizations, and individuals and how to service subscriptions of the above publications should be considered, these lists to be made available to interested publishers and distributors:
   a. USIA overseas posts determine recipients and make direct presentations;
   b. USIA make grants to American nonprofit institutions, such as the Asia Foundation and AMIDEAST, to identify recipients, purchase subscriptions, and handle mailings; and
   c. USIA provide direct funding to the ALA, Bowker, and publishers of academic and scholarly journals to permit them to make complimentary subscriptions.

6. To provide information to overseas readers on current books supportive of USIA themes, the agency might emulate the British Council book review journal, *British Book News*, which announces and reviews books supporting British national interests. Such a review journal would be distributed by USIA overseas posts to a large audience including booksellers, librarians, university professors, journalists, writers, other intellectual leaders, and general readers with an interest in the United States. Options include:
   a. The USIA bibliographic staff making selections and preparing and editing entries, with the journal being printed at its overseas printing facilities;
   b. USIA making a grant to a nonprofit organization already reviewing books and publishing review and bibliographic journals to select titles, prepare entries, and publish the former *American Book Review*; and
   c. USIA developing a review service that draws its reviews from commercial sources as authorized and as fits the needs of the agency.
7. USIA also should explore with the Library of Congress and some of the major book index and review publishers, such as Bowker, ALA, and Wilson, the need and resources required for providing a machine readable bibliographic tool kit for foreign users. Such a tool kit could include cataloging information, ISBN numbers, vendor information, prices, reviews or references to reviews in journals, acquisition by USIA libraries, etc. Such a kit also would provide a more comprehensive, one-stop mechanism to facilitate the awareness, selection, ordering, and cataloging of U.S. books in foreign countries. It could, in addition, be used by USIA posts to generate specialized lists, promote U.S. books within that country and assist foreign libraries and distributors to acquire or market U.S. books.

International Exhibits (Topic IV)

Approaches to disseminating more information on the content of American books are discussed elsewhere in this report. International exhibits are treated here under a separate topic heading because this is a distinct form of providing information on books themselves, as well as discussing the method to order the books.

The Reid Foundation concluded that American publishers, even those who regularly participate in major events such as Frankfurt, do not give sufficient priority to the less widely promoted book fairs, especially those of the Third World, such as Buenos Aires, Cairo, Jerusalem, and Mexico, nor do they attach importance to meetings of academic and professional associations around the world. Smaller commercial publishers, university presses, and "private" or "association" publishers, such as the American Enterprise Institute, Brookings, the Foreign Policy Association, Heritage Foundation, and Heldref—many with lists rich in serious works of American culture and policies—cannot afford to participate.

Opportunities abound for displaying American books in many countries, including developing countries. International and national book fairs have been organized and are held annually (for the most part) in Algeria, Argentina, Bahrain, Brazil, India, Iraq, Kuwait, Mexico, Nigeria, Poland, Senegal, Singapore, and Yugoslavia. The French government's Office of Promotion of French Publishing has prepared a 1985 Exhibit Program listing more than 60 events in which it will exhibit and promote French books. The Soviets are known to participate in many more.

The American national interest would seem to call—from a commercial, cultural, and policy viewpoint—for *direct participation* in international and national book fairs, as well as in meetings of academic and professional associations, and the *holding of exhibits independently* at organized events such as is done with USIA thematic exhibits, no longer active due to personnel shortages. Because of USIA's primary concern with the promotion of American books abroad, it probably will want to take the lead in overall U.S. government participation in international book fairs and in a program of independent book exhibits.

Recommendations

In keeping with the above, the Task Force believes that there is a critical need to improve both the quality and quantity of American participation in overseas book fairs and exhibits and recommends that:

1. There be the broadest private-public participation in more book fairs, including regional and local fairs and those fairs featuring special themes, such as children's books. Further, the government should give careful consideration to establishing and maintaining permanent display centers overseas to house American books in educational and development-related fields, in business and management subjects, and on American culture and society.
2. The government should harness and coordinate its exhibit programs with the expertise of private and nonprofit firms, organizing collective exhibitions, and permanent point of purchase exhibitions.

Donated Books and Presentations (Topic V)

Private donations of books, privately solicited and assembled and privately shipped abroad, have long been widely accepted as demonstrative overseas of the American traits of generosity, neighborliness, and volunteerism.

Donated books can supplement and enhance purchased presentations of books, but they cannot and should not be thought to replace them. Indeed, free distribution of U.S. books reach prospective buyers and they encourage and facilitate the study of English.

The government experience with donated books, however, has not been without problems. The Reid Foundation report discusses the history and status of donated books in considerable detail.

Recommendations

In view of the above and background provided in the Reid report, the Task Force believes that there is a valid need in the national interest overseas for a two-track approach in presentations: first, for the presentation of books donated by the private sector for needy recipients unable to obtain these books through normal commercial channels and, second, for the increased purchase by USIA and by private organizations of carefully selected titles for special presentation to influential foreigners. The Task Force also believes that the present USIA budget and staff for obtaining and distributing donated and presentation books is grossly inadequate and that the sum of $400,000 requested for FY 1986 for shipping costs and grants to private organizations also is seriously insufficient to meet the needs and opportunities. The one officer available to deal with donated books also must carry out a number of other duties, including the time-consuming task of arranging for exhibits. Therefore, the Task Force recommends that:

1. While U.S. publishers cannot designate recipient countries for donations, those engaged in donations should avoid distribution in countries of commercial potential, except as the donors agree.
2. USIA, USAID, and other public agencies should provide funding for handling and shipping costs to nonprofit organizations engaged in distribution of donated books abroad, taking into account quality, quantity, and the U.S. national interest. Local need and choice are of paramount importance in the development of this program.
3. Whenever possible and deemed desirable for political, economic and other reasons, the U.S. government should look first to the private sector for the implementation of overseas donated book programs, avoiding duplication and uneconomic competition.
5. USIA should actively pursue funding of special donation projects consisting of previously selected "shelves" or topical collections, such as those of "Books USA," "American Literature," and the Freedom House collections on U.S. life and institutions.
6. USIA, USAID, and nonprofit institutions donating books abroad should explore the availability of low or no-cost shipping services for both domestic and international transportation.

Copyright Law and the Protection of Intellectual Property (Topic I)

The Reid Foundation reports that copyright laws and the execution of them as protection for intellectual property is a concern that the book community shares with other media producers. The creative works of both are threatened by illegal use of new technology used to copy them. Thus, the book world has joined forces on copyright protection both here and abroad with motion pictures, television, music, journals, and all producers and distributors of creative works under varying and special circumstances. In the still larger picture, concerns are shared with patent and trademark owners and licensees.

The U.S. International Trade Commission has surveyed the larger worldwide picture of "counterfeiting," including book piracy, and has determined that an estimated $8 billion per year is lost to American industry from such activities.

The value and importance of individual and group creativity to society are inherent in both democracy and free market concepts, and this alone is a basis for more action in the minds of those interviewed by the Reid Foundation. This value is expressed in the U.S. Constitution as the rationale for authorizing Congress to enact copyright and patent laws and, indeed, is more or less embedded in the law of all developed countries, many Third World legal codes, and at the international treaty and convention levels. This concept, however, is not fully understood in the Third World nor is it fully accepted in much of the socialist world. The U.S.S.R. is a relative newcomer to international copyright responsibilities.

An ongoing educational effort abroad is thought necessary via both private and public channels, with USIA most often emerging as the logical agency, in view of its cultural mission, to communicate our American understanding of these concepts.

Copyright law has both criminal and civil legal implications. Where support for the former is neglected by government, the latter does not seem a practical avenue to be pursued by U.S. complainants. All Western countries with major publishing industries have a shared interest in civil as well as criminal laws of the Third World, and U.S. government agencies should coordinate with them to gain improved environments and procedures for civil suits. English-language books are, however, the prime resource of the pirates, and the U.S. and United Kingdom the most directly concerned parties. Criminal action, even where laws exist, is not always vigorously pressed by the government that enacted the laws. Persistent representation by American embassies should play a major role in the criminal area, seeking meaningful remedies and/or punitive action for American private interests. Individual property owners, authors, and the book community share an interest in having Washington direct embassies to act on piracy as a priority of some importance. In fact, as explained further in the Reid study, U.S. agencies responsible for economic functions already are working with industry to enhance their own attention to copyright as it intertwines with their programs or can be deterred by them.

The Task Force is well aware that compulsory licensing of reprints and translations, permissible under both the Berne Convention and the Universal Copyright Convention since the Paris Act of 1971, is expected by some to grow unless other means are found to make American books available in the developing countries which the Paris Act covers. (This practice consists of translating and reprinting without permission from the original copyright holder and without that holder stipulating the royalty.)

International copyright centers were established by major developed countries to facilitate the acquisition of rights short of the resort to compulsory licensing. The International Copyright Information Center (INCINC) in the U.S. is located in the Washington, D.C., office of the Association of American Publishers (AAP). Thus far, it has been under-utilized by foreign publishers, due in part to a lack of information about it in the developing world but also due to politicization of compulsory licensing in UNESCO. INCINC also is not meaningfully staffed. Funding by the government has been proposed by publishers at various times, as has location of the INCINC function at the Copyright Office, although neither approach has been pursued effectively.

Although piracy thrives in some regions simply because it is profitable to some entrepreneurs, and compulsory licensing is likely to grow simply because it is more economical for dollar-short governments, the basic rationale that is evoked in support of such steps is that foreign books are essential to the national development of the Third World and that it is the responsibility of the developed world to see that they get them. In one sense, therefore, the entire U.S. Books Abroad project can be viewed as a response to that Third World demand for American books. At the same time, improved availability of American books and reprint or translation rights moderates the demand for compulsory licensing and the validity of such licenses under the provisions of the Paris Act.

Recommendations

1. INCINC should be substantially enhanced through private-government funding to enable it to play a larger direct role in copyright acquisition by foreign publishers, bypassing the obstacles now raised by UNESCO. INCINC also should work closely with USIA and/or Commerce in the educational efforts of the former and the commercial policies of the latter. U.S. publishers not in the AAP, including those in the AAUP, as well as publishers overseas, should be informed through both public and private channels about INCINC activities on a regular basis as applicable to their concerns. Although a service provided by the AAP by default of others, INCINC is a separate institution capable of being transferred elsewhere if effectiveness made that appropriate.
2. There should be general acceptance of current efforts to make foreign protection of copyright a consideration in all U.S. economic, political, and cultural agreements and activities, such as trade agreements, aid agreements, and cultural negotiations (including those of the U.S. in

binational commissions); and all U.S. agencies with international interests should support these efforts.

3. Commendation should be given to the development of such tools as the Commerce handbook that will make commercial attachés informed and active on copyright adherence and piracy abroad; and USIA should be urged to become involved in this effort at the Washington and embassy levels.
4. USIA should carry out a sustained educational role on the purposes and importance of copyright as an element of American society among the publishing and educational audiences of that agency; and USIA should ensure that its own programs abroad carry the message of copyright protection in their execution.
5. The Task Force understands that the administration intends to submit the Berne Convention to Congress in 1985 and joins the many media associations in urging that Congress take positive action.

Financial Assistance (Topic VIII)

The lack of dollars with which to pay for their book orders and translation-reprint rights has brought much of the developing world's book trade with the United States almost to a halt. Currency is a problem in most countries of Latin America, Eastern Europe, and parts of Africa and Asia. For the first time in current memory, even Gulf oil states have discussed, if not promulgated, rulings on the dollars available for various commodity imports.

Substantial progress in moving U.S. titles abroad will require the coordinated use of various government agency programs presently available or adaptable to the purpose of U.S. Books Abroad. Taken together, their impact could be significant and justify a recommendation that their utility be adapted and made better known to the publishing industry.

From the standpoint of the end user of an American book, a critical problem is price, for American books—like many other commodities—are becoming more expensive, and are among some of the most expensive books in the world. Where transshipment points are involved, prices are marked up by the publisher's own branch offices through which the order is fulfilled, since the branch must pay for incoming freight, storage, and other fulfillment facilities. Nevertheless, the student overseas examining an American book at the shop of his local bookseller will find prices equivalent to double or more the original dollar retail price in the U.S. The solution usually is purchase of a few copies (if at all) by a university library or the selection by the faculty of another text—often an English-language text—from the U.S.S.R. The recommendations under Topic VIII would contribute to bringing down the cost of American books.

The proposed U.S. Information Agency's book publishing program (addressed in Topic IX) also would contribute toward a solution of the price problem, but it will take several years to gear up such low-priced publishing, even if appropriated funds are made available beginning in fiscal year 1986. Many publishers also are concerned with the problem of price and are producing international student editions at lower prices or are producing special export editions. This practice by some publishers should be encouraged among all publishers.

Recommendations

1. *Criteria for eligibility of books.* Financial incentives discussed in these recommendations should be construed in terms broad enough to encompass those titles which promote understanding of American foreign policy, culture, technology, society, and values. Any successful American book program abroad would have several benefits. On one level, these books would be central in the "war of ideas" with totalitarian countries hostile to democratic principles. On another level, an expanded program would support commercial objectives because it is well known that "trade follows the book." And on a third level, American books would make a signal contribution in the worldwide marketplace of ideas and advance our educational, cultural, and humanitarian goals.
2. *Currency convertibility.* A currency convertibility program should be established, to be known as the "Book Export Financing Program" (BEF) to distinguish it as much as possible from programs of the past. A multi-benefits program should be carried out to justify imposing export dollar costs of book exports on the taxpayer. In addition to moving books abroad for the sake of the U.S. national interest, additional public benefits must be derived (see subparagraphs g, h, and i below).
   a. BEF would be essentially a facility for converting local currency proceeds of book exports into dollars and harnessing the local currency thus generated. It would not protect U.S. exporters against currency devaluation or commercial credit risks.
   b. BEF in the first year should be limited to approximately half a dozen high priority target countries. Country determination should be made by the government and incorporated in the annual proposed appropriation bill; the one-time authorizing legislation, however, would leave it to the president to determine the countries and identify them with each appropriation request.
   c. There should be no dependence on revolving funds or recovery of funds. Appropriations, not public debt money, should be used. Whether the recovery takes the form of local currency use substituting for U.S. government expenditure of dollars for local currency or the form of a long-term low-interest loan to repay the dollars, the foreign government would view the cost of book imports as a current or future charge against its dollar reserves and sooner or later would drop out or

become a reluctant partner in the book program. Also, Congress would question prospects for success in recovering dollars, based on past experience. It follows that that program should be financed by appropriations, thus requiring a strong justification. Appropriations should be for no-year disbursement (or two-year funds as a fallback).

d. Appropriation requests should be estimated at $3 million for each country, with the expressed intention of adding similar amounts each year.

e. All titles would be eligible, except for specifically excluded categories, drawing on past experience to define the exclusions.

f. The criteria for local currency use should be broader than for convertibility guaranties, leaving the administering agency as much discretion as reasonably can be requested of Congress.

g. The guarantee program should be administered to the extent possible to create an incentive for U.S. publishers and exporters to lower U.S. costs and pass these savings abroad. For example, preferential treatment might be given to low-cost products.

h. The foreign government should be encouraged to make available matching dollar exchange to import U.S. books. This might be a way to *offer* the program to more than a few countries. Thus, a few more countries, somewhat better off financially, might agree to match.

i. Local currency generated by convertibility guarantee payments should be made available by a bilateral agreement to book programs designated by the U.S. government and approved by the importing government. Priority uses would be (1) to finance total distribution of the imported books; (2) to finance any local currency costs of transaction and financing the acquisition of local currency costs of rights of eligible U.S. titles; (3) to finance indigenous publishing of U.S. titles, and (4) to the extent that funds remain, to meet the expenditures of other USIA book programs, such as libraries, translation and exhibits.

j. The BEF program should be limited to books, in that other media are not similarly blocked from reaching target countries, have less continuing utility than books, and would siphon off a large amount of the limited funds needed for book exports. An exception, however, might be made for categories of journals meeting education and development needs.

3. *End user grants*. Recognizing that the high cost of U.S. books is at least as much of a barrier to serving foreign markets as foreign exchange blockage, a financial program paralleling the BEF program should be developed by USIA along the following lines, backed by a $5 million appropriation in FY '86 and expanded in future years if warranted by program performance.

a. The program should be designed to deal with the ultimate consumer—primarily national, university, and other major libraries, but also including scholars, professionals, and students. In the case of institutions, the USIA post might contract with a university or other library to reimburse it for a defined percentage—say 50%—of its increase in expenditure for the import of American books beyond any base year. By such a plan, the cost could be directly controlled, and by dealing with responsible institutions, the agency would be relieved of defining books not worth subsidy and would be assured that all books were needed and in a useful place. Applying the aid only to increases in American book purchases would mean that the institutions would not be able to use the subsidy to lower their expenditures for American books in order to have more money for books from other nations and would assure that the program was producing a real growth in the export of American books. Requiring the institutions to share the cost would give them an incentive to bargain hard with booksellers, while local wholesalers and booksellers would be protected in their markets and have an incentive to stock more American books.

b. Participating institutions would be encouraged to establish other educational and cultural programming related to American interests, such as lectures and American studies.

c. In the case of individual students, professors, independent scholars, professionals and others, USIA might issue coupons redeemable at local bookstores. The mechanics would require considerable exploration, and careful protection against fraud would be necessary.

4. *Local government-sponsored grants*. In addition, USIA should have the discretion to employ where desirable, a variation of the approach described above in which the target institutions would be approached through the national government. If an institution were unable to make the required local currency payment, the grant would be made through the government, which would assume the local currency obligation. Local currency would be generated (or paid as part of the cost) at a predetermined percentage—say 50%—of the dollar grant at prevailing exchange rates (to be realistically defined). This currency would be available for the distribution, publishing, translation, and local currency costs of acquiring rights and similar book activities by the grantee or other competent organization in that country. These grants would be made in the first year in selected countries important to U.S. foreign policy objectives and willing to cooperate with USIA book programs.
5. *Other financial assistance*. The Presidential Directive recommended above should explicitly direct interagency coordination to make available a number of existing government programs which might offer increased

financial assistance to the export, foreign distribution, or foreign publishing of U.S. originated titles without new legislation or new appropriations.

a. Commerce, the U.S. Trade Representative, OPIC, USAID, Treasury, and the Export-Import Bank all have been identified in the Reid Topic Paper as having programs which could be adapted to the special needs of book publishing. Such programs include export insurance, insurance against political losses (war, civil strife, arbitrary currency controls or valuation, etc.), and loan guaranties. OPIC insurance and loans are available for investment in publishing and distribution ventures in developing countries. Institutional and tax incentives, offered in the Domestic International Sales Corporation, Foreign Sales Companies and Export Trading Companies legislation identified by the Reid Foundation, might usefully be examined by book publishers and book exporters. The Small Business Administration should reconsider its "opinion molding policy," which makes media companies ineligible for SBA loans and other assistance. The experience of other agencies, such as USIA and USAID, relative to resolving content differences with the book publishing industry might provide guidance to SBA on modification of its media policy.

b. The relevant agencies and departments should explore the availability to book programs of local currency accumulations from U.S. programs in certain countries which give the U.S. government a voice in their use. The largest source is PL 480 agricultural exports, but there are other sources to be looked into. Unfortunately, there are only a few countries which might be targeted for a book program and which also have local currency accumulations (usable, perhaps, following negotiations). Even in those countries, despite agreement on the broad category of use, local currency book programs could not be conducted without some degree of approval or involvement of the local government.

Appropriations. The Task Force strongly recommends that the U.S. government appropriate approximately $20 million a year to finance the movement of U.S. books into difficult foreign markets in target countries and that two methods be available: subsidizing carefully selected institutional buyers and using currency convertibility guarantees to facilitate the availability of U.S. books at affordable costs. If there is conflict between this subsidy of the importation of books through grants and a less selective BEF program, the Task Force believes that the grant program more directly would serve the U.S. government's objectives and should prevail. However, there is a potential for using both programs to give the government maximum flexibility to meet the differing obstacles that may exist in different countries and possibly to integrate both programs in a single country, making common use of generated local currency. Furthermore, such an approach might enhance the prospects for congressional acceptance of a BEF program by emphasizing the primary objectives of reducing costs of U.S. books to the foreign buyers and that the BEF program and the grant program are a single two-part financial program for this purpose.

Exchange of Know-how (Topic VII)

The Task Force considers this a subject of considerable importance and sees two needs: (a) to increase American knowledge about overseas publishing, selling, buying, and reading habits and (b) to increase the knowledge of individuals overseas connected with various book activities about American publishing and distribution, with emphasis on the most effective ways to obtain American books.

We believe that all types of private and public sector exchanges must be considered. Special attention should be given to (a) participation by U.S. publishers, distributors, and librarians in professional meetings, seminars, and workshops abroad through both private and public support, including USIA AMPART and ACULSPEC programs; (b) the involving of publishers, editors, translators, authors, booksellers, librarians, and scholars of English and literature in both private and public exchange programs (including internships with publishers and the USIA International Visitors program); (c) education for foreigners in publishing in the U.S. at various institutions, such as universities and publishing houses; and (d) seminars and educational programs for Americans, such as the June program by Columbia University to familiarize participants with the foreign book market potential, funded by the Department of Education.

Recommendations

The Task Force recommends that:

1. USIA should take the lead in coordinating with USAID missions in identifying and selecting qualified middle-level people in publishing and in the book trade to come to the U.S. under International Visitor and participant training programs of the two agencies, both of which should increase sharply the number of book world participants to receive such grants.
2. USIA should select American participants and specialists from the publishing industry and book trade to go abroad as lecturers and seminar participants in order to provide information on American publishing and book selling.
3. USIA, whenever practical, should include on the agenda of its programs international book fairs, seminars, workshops, conferences, discussions, and the like to bring together American and overseas publishers and

book trade representatives to exchange information and know-how on publishing and book selling.

4. USIA, with guidance from the recommended advisory commission, should take the lead in coordinating efforts of all U.S. government agencies that have contributions to make in support of the two-way flow of persons and information, so vital to our book program. Grant mechanisms should be used, where appropriate, with institutions capable of organizing meaningful forums for training and exchange.

Statistics and Data (Topic II)

All evidence points to a serious book gap between the availability of substantive American and Soviet books abroad. The exact magnitude of the problem, however, is clouded by lack of reliable data and statistics.

Statistics essential to ongoing program planning and/or trade and market development are limited and, in themselves, inconclusive. Commerce Department statistics assembled for project researchers are based on required customs declarations for both exports and imports. Some considerations:

— Declarations are required only on book shipments valued at more than $500, albeit the quantity shipped is included as well as destination in compilations from these declarations.

— Statistics do not reflect trade transshipment, thus missing major trade data for Singapore, Hong Kong, London, and the Netherlands, which are locations for overseas branches of major publishers and export companies and/or subsidiary companies.

— Categories for reporting on customs forms are: Bibles and religious literature, dictionaries, thesauri, encyclopedias, textbooks, professional books, children's books, and "books not elsewhere classified."

Professionals believe that total book exports are at least double the declared shipments in both quantity and dollar value, because they believe from their experience that many orders for less than $500 are filled.

Transshipment statistics are necessary to identify the real markets as distinct from the market of customs record. For example, the current Indonesian market is impossible to compare to that of Korea when book exports to the latter are all direct sales, while Indonesian importers buy from Singapore offices as well as directly from U.S. publishers.

Commerce figures, those issued by the AAP each year, and those of the Book Industry Study Group (BISG) are based in part on each other, and none of them address U.S. book exports in the form of translation or English-language reprint rights. In sum, except for some dollar earnings information from subsidiary rights sales in the AAP report that include translation earnings, so little is known about American books available in translation that caution is in order in drawing comparisons relative to the books of other major producing countries.

Recommendations

1. The Commerce Department should convene a meeting of publishing professionals and others in the private sector concerned with U.S. books abroad and government agencies, such as USIA and USAID, to revise the content categories now used on customs reporting forms for export and import reporting so as to include more useful substantive breakdowns, such as social sciences, literature, and arts. Reporting and use groups could then identify problems that arise for subsequent bi-annual meetings.
2. A study group should be formed among publishers, other private sector groups, Commerce, USIA, etc., to identify ways in which statistics on exports under $500 in value might be acceptably estimated, ways in which ultimate destinations of transshipments can be established, and ways in which multinationals producing books in English abroad might provide at least quantitative information on those books of American origin. Funding should be provided by goverment and private institutions to enable such study(ies) on an annual basis.
3. A system should be developed within USIA or in the private sector to record U.S. titles on which rights for English reprints abroad and/or translation have been sold and those titles which are subsequently published. Catalogs of such books by language provide a resource for USIA in its programming and publishing abroad, which can promote sale of such translations to the benefit of U.S. rights holders in terms of enhanced royalties and to the benefit of the foreign publishers. Dollar value could be requested on an aggregate annual basis to maintain competition.
4. The results of these statistical studies should be widely promoted by a private sector institution so as to ensure their availability to newcomers to the international scene. The Reid Foundation established that discussants in publishing not in the international mainstream of publishing were not aware of the existence of those statistics already available nor that such compilations were the result of their customs reports.

Exports and Rights Facilitation (Topic VI)

The Reid Foundation discovered that foreigners trying to find information on buying American books are likely to be frustrated and, indeed, may turn to purchasing books from other nations instead. Traditional publishing and customs of the trade play a large role in this situation. While the books of all publishers in the Soviet Union can be purchased from a single governmental exporter, the American distribution system is fractionalized.

These purchasing problems do not apply as extensively in the case of multinationals with their own overseas sales offices, but a buyer in Nigeria who orders from the United States will have his order passed on to a London office, which may or may not have the titles ordered in stock or, in the best of circumstances, will charge a higher price for the service of providing them from London. In the case of export representatives who contract to handle the overseas sale of the books of specific publishers, service may be fairly reasonable as long as the order is for the books of a represented publisher and the buyer is not ordering from a country or region in which, for business reasons, a publisher may service himself, work directly with an overseas firm, or have one of a variety of other distribution channels.

Such problems are so long-standing they defy early solution, but a start must be made.

Recommendations

1. USIA, Commerce and the industry should develop material on how to buy American books, including institutions, payment requirements, where and how to address orders, etc., and distribute such material widely, the lack of know-how being less prevalent but still significant in the developed world.
2. Commerce and/or USIA should assume responsibility for foreign book market research on a country-by-country and regional basis using expertise of the USIA Regional Book Offices in book matters, as well as the cultural understanding of other USIA officers. The need also to include private sector experience may suggest a nonprofit institutional approach or a combination of government and industry resources.
3. Inwardly oriented promotion of a greater participation by U.S. publishers in direct export sales should be undertaken, as well as through export representatives, wholesalers, export trading companies, etc. Included should be experience with splitting market rights for English-language reprints, as well as other global and regional languages, such as Spanish. An expanded INCINC (Topic I) would play an effective role in the rights stage of market development.

A Book Publishing Program for USIA (Topic IX)

The Task Force unanimously agrees that the role of USIA in the U.S. Books Abroad effort is crucial. This is certainly true when considering substantive titles that responsibly treat foreign policy issues or American society, culture, and values.

Unfortunately, the USIA book and library program has virtually melted away over the past two decades. USIA-supported translations reached a peak year production of 10.2 million volumes in 1965 and then plunged to approximately half a million volumes today. A few decades ago, USIA supported translations into some 57 languages, whereas last year American books were translated into only 14 languages under agency programs. The staff of American book officers and foreign service local personnel dwindled. Only two American book officers were in place overseas in early 1984. Current agency budgets are but a fraction of those two decades ago—in terms of constant dollars, a tragically small fraction. The number of agency libraries and the size and depth of their collections and staffs also have been eroded. Nevertheless, the USIA library system in some 80 countries and its professional staff of Americans and foreign nationals represents a vitally important foundation for rebuilding the neglected book program of the agency. Still, by design and fiscal necessity, the agency came to rely increasingly on forms of communication other than books. Many of these were effective, but none replaced the unique quality of the book.

Meanwhile, other countries studied world communication needs and opportunities and forged ahead with their book programs. The Soviet Union, for instance, increased exports of its books more than 250 percent over the past decade, exporting more than 70 million books in 1982 alone. Today in bookstores and libraries in most countries—and especially in developing countries—Soviet books abound. Students, professionals and other influential citizens have no trouble finding cheap Soviet textbooks and books extolling Communism and Soviet society.

On November 29, 1982, Director Wick identified this serious problem and wisely set the stage for a comeback, announcing a new rationale or policy for USIA book progams, stating:

> Serious American books in English or in translation on themes of concern to USIS are essential to the Agency's mission in public diplomacy. Books have unique qualities enabling them to provide foreigners substantive perceptions and insight into American society and government policies which they can get in no other way.

Director Wick further stated:

> In itself, this rationale calls for no immediate new expenditures, although it provides the conceptual foundation for an expansion of our book programs as funds become available. Certainly, as soon as possible, we hope to amplify these programs to provide support to our posts' cultural and information activities and to compete adequately with other major powers.

Recommendations

1. USIA's overseas book publishing and promotion and library program should be expanded to at least the levels of the 1960s. In constant dollars, the budget exclusively for the book program would be approximately $15 million. A commensurate budget increase would be needed to upgrade library activities and expand the number of libraries by approximately 25%. The Task Force further recognizes that USIA's general promotion of American books circulating through regular chan-

nels of the book trade deserves attention parallel with the carrying out of the agency's own book activities.

2. All categories of book activities identified by the Reid Foundation should be upgraded: translations, English reprints, textbooks (P.L. 480 and dollar funded), English teaching materials, including Ladder Books, and foreign-authored works. Not all are right for all countries at all times. The agency must retain the discretion to determine the mix of programs for specific regions and nations, but certain generalizations are offered:

Books are efficient instruments for both short and long-term impact, although most books make their greatest contribution to public diplomacy in longer-run terms than do journalistic or telecommunication media; all books sponsored through USIA programs must be considered not only in terms of USIA program objectives, but also as to reader-interest in specific nations in order to assure maximum effectiveness.

3. USIA should assure that book-wise staff persons are assigned to the most important posts where book projects will be carried out, especially to those book offices dealing with French, Spanish, Arabic, Chinese, Portuguese, and overseas English language publication programs. Indeed, all USIA personnel in the field should have basic but adequate orientation in the book field. The Task Force supports the various personnel training and orientation approaches identified by the Reid Foundation, including training programs, temporary use of specialists from the industry, and the hiring of specialists for extended periods.
4. Before field posts are fully staffed with personnel skilled in book matters, the agency should arrange for special surveys, calling upon the expertise of specialists from the industry. Such surveys should develop operating plans and budgets, although we emphasize that the surveys must encompass the interests and attitudes of educators and intellectual leaders and other non-governmental specialists, thereby ensuring that the books USIA sponsors will actually get into the hands of readers.
5. Co-publishing, as explained by the Reid Foundation, should be pursued in some circumstances for getting books at lower-than-normal prices into various countries. Possibilities exist for particular titles in Spanish, French, Portuguese, Chinese, Arabic, and English, but this is not an across-the-board panacea and can be difficult for non-specialists to organize.
6. USIA should cooperate closely with those American publishers who have effective experience in developing countries, particularly in regard to co-publishing, since they are practiced already in this technique.
7. USIA may wish to explore the possibility of obtaining overruns of American books for program use. Although a number of problems may be expected, the Task Force believes that effective collaboration between the agency and publishers is possible and well worth the effort.

In addition to the above recommendations, the Task Force has the following comments:

— After full consideration, the Task Force believes this is not the time to recreate Franklin Book Programs which was prominent and effective in past years.

— The Task Force underscores the major contribution that can be made to the concerns of Topic IX by those matters dealt with under Topic III (dissemination of information on the content of U.S. books) and Topic VI (facilitation of acquisition of rights).

— We warn against the danger to the U.S. national interest should there be any effort at ideological change in the content of school textbooks overseas unless U.S. participation is welcomed by the host government. Better that USIA and the private sector increase the availability of quality American textbooks, thereby offering an alternative to those books biased against American society.

— Finally, we support a USIA working philosophy that financial arrangements with foreign (as well as American) publishers should, in general, be structured so as to provide real economic incentive for quality production and distribution. The agency, however, must retain the ability to promote the speedy publication and distribution of titles with limited commercial appeal in the event these are deemed of unusual importance to the national interest.

Operation Through Existing Organizations and/or Establishment of a Nonprofit Book Development Council (Topic X)

The National Security memorandum launching the U.S. Books Abroad effort asked a number of questions. One important query was this:

> Should we establish an International Books Council (or Foundation) as a Title VII entity under the State-USIA Authorization? If so, provisions should be made for public, quasi-public and private programmatic initiatives under this Title.

The NSC memorandum was explicit in pointing to the recent report by Curtis G. Benjamin, *U.S. Books Abroad: Neglected Ambassadors*, as a source of its questions and noting the fact that the Benjamin Report concluded with a recommendation that an international book development council be established. In its subsequent study, the Reid Foundation concluded that "the objectives of the proposed council are quite in harmony with the task presented by the NSC and this study, albeit it is necessary to determine whether existing institutions might not preempt it if the many recommendations made by the Task Force are accepted as responsibilities of particular existing agencies of government or existing industry organizations."

One foundation consulted on this issue is the Asia Foundation, which is experienced in East Asia and the Pacific in obtaining and distributing primarily donated books, as well as setting up seminars bringing together professionals, funding specialists in overseas trips, and supporting the translation and publication of American works by foreign publishers. Another was Freedom House, which is interested in reactivating its 1960s donated book program, and there are several other earlier private initiatives that might be revived, such as the CARE bookshelf, which received free advertising and monetary donations from individuals and groups to ship 20-title collections to institutions abroad.

The Tasks Force has deliberated this question with care, considering such models as the National Endowment for Democracy, the former Government Advisory Committee on Books and Libraries and the U.S. Advisory Commission on Public Diplomacy and believes that a true need does exist for a high-level body to be concerned with the diverse problems and opportunities offered in international book activities and the difficulty in the full exchange of information and coordination of efforts. In a pluralistic and dynamic entrepreneurial society, it is virtually impossible for any single organization to know what other organizations are doing and planning, how this might complement its own activities and what research is available or needed. Although we might wait for adequate individual initiative and cooperation among the many public and private groups involved in books abroad, experience shows this to be a promise unfulfilled. Simply put, this promise is too important to the national interest to be left to chance.

Recommendations

1. A non-partisan organization should be established in the form of a presidential advisory commission, reporting simultaneously to the president and to Congress.
2. This commission should be charged with the responsibility to provide advice in order to enhance collaboration among all U.S. government and private sector international book-related activities and have as major responsibilities recommending innovative book programs and maximizing communication and coordination among public and private organizations.
3. The commission should not have the authority to implement international book programs or to issue grants or funding (other than may be required for appropriate research).
4. The commission should be concerned with the reciprocal flow of books between the United States and other nations.
5. The commission should have U.S. government funding sufficient to provide for an adequate professional staff, member travel, and such matters as research. Commission members should have a demonstrated interest and/or expertise in books.

6. In parallel with the above recommendations, the president should establish a senior interagency group to meet at least bi-annually to assure appropriate government implementation of international book-related activities.
7. Motivated and experienced private and quasi-public organizations dealing with books abroad should be urged to increase and expand their activities as well as volunteering their knowledge and advice to the government. An example mentioned by the Task Force is the possible increase of the geographical scope of the Asia Foundation.

It bears special mention that the Task Force believes we should not establish an organization with authority to initiate or implement international book programs or to give grants or funding to those action organizations. We believe it fully sufficient to provide advice and act as a clearinghouse for information and research, leaving programmatic action to those private and public organizations now involved in books abroad and, perhaps, stimulating new groups to join this important endeavor.

USIA Book Program Content and Title Selection (Topic XI)

Without question, the Task Force urges expanded and improved USIA programs as a major part of the public-private effort to increase the flow of substantive American books abroad. Central to reinvigoraton of USIA's program is the question of content and title selection. This is a vexing subject that has been debated for decades, involving legal, ethical, and programmatic considerations. What is legal? What is ethical? What is most effective? And what is responsive to the NSC initiative?

Currently, USIA believes its book programs must strive for many goals: strengthening foreign understanding and support for U.S. policies and actions, promoting foreign awareness and knowledge of American society, culture, and values, countering hostile attempts to distort or frustrate U.S. objectives and policies, developing exchange programs that will strengthen international understanding, cooperating with private American institutions and interests to increase the quality and reach of the agency, and assisting in the development of a comprehensive policy on the free flow of communication.

The Task Force, in its deliberations, noted the inevitable conflict between public sector and private sector interests in this subject, but concluded that the fundamental question is the basis for selection of titles for the several book programs. It concluded that selection of titles should be based on three basic factors: (1) nature and content of the book; (2) purpose and function of the program; and (3) characteristics of the intended audience.

The Task Force believes the USIA book and library program, in its totality, should include books that reflect the best available works broadly reflecting American life, culture, arts and humanities, education, and science and technology. Sources for selection should be reputable reviewing tools, with some options for local choice. Central direction of the program requires some consistency of selection across the world; however, local needs and interests must be a consideration if the books are to be effective. A strong reference collection in libraries, with fiction and nonfiction works, as well as other materials, should be included.

While Task Force members place considerable emphasis on promoting those titles which strengthen understanding of U.S. policies, the majority of the members also argue for promotion of an even broader title selection than now in practice, to encompass children's literature (and substantive treatment of children's issues) and to place additional stress on science and technology. Science and technology offers a special problem. While USIA should be encouraged to use some of its book and library program resources in selective promotion of science and technology titles, the private sector should be called upon to expand its distribution of these materials, since USIA cannot be expected to meet the widespread worldwide demand. USAID also should be encouraged to increase its efforts to promote distribution of materials in science and technology.

The Task Force strongly believes that books can and must be used to support both short and long-term objectives, although, by their very nature, books generally will provide enforcement to medium to long-term objectives. However, when titles of clear relevance to short-term objectives become available, these deserve special attention and promotion.

Another consideration is the opportunity provided to USIA to build upon the accretion of generations of experience with the openness of access to information that characterizes American society.

Finally, the Task Force considers the problem of personnel as central to this subject, noting the pressing need for a revitalized corps of American book officers and librarians who must direct resurgence of the agency's book and library programs.

Recommendations

1. USIA book and library programs should be designed to reflect broadly the best works that inform and explain American society, culture, and values. Special attention should be given to titles which clearly strengthen foreign understanding of U.S. policies and actions.
2. USIA should make every effort to reinstate a strong corps of American book officers and librarians to guide the revitalization and expansion of the program.
3. USIA should develop effective methods to take into account local needs and interests in order to enhance their effectiveness.

4. USIA should reinstate its children's book programs, including books and programming intended to reflect the child in American culture.

A special concluding comment on this subject: the Task Force appreciates the difficulty at this time of obtaining additional personnel. Nethertheless, there is no way that effective content and title selection can be carried out without the worldwide placement of skilled and knowledgeable book officers and librarians. In addition, USIA must make every effort to improve its orientation and training programs, calling for assistance, where appropriate, from the private sector.

Editors' Note on Task Force Report

The foregoing report and recommendations prepared by the U.S. Books Abroad Task Force are based on the original Reid Foundation study which was comprised of eleven topic papers determined by the Task Force. In editing and expanding that study for publication, the editors converted the original topics to chapters, changed some topic headings, added additional chapters, and reordered the sequence. The following table lists the original topics in the order numbered at the outset of the Reid Foundation research and relates them to current chapters in this book.

Topic Papers Addressed in Task Force Report	*Corresponding Chapters in Reid Study*
Topic I—Copyright Law and the Protection of Intellectual Property	Chapter 3—Same Title
Topic II—Statistics and Data	Chapter 11—Statistics and Data for International Trade
Topic III—Dissemination of Information on the Content of American Books	Chapter 7—Same Title
Topic IV—International Exhibits	Chapter 8—International Book Fairs and Book Exhibits
Topic V—Donated Books and Presentations	Chapter 9—Seeding the Marketplace: Presentations and Donated Books

Topic VI—Export and Rights Facilitation	Chapter 12—Market Research for Export, Reprint, and Translation Rights Facilitation
Topic VII—Exchange of Know-how	Chapter 10—Education for Publishing: At Home and Abroad
Topic VIII—Financial Assistance	Part II—Economics and Finance (Chapters 4–6)
Topic IX—A Book Publishing Program for USIA	Chapter 14—Same Title
Topic X—Operation Through Existing Organizations and/or Establishment of a Nonprofit Book Development Council	Chapter 13—The Role of Private, Public, and Independent Organizations
Topic XI—USIA Book Program Content and Title Selection	Chapter 15—A Matter of Content: Title Selection and the National Interest

The following chapters were added to the published Reid Foundation study for purposes of providing additional information for a more general audience:

Introduction—America's "Neglected Ambassadors"
Chapter 1—The U.S. Book Industry Today
Chapter 2—U.S. Publishing on the International Scene
Chapter 16—International Book Programs of Major World Powers
Chapter 17—American Books Abroad: New Directions and Approaches

Overview and Recommendations of the U.S. Books Abroad Project

Leonard H. Marks

March 29, 1985

Introduction

On January 3, 1983, by S. Con. Res. 59, the Congress of the United States authorized the Librarian of Congress to conduct a "study on the future of the book." In that resolution, Congress noted that "the book is now among the least expensive and most widely accessible means to liberty and learning."

In fulfillment of that mandate, Dr. Daniel J. Boorstin, the Librarian of Congress, submitted a detailed report that recognized that what we do about book and reading in the next decade will have a critical impact upon our way of life.

Although his report dealt primarily with the impact of the printed word upon domestic audiences, the observations apply equally to literate people everywhere.

As an introduction, I thought it would be useful to repeat some of the observations made by the Librarian of Congress since they highlight the importance of providing and distributing books overseas.

The culture of the book has dominated civilization for ages; history is replete with illustrations of how the destiny of nations has been changed by the printed word. This is particularly true in religion and education. Each of our major religions is based upon a book—the Bible, the Koran, or other sacred texts which embody not only theology, but the principles of morality upon which society is based.

Our political life rests on books devoted to law, history, geography, and biography. "Books are the main source of our knowledge, our reservoir of faith, memory, morality, poetry, philosophy, history, and science." Dr. Boorstin points out:

> . . . Never since the discovery of fire and the invention of the wheel has any other innovation had so pervasive and so enduring an influence on ways of thinking, feeling, worshiping, teaching, governing and discovering. The revolution since Gutenberg is without precedent. Its consequences are yet to be seen in much of the world. . . .
>
> . . . It is no accident that people everywhere have considered books sacred and have made them the source and the vehicle of their religious faith. For the power of the book has been uncanny, mysterious, inestimable, overpowering, and infinite, just as the activity of reading has a unique individuality, intimacy, and privacy. . . .
>
> . . . The proverbial convenience, accessibility, and individuality of the book are unrivaled now or by any new technology in sight. The book is independent of outside power sources, and offers unique opportunities for freedom of choice.

> . . . Books are messengers of freedom. They can be hidden under a mattress or smuggled into slave nations.

At the risk of repeating the obvious, it is abundantly clear that the book is a vital instrument of our foreign policy and an eloquent interpreter of our way of life. We must not minimize the impact of the printed word. " . . . The very omnipresence of books leads us to underestimate their power and influence. One measure of their meaning to mankind is the desperate hunger of people in unfree societies to read everything that is not government-authorized pap."

These considerations lead to an obvious question—what are we doing to use the book as a messenger of our ideas and philosophy (outside of the United States)?

Background Data

Domestic expenditures for books rose from $3 billion in 1972 to nearly $9 billion in 1983. The increase has embraced fiction and non-fiction, biography, history, political science, sociology, economics, science, and technology. During this period, the number of new book titles published annually in the U.S. increased from 38,000 in 1972 to 53,000 in 1983—more than 1,000 new titles are published every week of the year. This increase is expected to continue.

But, when the overseas market is examined, we find a different picture.

The U.S. is the world's largest book exporter, but our share of the international market has declined from 26 percent five years ago to 21.8 percent in 1980.[1]

Our 1983 exports were off 5.3 percent from 1982 sales. When these statistics are analyzed, they reveal that 78 percent of our 1983 sales went to only 12 countries (Australia, Canada, Japan, Phillipines and Western Europe)—reflecting dramatically how underdeveloped our trade actually is with Eastern Europe and the Third World.

The U.S.S.R. is not included in international reports of book exports since the Soviets refuse to supply such to the United Nations. However, in 1984, a USIA study, "Soviet Book Exports, 1973–1982," showed that exports of books by the U.S.S.R. in that period *more than doubled*. Here are some of the details for 1982.

- the U.S.S.R. produced 3,951 foreign language titles in 56 non-Soviet languages—for a total of *74.5 million copies*.[2]

---

[1] This year is the most recently available for comparative purposes.

[2] The Soviet statistics do not include the non-commercial distribution of books, the sale of translation rights, co-publishing ventures, or the subsidized production of Soviet books abroad. No statistics are available for these activities, which some industry experts believe to be more important than the programs officially reported. A gauge of this effort is the claim of Kniga that it has 1,000 "trading partners" abroad and that Soviet exports have been increased by an average of 25 percent for each of the past ten years.

- this output consisted of 24.3 million copies in English, 11.6 million in Spanish, 10.9 million in German, and 6.6 million in French.

Now, let's compare the USIA effort.

Unfortunately, the USIA book and library program has virtually melted away in the last 15 years. In 1965—a peak year—USIA-supported translations reached 12.7 million volumes, using 57 languages. Last year, the production was 571,000 volumes translated into 14 languages.[3]

Similarly, the staff of book offices dwindled—only *two* American book offices were in place overseas in 1984. The number of agency librarians and the size and depth of their collections have also eroded. A further statistical comparison of this alarming disparity: while the Soviet export book publishing firm (Mezhdunarodnaiar Kniga) was displaying its wares at 1,500 events in 1982, U.S. books were displayed at less than 100 book fairs, none of which were international book events.

An examination of the book publishing efforts of European countries is also revealing.

The United Kingdom leads the West in promoting its publishing industry overseas. For many years, the British have supported the premise that "trade follows the book" and that where books go, exports will follow. In a recent report, the British Council, a quasi-public institution with a Royal Charter, celebrated its 50th anniversary in June, 1984, by reporting:

1. The sale of 1.5 million low-priced textbooks in 78 developing countries through subsidized publication exports.
2. The purchase of $5 million worth of books from U.K. publishers which were used to stock libraries in developing countries in support of U.K. programs.
3. Publication of *British Books News*, a monthly book review magazine that reviews more than 1,000 titles for the foreign book world.

As a final comparison, the efforts of a smaller nation, Spain, are significant. The Instituto Nacional del Libro Espanol in Madrid (INLE) broadly promotes Spanish books throughout the world with funding of book exhibits, provision of export insurance to the publishers, sponsorship of seminars and meetings in the book community, and a variety of other encouragements to book distribution. INLE also produces the basic reference works of the Spanish book world such as *Libros Españoles en Venta: ISBN* (Books in Print), and *El Libro Español* (The Spanish Book). Concerned that currency shortages might keep Latin Americans away from the Barcelona International Book Fair in September, 1984, INLE funded delegates to the Fair from almost all Spanish-speaking countries.

---

[3] This figure refers only to books distributed abroad with USIA assistance.

The NSC Directive

Based upon these and similar reports the National Security Council, in a memorandum of April 15, 1984, decided that the time had come for a review in depth of the U.S. book programs abroad. After listing specific questions, the National Security Council Directive stated:

> The book gap is serious. It is solvable by a national commitment. We are prepared to make that commitment.

The NSC requested that the USIA commence a comprehensive study addressing the need and the respective roles of the various private, public, and quasi-public sectors concerned with this issue and present a comprehensive package for legislative and administrative action.[4]

In response in June, 1984, you requested the USIA Book Advisory Committee to undertake a review in depth of these issues and, at the same time, you appointed me as a consultant to work with the Task Force and to prepare recommendations for further action.

Since that time, both the Task Force and I have worked in close cooperation with the Helen Dwight Reid Educational Foundation to prepare background information on the economics of book publishing and the distribution process abroad, the prior experiences of the industry and an assessment of the current problems. To this end, the policy background papers have been prepared and are attached as Appendix 2, together with the Task Force Report, Appendix 3. (Editors' Note: In this book, these two reports *precede* this commentary by Mr. Marks.)

The Problems

The Task Force Report identifies several aspects of the book export problem and recommends specific remedies.

Essentially, it is clear that the U.S. book publishing industry has been handicapped in exporting U.S. titles because:

1. Potential buyers are unable to pay in U.S. dollars due to governmental restrictions imposed upon them by central banks and by the lack of dollar exchange available to these countries;
2. The high costs of U.S. books are in competition with the subsidized importation for their countries, principally the U.S.S.R.; and
3. The normal promotion and sales efforts have lagged or been abandoned because the prospects for sales are dim due to the conditions described above.

These obstacles can be overcome.

---

[4] The text of this directive, NSCD-130, is attached as Appendix 1.

The Currency Convertibility Problem

The Task Force describes this problem graphically:

> The lack of dollars with which to pay for their book orders and translation-reprint rights has brought much of the developing world's book trade with the United States almost to a halt. Currency is a problem in most countries of Latin America, Eastern Europe, and parts of Africa and Asia. For the first time in current memory, even Gulf oil states have discussed, if not promulgated, rulings on the dollars available for various commodity imports.
>
> From the standpoint of the end user of an American book, a critical problem is price, for American books—like many other commodities—are becoming more expensive, and are among some of the most expensive books in the world. Where transshipment points are involved, prices are marked up by the publisher's own branch offices through which the order is fulfilled, since the branch must pay for incoming freight, storage and order fulfillment facilities.

This problem must be solved at the earliest possible date. To that end, *I recommend that the USIA establish a currency convertibility program to carry out this objective.*

No new legislation is required since Congress has previously supported this concept in the Information Media Guarantee (IMG) program, which was abandoned in 1968 because Congress had no control over the amounts spent for the convertibility of foreign currencies. That serious defect can be remedied by having the congressional appropriation specify:

> The USIA may expend not more than $__________ for the purchase of local currencies from book publishers who have received approval from the USIA for the distribution of books sold in countries specified by the USIA and for titles approved by the USIA in furtherance of the national interest of the U.S. The director of the USIA shall annually report to the Congress the amounts expended for this program with an explanation of the objectives achieved.

This effort can be successful only if (1) the host country approves and welcomes the importation of English language books; (2) established channels of distribution are employed, e.g., book publishers in the country or other book distribution outlets. If there are none, then the USIA might consider the opening of a book store where not only U.S. books, but radio tapes, records, and art are sold. In the past, book stores have been established in a few countries, some with considerable success; (3) proper promotion and publicity is given by USIA offices in the country.

A budget should be established for this exploitation by the publishers and the USIA, so that the effort will attract maximum support.

Because of the urgency, these innovations should be made in FY 1986 using such funds as may be available in the current appropriations bills. However, for the succeeding years, a much larger appropriation will be required if the U.S. is to regain its place in the international book world. To this end, other governmental agencies should be made aware of the need. The Task Force highlights this problem with the recommendation that:

> . . . The main thrust of the NSC memorandum be transformed into a Presidential Directive to relevant departments and agencies instructing them to adapt their programs, funds, and other resources to the extent consistent with their other responsibilities, to accommodate the U.S. Books Abroad objectives.
>
> This step is necessary in view of the cross-cutting nature of the challenge in promoting the increased flow of substantive American books abroad. It is particularly important in order to stimulate the development of financial assistance programs through USAID, the Departments of Commerce, Agriculture, Treasury and other agencies.

I endorse this suggestion and am attaching a proposed directive to accomplish this result, Appendix 4. (Editors' Note: Not available for reproduction at time of publication of this book.)

Lowering the Cost of Books

As previously noted, even when dollar exchange is available, U.S. titles are at a competitive disadvantage because of the high cost. The Task Force states:

> Nevertheless, the student overseas examining an American book at the shop of his local bookseller will find prices equivalent to double or more the original retail price in the U.S. The solution usually is purchase of a few copies (if at all) by a university library or the selection by the faculty of another text—often an English-language text—from the U.S.S.R.

This procedure will enable Congress to keep control over the funds and satisfy the private sector problem of selling in Eastern Europe and the Third World which today are foreclosed because of the currency limitation.

The Task Force recommends a new currency convertibility program—Book Export Financing (BEF)—to distinguish it as much as possible from programs of the past. I endorse this concept but do not believe that you should wait for Congress to pass new legislation to inaugurate the effort. The time to act is *now*—there is an urgency which must be addressed. The U.S. cannot sit by and allow the export market for U.S. books to disintegrate further.

The BEF program outlined by the Task Force has many attractive features which can be incorporated into a program now rather than when and if Congress acts. Such features listed below can be put into effect by you by internal administrative regulations. Specifically, I would make the recommendations listed below.

1. The guarantee program should be administered to the extent possible to create an incentive for U.S. publishers and exporters to lower U.S. costs. To this end, preferential treatment might be given to low-cost products.

2. Priority should be given:
   a. to finance local distribution of the imported books;
   b. to finance local currency costs for acquiring rights of eligible U.S. titles;
   c. to finance indigenous publishing of U.S. titles; and
   d. to meet the expenditures of other USIA book programs, such as libraries, translation, and exhibits.
3. The foreign government should be encouraged to make available matching dollar exchange to import U.S. books.
4. Local currency generated by convertibility guarantee payments should be made available by a bilateral agreement to book programs designated by the U.S. government and approved by the importing government.
5. All titles would be eligible, except for specifically excluded categories, drawing on past experience to define the exclusions.

Although these measures require no congressional action, I would recommend prior consultation with the House and Senate committees. They should welcome these restraints on the IMG procedures and the return to Congress of the appropriation authority.

> Donated books can supplement and enhance purchased presentations of books, but they cannot and should not be thought to replace them. Indeed, free distribution of U.S. books reaches prospective buyers and they encourage and facilitate the study of English.

Not all books available for donations will be useful in the overseas market, and caution must be observed to avoid shipping books that will have no appeal to the interested audience.

Participation by the Private Sector

Several private organizations have had extensive experience in distributing books abroad, particularly the Asia Foundation and Freedom House. Their expertise can prove valuable in enlarging the scope of the program and should be sought by the USIA staff in expanding the effort.

Similarly, American foundations have demonstrated their support for a book program. For example, the Andrew W. Mellon Foundation recently announced a $500,000 program of matching grants to enable public libraries in the U.S. to acquire 60-volume sets of the *Libraries of America*. The nonprofit *Libraries of America* publishes the collected works of America's major writers such as Herman Melville, Nathaniel Hawthorne, Walt Whitman, and Harriet Beecher Stowe. It was given the National Book Critics Circle Award in recognition of its "distinguished contribution to the enhancement of American literary and critical standards."

This or similar collections could be underwritten by nonprofit organizations and contributed to libraries throughout the Third World and in Eastern Europe as representative of American literature.

These authors have achieved worldwide recognition and are well-known to students everywhere. The wider distribution of their books would be a valuable addition to this project.

In this connection, we must not overlook the importance of distributing American books to Eastern Europe and the Soviet Union. Although those countries impose rigid restrictions on the importation, every opportunity should be explored for dissemination of this material either within the country or from outside. Mail received by the Voice of America and RFE/RL discloses a keen interest on the part of Eastern Europeans and Soviet citizens for more information about U.S. political and social institutions, our novelists and poets, and, particularly, contemporary arts. USIS posts are aware of the significance of this audience and should be encouraged to meet this demand.

In evaluating this problem, we must be mindful that the U.S.S.R. and other countries subsidize their books and in many countries distribute them without charge. Although the USIA has also made token grants to selected institutions, it has not been extensive.

It is my feeling that the student who purchases a book values it much more than one received as a gift. *To this end, I would not endorse a major "give away" program, but, instead, urge that the price in the local market be lowered*, either by:

1. a government subsidy to U.S. book publishers so that the retail price will be competitive with other suppliers; or
2. co-publishing by U.S. publishers with local counterparts in specific countries where production costs are lower than the U.S.

To illustrate the importance of co-publishing, one example should be impressive. I have been informed by the U.S. Ambassador to India that an American textbook costs $20–30, the equivalent of a week's salary for a university teacher. Obviously, American textbooks are not being sold in quantity to this important segment of the population. However, an Indian publisher can reprint the book for $3–4, including paying for the copyright. During the 1960s, when USIS reprinted in India over 1,800 editions, 8.2 million copies were published by Indian publishers using USIS seed money such as I am suggesting here.

If the reprint procedure is followed, it would appear that for $100,000, we could subsidize the sales in India of approximately 120,000 copies of 40 American textbooks. This calculation assumes a payment of a normal royalty to the U.S. publishers. Any reduction in this payment would, of course, increase the leverage. As part of this program, consideration should be given to resuming the Ladder Book Series that involves the editing of classic American books in simplified fashion for foreign audiences. Previous experience with this series has demonstrated its great value and universal appeal.

I strongly urge that you adopt a program using existing USIS appropriations for co-publishing ventures such as described. The possibilities are explored in detail in the Task Force report.

Donated Books

The Task Force notes:

> Private donations of books, privately solicited and assembled and privately shipped abroad, have long been widely accepted as demonstrative overseas of the American traits of generosity, neighborliness, and volunteerism.

Since shipping costs are an important element in the distribution of donated books, the Task Force recommends:

> USIA, USAID, and other public agencies should provide funding for handling and shipping costs to nonprofit organizations engaged in distribution of donated books abroad, taking into account quality, quantity, and the U.S. national interest. Local need and choice are of paramount importance in the development of this program.
>
> USIA, USAID, and nonprofit institutions donating books abroad should explore the availability of low or no-cost shipping services for both domestic and international transportation.

Both recommendations are necessary to the success of this effort. At the same time, *there should be consultation with the Internal Revenue Service to broaden the deductibility to the publishers of the donated books*. The very restrictive interpretation which now prevails has discouraged potential donors.

Promotional Efforts

It is well recognized that there is an American genius for the promotion and sale of consumer products. We know how to advertise our wares. Yet, in the book publishing field, we have fallen behind:

> Opportunities abound for displaying American books in many countries, including developing countries. International and national book fairs have been organized and are held annually (for the most part) in Algeria, Argentina, Bahrain, Brazil, India, Iraq, Kuwait, Mexico, Nigeria, Poland, Senegal, Singapore, and Yugoslavia.
>
> American publishers, even those who regularly participate in major events such as Frankfurt, do not give sufficient priority to the less widely promoted book fairs, especially those of the Third World, such as Buenos Aires, Cairo, Jerusalem, and Mexico, nor do they attach importance to meetings of academic and professional associations around the world. Smaller noncommercial publishers, such as the American Enterprise Institute, Brookings, the Foreign Policy Association, Heritage Foundation, and Heldref—many with lists rich in serious works of American culture and policies—cannot afford to participate.

The Task Force addresses this concern and urges that there be the broadest participation in more book fairs. Where it is uneconomical for publishers to display their wares, the USIA or Department of Commerce should provide assistance grants to "show the flag" and in the process "sell the book."

Following a period of neglect, recently the USIA participated in major book fairs at Frankfurt, Cairo, Calcutta, and other cities. This is a step in the right direction.

It is axiomatic that the prospective buyer should know what the U.S. has to sell—which titles are available and how to order them. For this purpose, at one time the USIA published *American Book Review*, which carried content reviews of new and current American and foreign-authored books on agency-related themes. The U.K. relies upon *British Book News,* produced for the British Council by the U.K. publisher and book export firm, B.H. Blackwell's. It has paid subscriptions and publisher advertising which enables it to be almost self-sufficient. The standard bibliographic tools such as *Books in Print, Publishers' Weekly* and book review publications, such as *Booklist, Choice, Library Journal,* and book review sections of major American newspapers, including the *N.Y. Times Book Review Section, New York Review of Books*, and the *Washington Post Book World*, are also vehicles for this purpose. These sales tools need to be revived if our dormant overseas market is to be awakened.

USIA Libraries

This report would be seriously deficient without a recognition of the value of USIA libraries.

In 1965, the agency operated 254 overseas libraries and reading rooms. Today, there are 131.

In my experience, these libraries are our best showrooms for American ideas. They open up the minds of foreign students to American ideas, aspirations and policies. In addition, they open up windows of opportunity for American business.

I have visited these libraries in all parts of the world. Invariably, they are crowded, and the books and magazines are well thumbed. They are a splendid investment and a wonderful showcase for American thinking and for the display of the newest books in science and technology, for the innovations in drama and the arts and certainly for our views on democracy and human rights. *For these reasons, consideration should be given to opening new libraries where needed with trained librarians and staff.*

The Task Force report contains observations and recommendations on related topics that should be considered in enlarging the scope of an overseas book program. I endorse the general objectives and urge careful consideration of the specific suggestions. To carry out the program, the Task Force believes that:

> . . . A true need does exist for a high-level body to be concerned with the diverse problems and opportunities offered in international book activities and the difficulty in the full exchange of information and coordination of efforts.

> In parallel with the above recommendations, the president should establish a senior interagency group to meet at least bi-annually to assure appropriate government implementation of international book-related activities.

The Task Force also proposes the creation of a presidentially appointed Advisory Commission to initiate or implement international book programs. *I concur in the objective, but do not believe that it is necessary to create a new body.* A new committee would overlap with the U.S. Book and Library Advisory Committee and the USIA Advisory Commission on Public Diplomacy, a presidentially appointed body. In the past, both have been concerned with the book program. The Book and Library Advisory Committee has just completed the excellent Task Force report on which this report is based and the USIA Advisory Commission in its 1985 report devotes a chapter to these questions (pages 39–40). I believe that in the future both are capable of fulfilling the mandate outlined and that it is not necessary to create a new body.

Conclusion

It is undeniable that our national security requires military preparedness. To that end, we seek the most advanced technology in tanks, guns, planes, and missiles.

Similarly, it is also undeniable that our national security dictates that people throughout the world understand our ideals, our national objectives, and our cultural heritage. To that end, we must use all "weapons" available to us in the "war of ideas."

For several centuries, books have been a staple in the arsenal of ideas, "for the power of the book has been uncanny, mysterious, inestimable, overpowering and infinite. . . . The activity of reading has a unique individuality, intimacy, and privacy. . . . "

The time to act is now. The need is great. Our arsenal of ideas overflows with a storehouse of books of great American authors. We must not hoard this treasure.

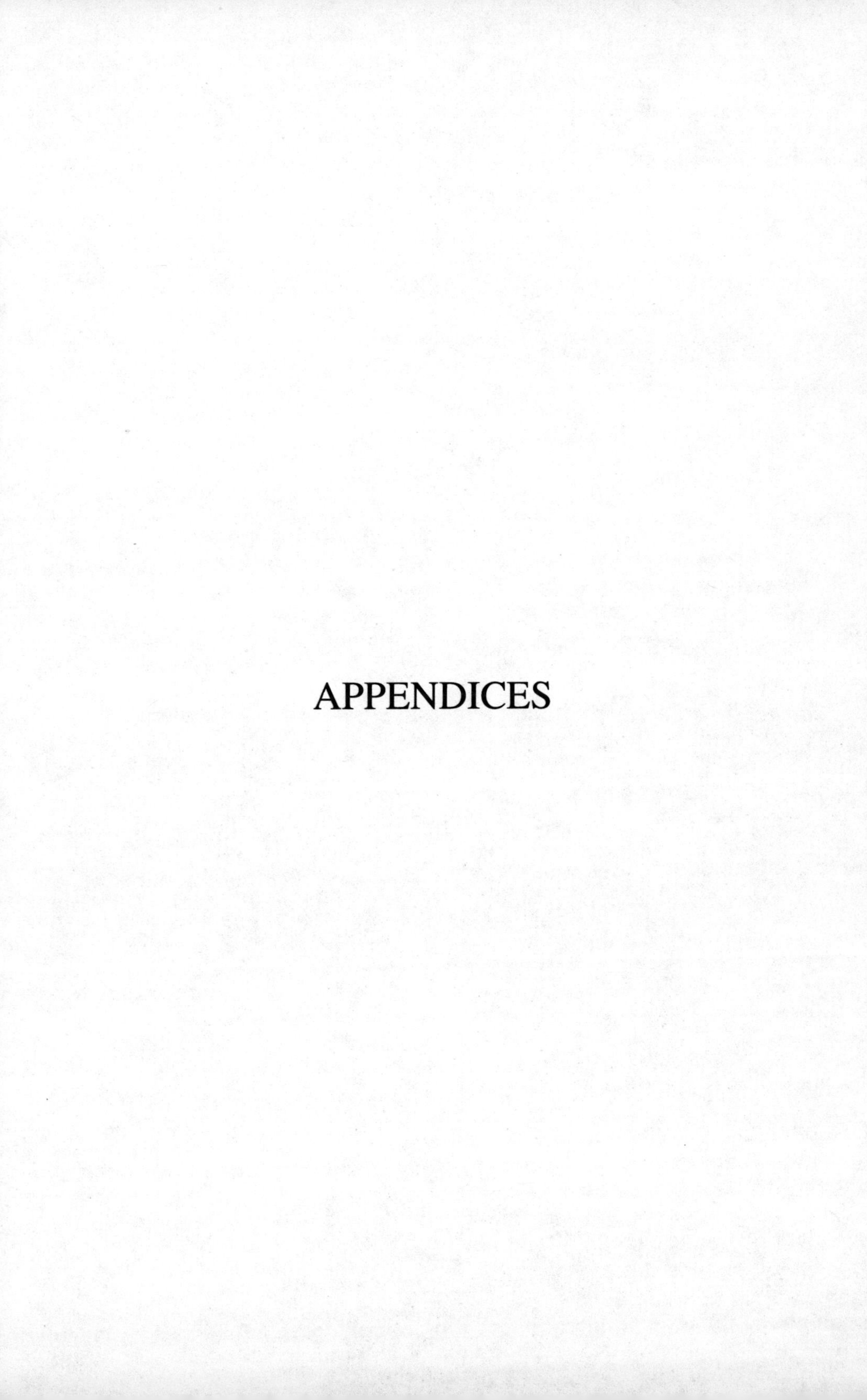

APPENDICES

Appendix 1

THE WHITE HOUSE
WASHINGTON

April 4, 1984

MEMORANDUM FOR THE HONORABLE CHARLES Z. WICK
Director, U.S. Information Agency[1]

SUBJECT: U.S. Books Abroad

The time is right for a major new commitment to the provision of U.S. books abroad. A distinguished American publisher has written that "The American book abroad is in the vanguard of all our battles to improve our nation's present position and its future relations with all countries of the world." The power of ideas has been projected through the written word. Whether we are dealing with the "war of ideas" or looking at the problem in terms of fostering the "infrastructure of democracy"—twin goals eloquently stated by the President in London on June 1982 (sic)—we must compete. Statistics have graphically demonstrated, in Curtis Benjamin's book, "U.S. Books Abroad: Neglected Ambassadors," that the United States has virtually unilaterally disarmed in this field. One simple statistic bears repeating: In 1983 the Soviet Union produced 83,000,000 highly-subsidized books for export overseas. In the same year, USIA brought out 581,000 volumes in its publishing and translation program.

The problem is not simply the weakness of current federal programs. Donation programs by private American publishers have been reduced. Funds

[1] National Security Council Directive No. 130.

handled by quasi-public/private organizations have been cut back. We need to renovate our total approach. The Benjamin study, The Asia Foundation, and the President's Advisory Commission on Public Diplomacy have all spoken forcefully about the problem. What is required now is a sharply-focused report to develop a coherent strategy for the long-term. This effort would best be undertaken by the establishment of a Task Force whose composition draws upon US Government expertise, the publishing sector, the academic world, and the experience of those quasi-public groups such as The Asia Foundation. The study should review a number of related issues, several of which are defined below:

— What should be the size and thrust of a USIA program?
— How much translation? What pattern of distribution?
— How can we best utilize the expertise and professionalism of existing organizations, such as The Asia Foundation, the Inter-American Foundation, and other groups to develop private distribution programs. We should build upon existing capabilities and experience whenever possible.
— How can we stimulate more direct involvement of the American publishing industry?
— What legislative and tax amelioration would be appropriate?
— What type of book selection process is appropriate?
— What international conditions prevail? Are programs better managed by official US involvement or by a non-government organization?
— Can we develop a book distribution program to reach totalitarian states, particularly the USSR and East Europe?
— Should we establish an International Book Council (or Foundation) as a Title VII entity under the State-USIA Authorization? If so, provisions should be made for public, quasi-public and private programmatic initiatives under this Title.

The "book gap" is serious. It is solvable by national commitment. We are prepared to make that commitment. I request that USIA: (1) take the lead in commissioning a comprehensive study which addresses the need and the respective roles of the private, quasi-public and public elements sectors concerned with this issue; and (2) present a comprehensive package for legislative and administrative action. I have in mind a commissioned study by an independent structure in much the same fashion as the American Political Foundation was asked to undertake the Democracy Study Project which led to the legislative package creating the National Endowment for Democracy. It would appear to be within USIA's charter to fund the Task Force/Commission. Two organizations worth consideration to undertake the study would be the National Endowment for Democracy and the Ad Hoc Advisory Committee of the Center for the Book (Library of Congress).

These organizations clearly have a role to play as does the President's Advisory Commission on Public Diplomacy and the quasi-public sector. The

Asia Foundation, for example, has done pioneer work in this field. Lastly, I would strongly urge that there be congressional representation on the Task Force. This is an issue with genuine bipartisan support and it would be best to start out with strong Congressional support for an initiative which will presumably have legislative and budgetary ramifications.

The study group should be formed immediately and I would like to see the study completed by 1 July with precise recommendations for budget, legislative actions and organization. In addition, a timetable for implementing actions should be included. I would request that USIA work the action in conjunction with the IIC.

Robert C. McFarlane

Appendix 2

U.S. Books Abroad Task Force Membership

Chairman:
Paul E. Feffer, President,
Feffer & Simons, Inc.

Leo N. Albert,
Chairman of the Board,
Prentice-Hall International, Inc.

Toni C. Bearman,
Executive Director,
National Commission on Libraries and Information Science

Simon M. Bessie,
Harper & Row Publishers, Inc.

Nazir A. Bhagat
Department of Commerce

Guy S. Brown
U.S. Information Agency

Maury Brown
Agency for International Development

Richard Bye, President,
Publishers Association of Southern California

Allen Choate, Vice President,
The Asia Foundation

John Y. Cole, Executive Director,
Center for the Book

Richard D'Azino
Department of the Treasury

Lewis S. Flacks
Copyright Office

Erwin A. Glikes,
President and Publisher,
The Free Press

Dorothy Gray
National Commission on Libraries and Information Science

Lois Spice Haig
National Council of Teachers of English

Townsend Hoopes, President,
Association of American Publishers

Robert Jordan
Overseas Private Investment Corporation

Dan Lacy
McGraw-Hill, Inc.

William S. Lofquist
Department of Commerce

James E. Lyons, Vice President,
University Press of America

Susan A. Mango
National Endowment for the Humanities

Anne Mathews
Graduate School of Librarianship and Information Management,
University of Denver

David McIntosh
Gunster, Yoakley, Criser & Stewart

Maurice Mitchell, Director,
Annenberg School of Communications

Carol A. Nemeyer,
Associate Librarian,
Library of Congress

Ralph G. Newman
Ralph Geoffrey Newman, Inc.

Fred Philipp,
Vice President (Retired),
Baker & Taylor Co.

Morris Philipson, Director,
University of Chicago Press

Steuart Pittman, Esq.
Shaw, Pittman, Potts & Trowbridge

Yale Richmond
National Endowment for Democracy

John S. Robling, Vice President,
Encyclopaedia Britannica, Inc.

Doyle Rogers
Alley, Maas, Rogers, Lindsay & Chauncey

Arthur Rosenthal, Director,
Harvard University Press

John T. Sargent,
Chairman of the Board,
Doubleday & Co., Inc.

Charles Scribner, Jr.,
Chairman of the Board,
Scribner Book Companies, Inc.

Datus C. Smith, Jr.
U.S. Committee for UNICEF

Lawrence M. Stone,
Vice President,
Thomas Nelson Publishers

Leonard Sussman, Director,
Freedom House

Deborah Szekely, President,
Inter-American Foundation

Mae Sue Talley
National Air and Space Administration

Theodore Waller, President,
Waller & Associates

Robert Wedgeworth,
Executive Director,
American Library Association

Hayden Williams, President,
The Asia Foundation

Observers

Max Celnick, President,
Max Celnick, Inc.

Edward Malinoski, President,
U.S.A. Book Expo

Richard Schmidt
Cohen & Marks

Reid Foundation Study Group

Evron M. Kirkpatrick, President
William M. Childs, Project Director
Donald E. McNeil
Howard R. Penniman
Cornelius W. Vahle, Jr.

U.S. Information Agency Advisers

Ronald L. Trowbridge, Associate Director
Howard Hardy
Robert O. Jones
Jerry L. Prillaman
Pamela K. Roe
Louise Wheeler

Consultant/Rapporteur

Richard D. Moore

Editorial Assistant

Cynthia M. Banks

Appendix 3

Restatement of USIA Mission[1]

The United States Information Agency (USIA) . . . an agency of the executive branch of the U.S. Government with headquarters in Washington, D.C., came into being in its present form on April 1, 1978. Its director reports to the President of the United States and receives policy guidance from the Secretary of State. The agency maintains 214 posts in 129 countries. Its director, deputy director, and four associate directors (Broadcasting, Educational and Cultural Affairs, Programs, Management) are appointed by the President and are subject to confirmation by the Senate. The director of the U.S. Information Agency is Charles Z. Wick. Overseas, USIA is known as USIS, the U.S. Information Service.

MISSION: The purposes of the U.S. Information Agency are to:

1. Strengthen foreign understanding and support for United States policies and actions;
2. Promote foreign awareness and knowledge of American society, culture and values so that other nations can better understand our policies and objectives;
3. Advise the President, the Secretary of State, members of the National Security Council and other key officials on the implications of foreign opinion for present and contemplated United States policies;
4. Counter hostile attempts to distort or frustrate the objectives and policies of the United States;
5. Develop and administer exchange programs which will strengthen international understanding, foster world peace, and further the national interest of the United States;
6. Cooperate with private American institutions and interests to increase the quality and reach of the United States Information Agency;
7. Assist in the development of a comprehensive policy on the free flow of information and international communication; and
8. Conduct negotiations on informational, educational and cultural exchanges with other governments.

[1] Reprinted from the "U.S. Information Agency Fact Sheet" issued June, 1985)

Appendix 4

Education for Publishing[1]

American Management Associations, New York, NY
American University, Washington, DC
Annenberg School of Communications, Washington, DC
Arkansas State University, College of Communication, Jonesboro
Association of American Publishers, Inc., New York, NY
Association of the Graphic Arts, New York, NY
Boston Center for Adult Education, MA
Boston College, Newton, MA
Boston University, MA
Cabrini College, Radnor, PA
California College of Arts and Crafts, Oakland
California Polytechnic State University, San Luis Obispo
California Publishing Institute, Berkeley
Case Western Reserve University, Cleveland, OH
Center for Book Arts, New York, NY
City University of New York, City College,
    Education in Publishing Program, NY
City University of New York, Graduate Center, NY
City University of New York, Hunter College, NY
City University of New York, Queens College, Flushing, NY
Coalition of Publishers for Employment, New York, NY
College of William and Mary, Williamsburg, VA
Columbia University, New York, NY
Council for Advancement and Support of Education, Washington, DC
Culver-Stockton College, Canton, MO
C.W. Post Center for Long Island University, Greenvale, NY
Douglis Visual Workshops, Swarthmore, PA
Drake University, Des Moines, IA
Dynamic Graphics Educational Foundation, Peoria, IL
Eckerd College, St. Petersburg, FL
Edinboro State College, PA
Editorial Experts, Inc., Alexandria, VA

[1] Copyright © 1985 Lois Spice Haig. All institutions and organizations listed here have engaged in some degree of education for publishing in recent years.

Fairfield University, CT
Florida State University, Tallahassee
Fordham University, Bronx, NY
Franklin and Marshall College, Lancaster, PA
Georgetown University, Washington, DC
George Washington University, Publication Specialist Program, Washington, DC
Graphic Arts Association, Graphic Arts Education Center, Philadelphia, PA
Hofstra University, The Publishing Studies Program, Hempstead, NY
Howard University Press Book Publishing Institute, Washington, DC
Jersey City State College, NJ
Johns Hopkins University, Baltimore, MD
Kent State University, Kent, OH
L/A House Seminars, Los Angeles, CA
La Roche College, Pittsburgh, PA
La Salle College, Philadelphia, PA
Lehigh University, Bethlehem, PA
Loyola University, Chicago, IL
Massachusetts Institute of Technology, Cambridge, MA
Miami University, Oxford, OH
National Composition Association, Arlington, VA
New School for Social Research, New York, NY
New York City Technical College, NY
New York Institute of Technology, Old Westbury, NY
New York University Book and Magazine Publishing Institute, NY
New York University, Center for Publishing, NY
New York University, Gallatin Division, NY
New York University School of Continuing Education, NY
North Carolina State University, Raleigh, NC
Northeastern University, Center for Continuing Education, Graphics Arts Program, Dedham, MA
Northern Arizona University, Flagstaff, AZ
Northern Michigan University, Marquette, MI
Ohio University, Athens, OH
Pace University, New York, NY
Pacific Lutheran University, Tacoma, WA
Parsons School of Design, New York, NY
Performance Seminar Group, Norwalk, CT
Philadelphia College of Art, PA
Printing Industries of America, Arlington, VA
Publishers Association of Southern California, Manhattan Beach, CA
Radcliffe College/Harvard University, Radcliffe Publishing Procedures Course, Cambridge, MA

Ragan Report Workshops, Chicago, IL
Rene Gnam Consultation Corp., Holiday, FL
Rensselaer Polytechnic Institute, Troy, NY
Rice University, The Rice Publishing Program, Houston, TX
Rochester Institute of Technology, School of Printing, NY
Sarah Lawrence College, Bronxville, NY
School of the Ozarks, Point Lookout, MO
School of Visual Arts, New York, NY
Simmons College, Boston, MA
Smithsonian Institution, Smithsonian Resident Associate Program, Washington, DC
Smith College, Northampton, MA
Society for Scholarly Publishing, Washington, DC
Southern Illinois University at Carbondale
Spring Hill College, Mobile, AL
Stanford University, Stanford Alumni Association, Stanford Publishing Course, CA
State University of New York at Albany
State University of New York at Buffalo
Syracuse University, NY
Temple University, Philadelphia, PA
Texas Woman's University, Denton
United States Department of Agriculture, The Graduate School, Washington, DC
University of Alabama, University
University of Arizona, Tucson
University of California, Certificate Program in Publishing, Berkeley
University of California, Davis
University of California, Irvine
University of California, Santa Cruz
University of Chicago, Office of Continuing Education, Publishing Program, IL
University of Connecticut, Storrs
University of Denver, Graduate School of Librarianship, Publishing Institute, CO
University of Illinois, College of Communication, Urbana-Champaign
University of Illinois, Graduate School of Library and Information Science, Urbana-Champaign
University of Maryland, College Park
University of Iowa, Iowa City
University of Kansas, Lawrence
University of Nebraska at Omaha
University of North Carolina at Chapel Hill

University of Notre Dame, IN
University of Oregon, Eugene
University of Pittsburgh, PA
University of South Florida, Tampa, FL
University of Southern California, Los Angeles
University of Tennessee at Knoxville
University of Tulsa, OK
University of Utah, Salt Lake City
University of Wisconsin, Extension Communication Program, Madison
Vermont College, MFA Writing Program, Montpelier
Warren Wilson College, MFA Program for Writers, Swannanoa, NC
Washington University, The Writers' Program, St. Louis, MO
Western Michigan University, Kalamazoo, MI
Western Wisconsin Technical Institute, La Crosse, WI
Wichita State University, KS
Wofford College, Spartanburg, SC
Writer's Center, Bethesda, MD
Writers Community, New York, NY
Writer's Digest School, Cincinnati, OH

Appendix 5

Professional Publishing Associations[1]

Agricultural Communicators in Education
Agricultural Publishers Association (1915)
American Book Producers Association (1980)
American Booksellers Association (1900)
American Business Communication Association
American Jewish Press Association (1943)
American Library Association (1876)
American Medical Publishers' Association (1961)
American Printing History Association
American Society for Information Science (1937)
American Translators Association
Association for Educational Communication and Technology
Association of American Publishers (1970)
Association of American University Presses (1937)
Association of Book Travelers (1883)
Association of Jewish Book Publishers (1962)
Association of North American Directory Publishers (1898)
Association of (Spanish) Christian Publishers and Booksellers (1982)
Baltimore Publishers Association (1981)
Bibliographical Society of America
Book Industry Study Group (1976)
Bookbuilders of Boston
Bookbuilders West
Book Industry Systems Advisory Committee
Book Manufacturers Institute (1920)
Books for the People Fund (1961)
Catholic Press Association (1912)
Center for Book Arts (1974)
Center for Book Research (1983)
Center for the Book (1977)

---

[1] Copyright © 1985 Lois Spice Haig. Only those organizations immediately representative of book publishing and international concerns in this area are excerpted from the author's much larger planned directory that includes writing, graphic arts, etc. Founding dates given where known.

Chicago Book Clinic (1936)
Chicago Women in Publishing
Children's Book Council (1945)
Children's Literature Association (1972)
Christian Booksellers Association (1950)
Club of Printing Women in New York (1930)
Connecticut Book Publishers Association
Copyright Society of the U.S.A. (1953)
Council of Communication Societies
Council on Interracial Books for Children (1965)
Educational Paperback Association (1975)
Educational Press Association of America (1895)
Evangelical Christian Publishers Association (1974)
Graphic Arts Technical Foundation (1924)
Graphic Communications Association (1970)
Gravure Research Institute (1947)
Gravure Technical Association (1949)
Guild of Book Workers (1906)
Independent Publishers Association
Independent Publishers League
International Association of Scholarly Publishers (1972)
International Booksellers Federation (1956)
International Board on Books for Young People (1953)
International Communication Association
International Periodical Distributors Association (1972)
International Reading Association
International Standard Book Numbering (ISBN) Agency
International Typographical Union (1852)
JWB Jewish Book Council (1942)
Livestock Publications Council (1974)
Magazine and Paperback Marketing Institute (1946)
Manhattan Publishing Group (1979)
Minnesota Book Publishers Roundtable
Music Publishers Association of the United States (1895)
National Association of Book Manufacturers (1977)
National Association of Publishers' Representatives (1950)
National Composition Association (1961)
National Information Standards Organization (1939)
National Music Publishers Association (1917)
New Mexico Book League
New York Publishers Rights and Permissions Group (1960)
Periodical and Book Association of America (1965)
Philadelphia Book Clinic
Philadelphia Publishers Group

Printing Industries of America (1887)
Professional Publishers Marketing Group (1980)
Protestant Church-Owned Publishers Association (1951)
Publishers Alliance (1978)
Publishers Association of Southern California
Publishers Association of the South (1985)
Publishers' Library Marketing Group (1965)
Publishers' Publicity Association (1963)
Religion Publishing Group (1973)
Rocky Mountain Book Publishers Association, Inc.
Society for Scholarly Publishing (1978)
Society for Technical Communication (1953)
Society of National Association Publications (1963)
Texas Publishers Association
Typographers International Association (1920)
United States Board on Books for Young People (1920)
Washington Book Publishers
Women in Scholarly Publishing
Women's National Book Association (1917)

GLOSSARY OF ACRONYMS

AAP	Association of American Publishers
AAUP	Association of American University Presses
ABA	American Booksellers Association
AID	Agency for International Development (also USAID)
ALA	American Library Association
AMCULSPEC	American Cultural Specialists Program, USIA
AMIDEAST	American Mid-East Educational & Training Services, Inc.
AMPART	American Participant in USIA Exchange Program
BBC	British Broadcasting Corporation
BDC	Book Development Council (United Kingdom)
BEF	Book Export Financing Program
BILE	*Bureau d'Information et de Liaison l'Exportation* (French Publishers Association International Division)
BISAC	Book Industry Systems Advisory Committee
BISG	Book Industry Study Group
CABP	Campaign Against Book Piracy
CBI	Carribean Basin Initiative (U.S. Government Assistance Plan for the Carribean region)
CIP	Commodity Import Program (AID)
DAPS	Development Aid Project Service (United Kingdom)
DISC	Domestic International Sales Corporation
EEC	European Economic Community
ELBS	English Language Book Society or Scheme (British Council Program)
ETC	Export Trading Company
Eximbank	Export-Import Bank of the United States
FCIA	Foreign Credit Insurance Association
FCS	Foreign Commercial Service, Department of Commerce
GAC	Government Advisory Committee on Book and Library Programs (abolished in 1977)
GATT	General Agreement on Tariffs and Trade
GPO	Government Printing Office
GSP	General Schedule of Preferences (U.S. tariff concessions to developing countries)
HICOG	Office of the High Commissioner (U.S.) for Occupied Germany
IBF	International Booksellers Federation

IBIS	International Book Information Service
IBP	International Book Project
ICIC	International Copyright Information Center
ICPIPR	International Committee for the Protection of Intellectual Property Rights
IFLA	International Federation of Library Associations
IIA	International Information Administration (predecessor agency of USIA)
IIC	Interagency Information Committee
IMG	Informational Media Guarantee Program (terminated in 1968)
INCINC	(U.S.) International Copyright Information Center
INLE	*Instituto Nacional del Libro Español* (Spain)
IPA	International Publishers Association
IRA	International Reading Association
IRS	Internal Revenue Service
ISBN	International Standard Book Numbering System
ISE	International Student Edition
ITA	International Trade Administration, Department of Commerce
ITC	International Trade Commission (U.S.)
LC	Library of Congress
Liber	*Salon del Libro* (Spain's International Book Fair)
Libraexport	French Book Exporting Agency
NAL	National Agricultural Library
NLM	National Library of Medicine
NSC	National Security Council (U.S.)
NSCD	National Security Council Directive
OPIC	Overseas Private Investment Corporation
OWI	Office of War Information (World War II-era predecessor agency of USIA)
PA	Publishers Association (United Kingdom)
PAO	USIA Public Affairs Officer
RFE	Radio Free Europe
RL	Radio Liberty
SBA	Small Business Administration
SIG	Senior Interagency Group
SITC	Standard International Trade Classification
SNE	*Syndicate National d'Edition* (French Publishers Association)
Sodexport	French Scientific and Technical Book Exporting Association
SSP	Society for Scholarly Publishing

UCC	Universal Copyright Convention
U.K.	United Kingdom
UNESCO	United Nations Educational, Scientific and Cultural Organization
USAID	U.S. Agency for International Development (also AID)
USBE	Universal Serials and Book Exchange, Inc.
USIA	United States Information Agency
VAAP	Soviet Copyright Agency
VAT	Value Added Tax
WIPO	World Intellectual Property Organization

Selected Bibliography

Albert, Leo N. "In Response to Helsinki." *A Proposal to the Commission on Security and Cooperation (on Currency Convertibility) by the Association of American Publishers*. Multilith. New York: Association of American Publishers, 1978.

Altbach, Philip G., Arboleda, Amidis G., and Gopinathan, Saravanan, eds. *Publishing in the Third World: Knowledge and Development*. Portsmouth, NH: Heineman, 1985.

Asia Foundation. *Annual Report*. San Francisco: Asia Foundation, 1983, 1984.

Asia Foundation. *Books for Asia Program Annual Report*. San Francisco: Asia Foundation, 1981, 1982, 1983.

Asia Foundation. "Expansion of the Asia Foundation's Books for Asia Program in FY 1986." Unpublished report to the United States Information Agency. San Francisco: Asia Foundation, 1984.

Asia Foundation. "Books for Asia." Unpublished paper prepared for the Helen Dwight Reid Educational Foundation. San Francisco: Asia Foundation, 1984.

Baker, John F. "The Frankfurt International Book Fair." *Small Press*, November-December, 1984.

Benjamin, Curtis G. *U.S. Books Abroad: Neglected Ambassadors*. Washington, DC: Center for the Book in the Library of Congress, 1984.

"Berne Convention for the Protection of Literary and Artistic Property, 1896 (Paris Act, 1971)." *Copyright Laws and Treaties of the World*. UNESCO-WIPO. Paris: UNESCO, n.d. (Distributed by Unipub, New York).

Book Program Division, USIA. "Books Published Abroad in Translation and in English." *Annual Report*. Multilith. Washington, DC: U.S. Information Agency, 1950–1984.

British Council. *Annual Report*. London: British Council, 1982–83, 1983-84.

Carter, Robert A. "The Center for the Book: Seeking Outreach." *Publishers Weekly*, 4 January, 1985.

Chapin, Russell, ed. *Renewal of the General System of Preferences*. Washington, DC: American Enterprise Institute for Public Policy Research, 1984.

Cole, John Y., ed. *U.S. International Book Programs, 1981*. Washington, DC: Center for the Book in the Library of Congress, 1982.

Delphos, William A., ed. *Washington's Best Kept Secrets: A U.S. Government Guide to International Business*. New York: John Wiley & Sons, 1984.

Dessauer, John P. *Book Publishing: What It Is, What It Does*. 2nd ed. New York: R. R. Bowker & Co., 1981.

Dessauer, John P. "Founding the Center for Book Research." *Scholarly Publishing*, October, 1984.

Drabelle, Dennis. "University Presses Moving into the Mainstream." *The Washington Post Book World*, 6 January, 1985.

Drew, Joseph S. *A Bowl of Burning Gold: American Publishers at the Moscow Book Fair*. Multilith. Washington, DC: Political Science Department, University of the District of Columbia, December, 1983.

Drew, Joseph S. *Through American Eyes: The Moscow Book Fair. A Survey of U.S. Publishers Who Have Attended*. Multilith. Washington, DC: Political Science Department, University of the District of Columbia, January, 1983.

Freeman, William E., with Righetti, Scott. "Soviet Book Exports 1973–82." *USIA Research Report R-5-84*, March, 1984. Washington, D C: U.S. Information Agency, 1984.

Freeman, William E. "The Moscow Book Fair." *USIA Research Report R-29-84*, November, 1984. Washington, DC: U.S. Information Agency, 1984.

Gardner, Richard N. "Selling America in the Marketplace of Ideas." *New York Times Magazine*, 20 March 1983.

Ghai, O. P. *International Publishing Today: Problems and Prospects*. Delhi, India: The Bookman's Club, 1984.

Geiser, Elizabeth A. with Arnold Dolin, eds. *The Business of Book Publishing*. Denver: Westview Press, 1985.

Graham, W. Gordon. "The Shrinking World Market." *Publishers Weekly*, 4 May 1985.

Grannis, Chandler B. "U.S. Exports, Imports, UNESCO Reports." *Publishers Weekly*, 4 May 1985.

Hanson, Allen C. *USIA: Public Diplomacy in the Computer Age*. New York: Praeger Publishers, 1984.

Hellemans, Alexander. "Science for General Readers." *Publishers Weekly*, 17 August 1984.

Hingson, Luke. "Private Efforts to Provide Book Donations." Unpublished memorandum to Donald E. McNeil, Helen Dwight Reid Educational Foundation. Pittsburgh: Brothers Brothers Foundation, 1984.

The Huenefeld Company. "Resources for Book Publishers, 21, January, 1985." Bedford, MA: The Huenefeld Company, Inc.

International Division, AAP. "Profiles of Major International Book Fairs." Multilith. New York: Association of American Publishers, 1984.

International Literary Marketplace 1984–85. New York: R.R. Bowker & Co., 1984.

Kobrin, Stephen J. *International Expertise in American Business*. Institute for International Education Research Report No. 6. New York: Institute for International Education, 1985.

Levin, Martin P. "Soviet International Copyright: Dream or Nightmare?" Unpublished. New York, 1982.

Librarian of Congress. *Books in Our Future*. Washington, DC: Joint Committee on the Library, Congress of the United States, December, 1984.

LMP 1985: Literary Marketplace—The Directory of American Book Publishing. New York: R.R. Bowker & Co., 1984.

Lottman, Herbert R. "A Calm Fair—But a Mighty Useful One." (Bologna) *Publishers Weekly*, 3 May 1985.

Lottman, Herbert R. "Growing Pains—But Still 'A Business of Optimists.'" (Frankfurt) *Publishers Weekly*, 2 November 1984.

Lottman, Herbert R. "Spain's Second Fair Attracts Latin American Publishers, Retailers." *Publishers Weekly*, 9 October 1984. (See *Publishers Weekly* Index for regular overviews by Mr. Lottman, International Editor, on book fairs and foreign publishing industries.)

McNeil, Donald E. "Book Program Review—1950 to 1980." Memorandum to Richard Moore, Director, Cultural Centers & Resources, U.S. Information Agency. Multilith. Washington, DC: U.S. Information Agency, 1981.

Mirza, M.H. "Combating Book Piracy in Pakistan." The *Pakistan Times Magazine Section*, 3 February 1984. Karachi, Pakistan.

National Inquiry Into Scholarly Communication. *Scholarly Publishing: The Report*. Johns Hopkins University Press: Baltimore, 1979.

President's Commission on Industrial Competitiveness. *Global Competition: The New Reality* (2 vols.) Washington, D.C.: Government Printing Office, 1985.

Price, Paxton P., ed. *International Book and Library Activities: The History of a U.S. Foreign Policy*. Metuchen, New Jersey: The Scarecrow Press, 1982.

Price Waterhouse and the Council for Export Trading Companies. *The Export Trading Company Guidebook*. International Trade Administration, Department of Commerce: Washington, D.C., March, 1984.

Prillaman, Jerry. *The French Book Trade and Book Policies in Sub-Saharan Francophone Africa*. Unpublished. Washington, D.C., 1982.

The Publishers Association. *Annual Report*. 1983–84, 1984–85. London: The Publishers Association, 1984, 1985.

Publishers Weekly. Staff. *Publishers Weekly Yearbook 1983*. R.R. Bowker & Co: New York, 1983.

Rosenberg, Emily. *Spreading the American Dream: American Economic and Cultural Expansion. 1890–1945*. New York: Hill & Wang, 1982.

R.R. Bowker Company's Technical Development Department. *Who Distributes What and Where: An International Directory of Publishers, Imprints, Agents, and Distributors* (3rd ed.), New York: R.R. Bowker & Co., 1983.

See, Lisa. "Literacy, Freedom to Publish, Survival of the Book." (AAP 1985 Annual Meeting). *Publishers Weekly*, 29 March 1985.

Shatzkin, Leonard. *In Cold Type: Overcoming the Book Crisis*. Boston: Houghton Mifflin, 1982.

Thompson, Nicolas. "Book Piracy—an Overview." *International Media Law*. London: Oyez Longman, October, 1983.

Turner, Mary C., Compiler. *Libros de los Estados Unidos al Idioma Espanol*. Buenos Aires: USIA, 1985.

UNESCO Statistical Yearbook 1983. Paris: UNESCO, 1984. (Dist. by Unipub, New York.)

"Universal Copyright Convention, 1952 (Paris Act, 1971)." *Copyright Laws and Treaties of the World*. UNESCO-WIPO. Paris: UNESCO, N.d. (Dist. by Unipub, New York.)

U.S. Copyright Office. *To Secure Intellectual Property Rights*: A Report to the Subcommittee on Patents, Copyrights, and Trademarks of the Committee on the Judiciary of the U.S. Senate and to the Subcommittee on Western Hemisphere Affairs of the Committee on Foreign Affairs, U.S. House of Representatives, September 21, 1984. Multilith. Washington, DC: U.S. Copyright Office, 1984.

U.S. Copyright Office. "Copyright Relations of the U.S." Copyright Office Circular R 38 A, July 31, 1983. Washington, DC: U.S. Copyright Office, 1983.

U.S. Advisory Commission on Public Diplomacy. *Annual Report to the Congress and the President*. Washington, DC: Government Printing Office, 1984, 1985.

U.S. Information Agency. *A History of the Informational Media Guarantee Program*. Unpublished. Washington, DC: U.S. Information Agency, 1970.

U.S. International Trade Commission. *The Effects of Foreign Counterfeiting on U.S. Industry*. USITC Publication 1479. Washington, DC: Government Printing Office, January, 1984.

Vahle, Cornelius W. Jr. "The Heldref Experience." *Scholarly Publishing*, April, 1982.

Wiarda, Howard J. *Ethnocentrism in Foreign Policy: Can We Understand the Third World?* Washington, DC: American Enterprise Institute for Public Policy Research, 1985.

Wick, Charles Z. "Rationale, USIA Book Promotion and Translation Programs." USIA Policy Statement. Washington, DC: U.S. Information Agency, November, 1982.

Wick, Charles Z. "USIA Library Program." USIA Policy Statement. Washington, DC: U.S. Information Agency, June, 1982.

Yen, Marianne. "American Books in China." *Publishers Weekly*. 31 May 1985.

Zecchini, Alain. "La Situation du livre Francais dans 140 pays etranger." *Livre hebdo*, 5 September, 1983.

CONTRIBUTORS

William M. Childs served as a Foreign Service Officer with USIA overseas book publishing programs in Latin America, the Middle East, and India and brings some 30 years experience to this study in international publishing including marketing, translations, reprints, and co-publishing. He has served as consultant to the American Enterprise Institute for the past 10 years advising on and directing activities in promotion and exhibits, international marketing, co-publishing and translations. Beginning June, 1984, he has worked full time as project director of the U.S. Books Abroad study project at the Reid Foundation and is co-editor with Donald E. McNeil of this volume.

John P. Dessauer is Director of the Center for Book Research, University of Scranton, and editor of that center's *Book Research Quarterly*. He formerly operated a statistical consulting firm, was Director of the University Press of Kansas, and Associate Director of the Indiana University Press. He is the author of the annual study of the Book Industry Study Group, *Book Industry Trends*, as well as *Book Publishing, What It Is, What It Does*. He is contributing editor to *Publishers Weekly*, and his writings have appeared in numerous books and journals.

Lois Spice Haig of Book Associates has been in publishing for over 35 years. She is the former Director of Periodicals and Special Publishing Projects for the National Council of Teachers of English. A member of many professional societies and committees, including the U.S. Books Abroad Task Force, her present interests, and personal efforts, are directed toward stimulating cooperative education in the publishing and related professions.

Kenneth Thurston Hurst is the former President of Prentice-Hall International (being in charge of Prentice-Hall's overseas operations) which included subsidiary publishing companies in England, Japan, India (which he founded in 1962), Singapore, Brazil, Mexico, and Australia, as well as branch offices spanning the world from Europe to South America and Africa. Mr. Hurst served as Chairman of the International Division of the Association of American Publishers for two years and chaired its delegations to India and Southeast Asia in 1979, 1981, and 1983. He also organized its training seminar in New Delhi in 1980 under USIA auspices. Additionally, he has served as adviser to the AID book program in Brazil in 1966–68, and participated on the AID teams to Turkey in 1964 and Morocco in 1965. He was a consultant to the Burmese publishing industry in 1960 under the American Specialist Program.

Evron M. Kirkpatrick is a political scientist, publisher, teacher, writer, and lecturer. He is the former Executive Director of the American Political Science Association. He is President of the Helen Dwight Reid Educational Foundation and the American Peace Society, and a resident scholar at the American Enterprise Institute for Public Policy Research. He has served on numerous public commissions and advisory committees and is currently a member of the USIA Future Directions Advisory Committee. As a scholar, writer, publisher, and foreign policy advisor, Dr. Kirkpatrick has been keenly interested in the availability to overseas scholars and intellectuals of serious books on American society, institutions, and policies.

Jeane J. Kirkpatrick is a political scientist, teacher, writer, and lecturer. She is the former United States Representative to the United Nations. Appointed in 1981 by President Reagan as the first woman ever to serve in that post, she returned to private life in 1985. Currently, she is Leavy Professor of Political Science at Georgetown University and Senior Fellow at the American Enterprise Institute for Public Policy Research as well as a member of the board of the Helen Dwight Reid Educational Foundation. Ambassador Kirkpatrick was born in Duncan, Oklahoma. She is a graduate of Barnard College, obtained her M.A. and Ph.D. in political science from Columbia University, and studied at the University of Paris Institute of Political Science.

Dan Lacy was until recently Senior Vice President and Executive Assistant to the Chairman of McGraw-Hill, Inc., and currently continues with that firm as a consultant. He has held a number of senior government and book industry positions, serving as Assistant Archivist of the United States, as Deputy Chief Assistant Librarian of the Library of Congress, as assistant administrator of the International Information Administration in the Department of State, and as Managing Director of the American Book Publishers Council. He is the author of *Books and the Future: A Speculation, Freedom and Communication*, and *The Meaning of the American Revolution* among other works for adults, as well as a number of juveniles including *The Colony of Virginia* and *The Lewis and Clark Expedition*.

William S. Lofquist is an economist serving as an industrial specialist in the International Trade Administration of the U.S. Department of Commerce with responsibility for U.S. statistics and data on the book publishing and related industries. He has been an industry economist with the U.S. Postal Rate Commission and a U.S. delegate to a GATT panel examining the manufacturing requirements of the current copyright law. Other international activities with the Department of Commerce include U.S. export promotion missions to Kenya, Liberia, and Japan. Prior to entering government service in 1966, he held industrial and consumer research positions with the G.M. Basford and Young & Rubicam advertising agencies. He is the author of numerous articles appearing in U.S. business journals and has written sections for several books including the *R.R. Bowker Annual of the Library and Book Trade Information* and the *Encyclopedia of Library and Information Science*.

Leonard H. Marks, currently Chairman of the U.S. Reform Observation Panel for UNESCO, was personal representative of USIA Director Charles Z. Wick on the U.S. Books Abroad project. In addition to his own overview and perceptions on the Task Force recommendations included in this study, Mr. Marks gave the Reid Foundation Study Group the benefit of his prior service as Director of USIA (1965–69), and as Chairman of the President's Advisory Commission on International Education and Cultural Affairs (1974–78). He also has chaired a number of U.S. delegations to international meetings concerned with telecommunications and communications satellites, and served as Incorporator of the Communications Satellite Corporation. Mr. Marks has practiced law since 1939, and has been a member of the firm of Cohen and Marks of Washington, D.C., from 1946 to 1965, and from 1969 to date.

Donald E. McNeil is a consultant to the Reid Foundation's International Education Division, as well as a practicing copyright attorney in Washington, D.C., with special interest in international and comparative copyright law. He retired from the U.S. Information Agency in 1984 after 28 years in various editorial, promotional, and managerial positions in that agency's book publishing programs. He was chief of the USIA Book Programs Division during his last 11 years of service, from 1973–1984, developing a U.S. national presence at the major international book fairs and the present structure of the agency's book publishing programs in French, Spanish, and Arabic. He is co-editor with William M. Childs of this volume, and has previously edited a number of books in literature and the social sciences published in the U.S. and abroad.

Howard R. Penniman is a political scientist at the American Enterprise Institute for Public Policy Research as Co-director of the Political and Social Processes research division and general editor of AEI's major series of studies on national elections in democratic societies. He on the board of the Helen Dwight Reid Foundation. Dr. Penniman is a former chief of the USIA book publishing program and book review specialist and has lectured and participated in USIA seminars overseas. He brought a rich knowledge and understanding of the activities and purposes of that agency's book and library programs to the work of the foundation's U.S. Books Abroad Study Group. As a writer or editor of over 24 works, most dealing with comparative politics, he is concerned over deterioration of the flow of American books abroad.

Theodore M. Waller is presently a management and political consultant in Washington, D.C. Active in book publishing for 30 years, he was most recently Executive Vice President of Grolier, Inc., and President of Grolier Educational Corporation. He has had extensive experience with book and library programs in the developing world, at UNESCO, and in a variety of professional and scholarly organizations. He was a member of the Government Advisory Committee on Book and Library Programs, and is a member of the Executive Committee for the Library of Congress Center for the Book.

Index